Kafka's Indictment of Modern Law

DOUGLAS E. LITOWITZ

University Press of Kansas

Published by the University Press of Kansas (Lawrence, Kansas 66045), which was organized by the Kansas Board of Regents and is operated and funded by Emporia State University, Fort Hays State University, Kansas State University, Pittsburg State University, the University of Kansas, and Wichita State University

Library of Congress Cataloging-in-Publication Data

Names: Litowitz, Douglas E., author
Title: Kafka's indictment of modern law / Douglas E. Litowitz.
Description: Lawrence : University Press of Kansas, 2017. | Includes index.
Identifiers: LCCN 2017020137
ISBN 9780700624737 (hardback)
ISBN 9780700624744 (ebook)
Subjects: LCSH: Kafka, Franz, 1883–1924—Knowledge—Law. | Law in literature. | BISAC: LAW / Criminal Law / General. | LAW / Legal History. | POLITICAL SCIENCE / Political Freedom & Security / Human Rights.
Classification: LCC PT2621.A26 Z769174 2017 | DDC 833/.912—dc23
LC record available at https://lccn.loc.gov/2017020137.

British Library Cataloguing-in-Publication Data is available.

Printed in the United States of America

10 9 8 7 6 5 4 3 2 1

The paper used in this publication is recycled and contains 30 percent postconsumer waste. It is acid free and meets the minimum requirements of the American National Standard for Permanence of Paper for Printed Library Materials z39.48-1992.

"You know, a long time ago being crazy meant something. Nowadays, everybody's crazy."

—Charles Manson

CONTENTS

KAFKA'S INDICTMENT OF MODERN LAW

Introduction: An Outline of the Project

The Two Aims of This Book

The first half of this book is *expository*. The second half is *interpretive*.

The first half attempts to identify, categorize, and summarize all of Kafka's fiction about law and legal systems. This includes all of his published and unpublished works that deal squarely with the law as a central motif, as well those stories that might be described as law-related for dealing with subjects that indirectly touch on law, such as matters that are political, administrative, and quasi-judicial. I will refer to this corpus of texts as "Kafka's legal fiction."

It's surprising that no one has done the housekeeping task of assembling all of Kafka's legal fiction in one place. But when it comes to Kafka, the secondary literature tends to focus exclusively on one or more selected pieces of fiction chosen by a scholar to support a particular point about some specialized aspect of law, without taking account of his legal writings as a whole. My project cuts against the grain by assembling all of Kafka's legal fiction and then asserting that there is a common, central message.

In other words, I suggest that we begin anew, by laying the relevant texts on the table and examining them as a whole to see if there is a metamessage running through this body of work. To inform this effort, I also look at certain aspects of Kafka's life that influenced the fiction, such as his legal education, his work as a lawyer, his interactions with other lawyers and authorities, his pen-and-ink drawings, and his involvement in a family-owned asbestos business.

By the time the reader has finished the expository part of this book, she will have a list of all the stories that bear on law, classified in a core-and-periphery schematic in terms of how centrally they bear on the topic of law, and she will have an understanding of how these stories were informed by Kafka's life. This sets a common ground from which we can move forward to discuss whether Kafka's legal fiction contains an overarching theme or metamessage about law.

The second, interpretive part of the book sets forth my position that Kafka's legal fiction does indeed contain a single overriding theme, to wit: modern legal systems cannot make good on their stated pretensions, and worse, they often embody the opposite of their promises. Kafka's depressing message is that modern people are put in an impossible double bind, where they expect and demand their full rights under the law, only to discover that the promise is illusory and the law is empty. Their dogged insistence on getting a day in court, finding justice, and setting matters straight only leads to an interminable nightmare of horizontal shifting within a legal maze, rendering their fate absurd, farcical, and tragicomic. My interpretation is set forth in a series of "indictments"—that is, a series of distinct ways that modern law fails by its own standards.

Here we must be careful to distinguish the writer from his texts. Kafka, the *man*, was a highly competent lawyer who functioned within the legal system and championed some progressive ideals, particularly in the areas of workers' compensation, insurance reform, and treatment for soldiers with mental injuries. He was consistently promoted at the state-sponsored workers' compensation agency where he spent the majority of his adult life. He was neither a revolutionary nor a "cause lawyer" devoting his life to putting the system on trial; if anything, his personal life was rather bourgeois. But Kafka, the *writer*, was an extreme skeptic about progress in the law, and he was also silent about the emancipatory and progressive elements within modern law. It does not go too far to say that he was a legal nihilist.

I say that Kafka was a nihilist because his fiction appears to reject the more nuanced positions found among contemporary critics of modernity (for example, Jürgen Habermas, Jeffrey Alexander, and Anthony Giddens), who acknowledge that there is a dark side to modernity and modern institutions such as law, but this dark side can be offset by countervailing advancements and emancipations that are themselves reflected and facilitated by modern law itself. Kafka's fiction does not square with Habermas's notion that modernity (and by extension, modern law) is "an unfinished project," or as Alexander says, that modernity is a Janus-faced dialectic of good and evil, a struggle of reason and barbarism.[1] Kafka is far more pessimistic. He did not write a single story where a person finds justice or is able to successfully navigate the law. When it comes to his legal fiction, we have to take seriously his admission that his work is a reflection of everything *negative* in his time but lacking in the extreme negativity that can turn the corner toward a positive program of emancipation;[2] his work is negative enough to reject any hope, but doesn't take the next step of offering any redemption. Even when we compare Kafka's writings to past legal theories that have been deemed excessively nihilistic—for example, legal realism, critical legal studies, Marxism, and deconstruction—we still discover that each of these contains a germ, however tenuous, that can point toward a countervailing positive movement in modern law. Kafka's legal fiction is more nihilistic. He does not, for example, make the claim that there is a difference between "the law on the books" and the "the law in action";[3] instead he asserts that there is no consistent law in action, period.

My own verdict on Kafka's legal fiction—set forth in the conclusion of this book—is that Kafka's take on modern law is flawed. He misses the emancipatory power of modern law and the internal dialectic of control and freedom played out in the law, which sometimes comes down on the side of freedom, emancipation, and vindication of rights. To say—as I do—that modern law has a bright side is not to take anything away from Kafka's achievement of capturing the other, darker side of modern law better than any other author who comes to mind, including Dickens, who wrote *Bleak House*, a massive novel about how a single case in probate court destroys everyone connected to it. For Dickens, at least there is a court, a judge, lawyers, and some kind of legal system; it may be slow and corrosive, but at least it exists. Kafka's characters never even make it to court.

Personally speaking, Kafka's pessimism resonates with me, especially on dark days. I have seen the underside of modern law, both in my personal life and in my professional life as a lawyer in Chicago. I have seen the frightened and crippled looks on the faces of regular people who find themselves summoned to Cook County Courthouse for a lawsuit. I have no illusions that the law is a permanent bulwark against totalitarianism or racism or anarchy, nor do I revere the judiciary or its pretenses, and I see how the law can be bent and twisted to the point of ridiculousness, making me ashamed to be a lawyer, and shooting waves of embarrassment through me when I have to stand up and explain a nonsensical rule of law to my students. This makes me a sympathetic critic of Kafka. I see where he is headed, and I often agree with him, but my considered position is that he takes nihilism to an untenable extreme.

To support my interpretation that Kafka's legal fiction is a sustained critique of modern law, I have to specify what I mean by "modern law." I devote a whole chapter to this, but for now let me say that "modern law" denotes the highly rationalized legal systems that emerged within industrialized Western societies in the nineteenth century, including the Austro-Hungarian legal system of Kafka's day. Modern law was supposed to replace the medieval and premodern legal systems built upon the divine right of kings and subject to the whims of judges. Instead of these empty traditions and superstitions, the legal system would be founded on rational laws grounded in Enlightenment assumptions about reason, truth, selfhood, and justice. Modern legal systems were supposed to guarantee basic rights within a public framework where all citizens could be fully apprised of their rights. Even if particular laws were unfair, the law as a whole could be characterized as clear, publicly available, impartial, fair, and rule-governed. This was the view of modern law that Kafka learned in law school, and it is this perspective that we still teach our law students and that our statesmen and judicial officials herald as an achievement of world-historical proportions. And—here is the catch—this is precisely the view of law held tenaciously and indignantly by the protagonists in Kafka's legal fiction, and it is this optimism that destroys them. Kafka's message is that modern persons carry these expectations to the bitter end, and the more they seek the law and demand justifications for its failures, the faster they plummet to their own death by exhaustion or violence.

Kafka's literary project was to problematize, satirize, undermine, and destabilize modern law and its apologists and flatterers, to show that modern legal systems give rise to horrible and unintended absurdities. Again and again, Kafka's legal fiction raises the question of whether modern legal systems are truly an advance over premodern systems, where people were subject to the whims of emperors, the caprices of luck, or the misty and circular machinations of oracles and priests. Modern law has its own set of problems that are just as bad. In modernity, law becomes so complicated that it is rendered unknowable and unnavigable, creating a condition of legal alienation where no one understands legal doctrine or legal procedure, rendering the law just as subjective and arbitrary as in premodern times. Kafka didn't write a single story where the legal system was clear, nor did he write a single story from the perspective of a legal insider such as a judge or a lawyer. Most of his fiction takes place in societies where the law is uncertain or nonexistent, and this fact is discovered by a person who expects the law to fulfill its promise. These are stories of disappointment without redemption.

Beneath the darkness is a strong current of black humor. Everything that he wrote about law centers on a hapless person who carries the fatal disease of modernity: he earnestly believes the rhetoric surrounding the guarantees and protections of modern legal systems. This very belief is their undoing. In other words, they believe that there can be found a clear body of law that will be applied by an independent judiciary; they believe that the courts will be accessible; they believe that they are due a fair hearing on the merits; they believe that courts should be places of solemn order; they put their faith in lawyers and court officials; they demand a consistent and clear explanation of why they are being treated in a particular way; and they pursue their rights with relentless determination. To their shock, they find out too late that they will not have their day in court, that their paths will always meander sideways and never forward, and that what awaits them is not a legal hearing on the merits of their case but purgatory, lawlessness, or death. This is the modern predicament—we are condemned to believe in modern law, yet we constantly find it ephemeral, an ideological concept that evaporates when we need it. Law is not a Kantian regulative idea toward which we strive imperfectly, nor some Hegelian unfolding of historical spirit, nor a practical method of limiting state power; it is rather a tool of abject power in the hands of people who do not care about us. The ideal of modern law is comforting—it allows us to go about our lives until that fateful day when we are called to the law and realize that its promises are empty, its officials are self-serving, its logic is circular, and its endless procedures lead nowhere.

Kafka seems to argue that a person will suffer proportionally to the extent that he believes in the system. As we will see, his best-known short story about law, the parable "Before the Law," is about a man who wishes to enter the law and believes that it should be accessible to everyone, but his entry is prohibited by a gatekeeper, and he ends up waiting for admission until his death. He is paralyzed by his belief in the system. In Kafka's best-known novel, *The Trial*, a man is summarily examined at his home without a warrant and without specific charges being filed, then is told to appear for an examination at an attic courthouse where no judge can be found, and ends up dependent on a useless lawyer, twisted into impossible directions by alleged court officials, and ultimately executed without ever being formally charged with a crime. He propels his case forward out of earnest righteousness, but his demand for the protection of modern law merely earns him the resentment of everyone in the system. In the novel *The Castle*, a purported land surveyor enters a village ruled by a Castle bureaucracy and spends his days shuffling among subservient villagers who are alienated from the Castle. Unlike these submissive villagers, he stubbornly insists on recognition by the Castle, until he becomes a vagrant and pariah in the village and never reaches the Castle. In stories like "The Problem of Our Laws," the people are not even sure if there is a legal system in the first place or whether it is an elaborate fiction; in stories like "The Refusal," the villagers are so accustomed to having their requests refused without explanation by a lowly official that they begin to take pleasure in the assurance that they will be denied. In the rare instances when a protagonist gets to speak at a tribunal, such as in the short story "The Stoker," he fumbles incoherently, too filled with rage to speak.

This, then, is my interpretation of Kafka's legal fiction. But the two aims of this book are conceptually independent. A reader can appreciate my expository effort while insisting that I have misread Kafka's legal fiction. I welcome disagreement. My goal is simply to turn the conversation to a more global or metaperspective on Kafka's legal writing.

A Literalist Reading

Unlike that of most scholars, my reading of Kafka is literalist. When he uses the word "law," I take him to mean "law," that is, positive law as a set of rules. Since he does not refer to particular laws of his time (say, the laws of Austro-Hungary or the Czech Republic), I do not take him to be referring to these particular laws.

This may seem hardly worth mentioning, but in fact my approach is atypical in the voluminous secondary literature on Kafka's writings on law. There are literary critics with stronger credentials than myself, who know Kafka better than I do, and they have put forth some ingenious readings where Kafka's use of the term "law" is polyvalent. In their readings, Kafka uses the term "law" to refer to religious and moral laws, or Oedipal laws, or the laws of fiction as a genre, or an indictment of bourgeois law in the Marxist sense, or as a commentary on the specific laws enacted in Austro-Hungary during Kafka's lifetime. As Jacques Derrida said of Kafka, "One does not know what kind of law is at issue—moral, judicial, political, natural, etc."[4] The polyvalence has been echoed by scholars who have catalogued a short list of approaches to Kafka: psychoanalytic, religious, literary, historical, Marxist, modernist, postmodernist, postcolonial, and a host of others.[5]

I applaud multiple readings, and I am willing to go some distance with these interpretations, but when it comes to Kafka's *legal* fiction, the literalist approach seems most reasonable for one simple reason: none of the other ways of reading his legal fiction can explain why Kafka's work remains so vital to so many different people. Kafka's popularity demands an explanation. Why do so many people all over the world read an author who wrote in the German language a century ago? Why does Kafka's legal fiction resonate with people of different historical backgrounds, of different political bents, of different religions, different genders, and different classes? Why do those of us in the common law tradition (that is, the system of precedent and stare decisis dominant in English-speaking countries) find his work compelling, even though he practiced in a civil law system dominant in other parts of the world?

Kafka's enduring popularity can be explained only by the notion that he touches a nerve in so many diverse people because they have something in common. And that one thing is that no matter where they live, they live under a modern legal system.

We continue to be fascinated with Kafka because he exposed the empty promise of modern law, and it is this emptiness that haunts all modern persons regardless of gender, ethnicity, nationality, or religion. We will lose sight of Kafka's point if we are too reductive: for example, if we see Kafka's legal writing as a reflection solely of, say, Judaism, or read him as a critic of Austrian law, or view him solely through a psychoanalytic lens. Whatever else is going on in Kafka's legal writings, the central message is about the failures and contradictions of all modern legal systems. There is a time and place to read Kafka as using "law" in a polyvalent sense, but I think the proper logical sequence is to trace out the literal reading, and then pass to more ephemeral readings.

By reading Kafka literally we can more easily explain why judges and lawyers in America continue to use the word "Kafkaesque" to describe situations arising under our legal system. We can explain why federal appellate judges like Richard Posner immerse themselves in Kafka's texts. And we can understand why Justice Kennedy of the US Supreme Court recommends that all lawyers should read Kafka, saying, "*The Trial* is actually closer to reality than fantasy *as far as the client's perception of the system.*"[6]

This quote by Justice Kennedy is a backdoor indictment of the legal system, whether he meant it or not. Look again at the quote, keeping in mind that *The Trial* is a book about a man arrested without reason, who never gets to court, has a useless lawyer, and is brutally executed. Let this sink in. A senior judge on the highest court in America is saying that *this* is how Americans view the legal system. And let's look at the numbers: by the American Bar Association's own figures, lawyers are only 0.4 percent of the population, which means that the other 99.6 percent of the population are "clients" who see the law the way that Kafka presents it—a series of dead ends, disappointments, illegitimacies, and ruinous delays. This sets up the tragicomic dynamic of Kafka's legal fiction, where the protagonist believes that he is owed his day in court, that he is owed a rational procedure leading to a decision on the merits, and he pushes this belief until he finds the horrible truth, which is that the law is an empty promise, a dead god. These men are victims, but there is something comical in the earnestness with which they demand (and expect) their rights. We—the reader—suspect that they are insisting on rights and procedures that the system cannot deliver, and we cannot help but feel sorry for these victims even as we laugh at their meandering path toward defeat.

Popular legal fiction from genre leaders such as Scott Turow and John Grisham has one thing in common: it holds out the promise that there is some justice to be had, if not in the case at hand, then in the future. Justice may be hard to find, it may be obscured by corruption and influence peddling, but there is always some hope that the legal system can be navigated and some chance of vindicating oneself in court. In most of these novels, there is a crusader, a truth, a vindication of justice or a clear indictment of the justice system, and a courtroom drama in which the system is itself put on trial.

Kafka will have none of that. Kafka sees disappointment as central to our dilemma as modern persons. We are misled to believe that beneath the law there is legitimacy, autonomy, due process, deliberation, access, fairness, and notice—and so we expect these things. But this expectation is precisely what leads to our downfall. James Hawes captures the point in his book on Kafka:

> What makes us feel so sympathetic to Kafka's characters is that they—like us, his readers—*think* they live in a world that is run on grounds of morality and rationality, a world where there is some connection between what we *deserve* and what we *get*. They expect a mysterious bureaucracy to be accessible . . . or a court to be fair . . . or an argument to be settled by appeals to factual truth. . . . He takes us so far with his deluded heroes that we all but accept their delusions. We find ourselves, too, longing for the code to the Door of the Law, for the Absolute Acquittal, the pass to the Castle, the Father's approval, and the Emperor's message.[7]

This is what makes Kafka's legal fiction so horrifying. By a cruel twist, if we ask for the law to make itself real, we only expose its unreality, and that makes us an intolerable pariah and an outcast.

The Failures of Contemporary Law

At this point, some readers (especially in America, which is steeped in rhetoric about the superiority and integrity of our legal system) may object that Kafka's take on modern law is wildly off the mark. After all, we are repeatedly told by our public figures that we have the best legal system in the world and that we adhere strictly to the rule of law; indeed, this is our major contribution and intellectual export to other nations.

For a person who has been trained to think in such laudatory ways about our legal system, it can be difficult to read Kafka as a critic of the system as it *currently* exists. Many will grudgingly concede that Kafka's legal fiction was a prescient depiction of a dark episode of modern law in the mid-twentieth century, marked by the Nazi legal system and the Soviet show trials, but that is where Kafka's critique ends. In other words, he predicted a nightmare that came true in his corner of Europe (let us remember in this connection that many of his family members and friends died in concentration camps and his work was restricted and censored in his own country, first by the Nazis and then by the Communists), but, so this view holds, his critique no longer applies to the quotidian functioning of our American legal system. In other words, we have come through the tunnel, and Kafka's legal fiction can be relegated to a negative utopia and not a contemporary critique. This is a comforting thought, perhaps too much so. But if I am correct, Kafka's critique does not apply merely to dark episodes of the past or to extreme outbreaks of lawlessness, but also covers the ordinary injustices and disappointments that are countenanced and facilitated by contemporary law. This is why his writing is still current.

To see this point, and to reinforce why Kafka's writings remain relevant, let's look briefly at a few recent developments in modern law in America that can only be described as Kafkaesque. Please keep these in mind during your reading of this book.

Mass Arrests. In Baltimore, Maryland—in a single year—108,000 arrests were made in a city with a population of 640,000 persons.[8] The offenses included dropping a candy wrapper on the street and sitting on the steps of a relative's house.[9] Other large cities like Austin, Texas, have adopted "take no chances" policies where people can be arrested for drunk driving while having a 0.00 percent alcohol level.[10] During large (and constitutionally protected) street protests, police simply cordon off groups of protestors and arrest them, or pepper spray them for "disturbing the peace."[11] Although the US Constitution specifically allows for citizens to gather peaceably and seek redress from the government, virtually any significant protest is met with military-level response because the Pentagon has been supplying police departments with armored vehicles, grenade launchers, shields, heavy ammunition, and even bayonets.[12]

Discretionary Stops. In cities like Chicago, the police can stop anyone at any time to fill out a "contact card" with the person's name and defining characteristics (physical description, tattoos, gang affiliations), even if there are no charges and no cause for stopping the person. In Chicago alone, the police wrote 600,000 contact cards in the first ten months of 2013 and stopped 250,000 people in the summer of 2014, according to the American Civil Liberties Union. Police insist that the information is given voluntarily because any person is free to walk away from a uniformed police officer, but it creates a pervasive sense that anyone can be stopped for any reason at any time. The information is placed into a massive database.[13] The Chicago police are now using a supercomputer to predict who will commit a crime in the future and visiting this person in the hope of preventing a *future* crime.[14]

Domestic Spying. The National Security Agency, empowered by a secret court under the Foreign Intelligence Surveillance Act, presumably acting under a mandate to provide security to Americans, has been keeping secret records of Americans' phone calls and their online activities (including online games), and when whistleblower Edward Snowden revealed this massive and unwarranted invasion of privacy, he was excoriated by elected officials and forced to defect.[15] It is now well settled that the government and the police apparatus have warrantless access to all of our communication, regardless of whether we are suspected of wrongdoing, and that the persons running this security apparatus have lied to Congress that it does not conduct warrantless spying on US citizens. President Obama referred to the secret court—where only one side is allowed to appear (namely the government)—as "transparent."[16]

Black Sites. In many cities, people are picked up by the police for alleged violations, then taken to private "black sites" where they can be held without charges, beaten, threatened, and denied access to counsel. In a single Chicago location, 7,000 persons were detained over an eleven-year period, without access to lawyers, some held in isolation, shackled, and abused.[17]

Indefinite Detentions. The National Defense Authorization Act of 2012 contains provisions allowing the government to indefinitely detain anyone "who was a part of or *substantially supported* al-Qaeda, the Taliban, or associated forces that are engaged in hostilities against the United States or its coalition partners, including any person who has committed a belligerent act or has directly supported such hostilities in aid of such enemy forces."[18]

This law was challenged by journalists who were rightfully afraid that merely conducting an interview with "evildoers" might be deemed a violation of federal law and trigger indefinite detention. A federal trial judge agreed with them that the law was overbroad, but the decision was quickly appealed by the government and then reversed, reinstating the law. Experts cannot reach an agreement on whether this law would allow US citizens to be held indefinitely without a hearing merely for donating money to an organization that is (unknown to the donor) on a secret list; in federal court proceedings, the US government refused to opine as to whether the very act of journalism itself might be considered support of the enemy sufficient to trigger indefinite detention of the journalist.[19] This is no idle threat when many defendants have to wait seven years between arrest and trial,[20] while others are simply held for years—sometimes in solitary confinement—without a trial.[21]

Wiretapping. A federal appellate court held that a person could sue the government for illegal wiretapping only if the victim can prove that she was specifically wiretapped, but the list of persons who were wiretapped must remain a state secret.[22] In other words, you can sue for unconstitutional invasion of privacy only if you can establish that you were wiretapped, but you are never allowed to know if you were wiretapped except in the rare case where a person is charged with a crime that reveals the content of the wiretap; the rest of us who are wiretapped never get to know; this Catch-22 was left untouched by the Supreme Court. Similarly, the FBI maintains a "No Fly" list, but the government has no mechanism for removing an erroneously named person from the list. So a person has no way to know if she is on the list, no forum in which to appeal being placed on the list, and the Department of Homeland Security admits that the list is composed almost entirely of innocent people who have names similar to persons who truly belong on the list.[23] When a hacker broke into the database of a government contractor and found that the Federal Bureau of Investigation was fraudulently infiltrating various protest groups to fish for information tying the protestors to alleged terrorist activity, thereby mislabeling them as criminals, the hacker was sent to prison and chastised for "total lack of respect for the law."[24] Yet the hacker who showed this "disrespect" for the law by exposing the truth explained to the Court that there was no way to expose government abuse other than to go around the law. As he told the judge:

> Could I have achieved the same goals through legal means? I have tried everything from voting petitions to peaceful protest and have found that those in power do not want the truth to be exposed. . . . We

> are confronting a power structure that does not respect its own system of checks and balances, never mind the rights of its own citizens or the international community. . . . I took to the streets in protest naively believing our voices would be heard in Washington and we could stop the war. Instead, we were labeled as traitors, beaten, and arrested.[25]

Torture. In connection with the treatment of prisoners captured in the Afghanistan and Iraq wars (or rather, "conflicts"), the Department of Justice wrote a secret memorandum redefining the word "torture" to exclude any procedure commonly understood as torture—no matter how violent or gruesome—so long as the torturer subjectively believed in his own mind that he was not committing torture.[26] This redefinition allows the government to claim that it does not engage in "torture," only "enhanced interrogation." Key members of the president's inner circle held secret meetings where agents of the Central Intelligence Agency demonstrated "enhanced interrogation" techniques that would be imposed on so-called enemy combatants, a newly invented category of persons who could be held indefinitely. In this way, the United States has redefined its way out of the Geneva Convention.[27]

Authorities without Authority. Many governmental agencies now do the exact opposite of what they are supposed to do. The Comptroller of the Currency, a federal agency created to control *abuses* by banks (such as rein in excessive fees and predatory lending), promulgated new rules specifically to exempt banks from prosecution for predatory lending. Instead of protecting the customers from banks, it was protecting the banks from customers.[28] Similarly, the Environmental Protection Agency argued before the Supreme Court that it lacked the authority to regulate greenhouse gases that are destroying the environment, while it simultaneously prevented the State of California from enacting its own stringent tailpipe emissions standards.[29] Even the head of the Justice Department said that he hesitated to pursue financial crimes conducted on a massive scale because they might have a chilling effect on the economy; in other words, some banks are "too big to fail" and "too big to jail," while for regular persons, there is no hesitancy to jail.[30]

Assassinations. During President Obama's tenancy, it was revealed that he reviewed a "kill list" on "Terror Tuesday," when he authorized unmanned drone attacks in foreign countries where we are not at war, in some cases targeting US citizens who have not been charged or tried in a court of law. All persons in the "strike zone"—including US citizens and children—are considered enemy combatants by virtue of being near the targeted person. The *judicial* determination of whether the summary execution of such people is consistent with their due process rights is deemed satisfied, according to a Justice Department memorandum, by informal internal deliberations in the *executive* branch. That is, a US citizen who is killed by an unmanned drone without any right to a hearing has received his constitutional due process if the president says so: "In other words, it's due process if the president thinks about it."[31]

Autocratic Rulings. The Supreme Court made a ruling that essentially selected a winner in the 2000 presidential election, then added a note saying that its decision is nonbinding in the future. Supreme Court decisions are by definition precedential, and this was a special exception. Similarly, presidents have gotten in the habit of appending "signing statements" to bills that they sign, announcing that they have no intention of having the executive branch enforce certain aspects of the very legislation that they are signing into law. The American Bar Association says that the use of signing statements means that "the President is effectively usurping the power of the legislative branch," essentially allowing a single person to decide which laws shall be enforced.[32]

Corporate Persons. The Supreme Court now recognizes corporations as persons with rights to free expression and virtually unlimited political contributions. And business law, at the highest levels, is now a dizzying mixture of tax avoidance schemes and paper entities, many of which are allowed to, for example, change their residency to Ireland to avoid massive tax liabilities, while natural persons cannot. Meanwhile, in a return to Dickens's England, a person can be jailed for failure to pay a debt, creating a specter of debtors' prisons in modern America.[33]

Lack of Access. The average person currently earns roughly $25 per hour before taxes, while the median hourly rate for a lawyer is $350 per hour, and this gulf means that most Americans cannot afford a lawyer.[34] It is true that lawyers will take certain types of cases on a contingency basis (that is, paid from the recovery, if any), but most cases have to be paid as the case progresses. Most ordinary matters involving divorce, contract disputes, and criminal defense require cash payment, which is why some surveys show that nearly 80 percent of parties are without lawyers in family court cases, a statistic (among others) that prompted the *Atlantic* to ask, "Is there such a thing as an affordable lawyer?" and to assert, "One of the most perplexing facts about our perplexing legal market is its failure to provide affordable services for just about anyone but rich people and corporations."[35] But with a majority of Americans holding little or no savings, legal representation for the bulk of people is limited to legal aid, which has been severely cut by state and federal governments. Most people in America cannot afford a lawyer, and if they find one, they will have to go deep into debt to have the most basic representation. Speaking personally, I have walked through the Cook County Courthouse in Chicago and been stopped by poor people who pull at my sleeve and shove documents into my face, pleading, "Help me!" The much-heralded notions of "justice for all" and "equal justice under the law" are belied by vast and burgeoning income inequalities. This forces litigants to either refrain from bringing a claim, risk bankruptcy to hire a lawyer, or throw themselves into a maze that they have no way to navigate. And make no mistake, it is a maze. Each judicial circuit and each court is a fiefdom, with multiple departments, branches, separate forms, local rules, timetables, and publication requirements. These are puzzling enough for lawyers and simply impossible for laypeople. The massive delays make a mockery of the legal system. On this point, the Supreme Court recently had to engage in preposterous verbal gymnastics to redefine the word "trial" to assert that the constitutional right to a "speedy trial" allowed a fourteen-month delay between a man's trial and his sentencing, presumably even if his sentence was less than fourteen months.[36] In cases like this and many others, the law is bent in ridiculous directions to fit the woefully inadequate legal system, instead of being used as a sword to fix the system.

The Incarceration Apparatus. America has 5 percent of the world population but 25 percent of its prisoners. It has an incarceration rate five to ten times higher than other Western democracies. According to the latest available statistics from the Department of Justice, one in thirty-five Americans is in prison, in jail, on probation, or on parole.[37] There are now more people under "correctional supervision" in America than were in the Gulag Archipelago under Stalin.[38] Even *Time* magazine pointed out that the State of California has built one college campus versus twenty-one prisons in the last thirty-five years, forcing a journalist for the mainstream publication to conclude, "The results are gruesome at every level. We are creating a vast prisoner underclass in this country at huge expense, increasingly unable to function in normal society."[39]

This Modern Dream

It would be easy to multiply further examples, but what is the point? The American legal system is riddled with problems that cut against the promises of liberty, freedom, common welfare, public safety, and the right to be left alone. Instead we find secret government memoranda, illicit wiretapping, illogical and subjective definitions of ordinary terms, blatant assassination of innocent persons, government agencies that act in diametric opposition to their mandates, courts and presidents proclaiming their own decisions nonbinding, a business system that virtually no one can comprehend, lawyers who people cannot afford, courts that take forever to reach, a president who instructs the executive branch not to enforce the laws that he signs, and a runaway police apparatus, all sitting atop an economic system where lawyers are overpriced and inaccessible. And all of this is on top of a legal system where the content of the law is tilted toward the powerful economic and political forces who can lobby the lawmakers, so that even if a person can get to court on a simple contract dispute, there is a strong likelihood that the applicable law will have been influenced against her by corporate lobbyists.

Here is a quote, and I want the reader to pause for a moment and speculate on who said it: "The whole system of justice in America is broken. The entire legal system is largely structured to be labyrinthine, inaccessible, and unusable."[40]

Who said this—a rebel, an outlaw, a convict, a psychopath?

No. It's from Harvard Law School's Professor Laurence Tribe, who taught President Obama, who clerked at the US Supreme Court, who has argued dozens of cases before the Supreme Court, who had Supreme Court justices as his assistants when they were law students, and who served as senior counselor to the US Department of Justice. If this reasonable man—a highly educated oracle of the law and a consummate *insider*—says that the legal system is broken, then something must be drastically wrong.

Another way of saying this is that the law fails on its own terms. Not according to some inherent standard of natural law, or some idealized vision of law drawn from an abstract concept of human essence, but from its own promises. Internally, it cannot live up to itself.

This way of looking at the law, namely as a failure, is anathema to what lawyers, law students, judges, and legal scholars have been taught. We tend to see the legal system from the perspective of insiders who know what is going on: those who enact laws, represent clients, decide cases, and participate in the system. The iconography of the system papers over its contradictions; there is a certain awe-inspiring feeling from massive marbled courthouses and judges in robes. Yet the genius of Kafka (who was, as we shall see, a legal insider) was to describe the legal system from the perspective of the people on the losing end, that is, those who are outside the system. His message is that if we are to understand the law, we cannot restrict ourselves to an internal perspective where the law is deemed *legitimate*, but we have to see the law from the outsider perspective as *delegitimized*. This means that Kafka is a realist, in the sense that he depicts how the law appears to outsiders, or as Anaïs Nin said to her critics, "How can one spend the length of a novel making something real which appears unreal to the central character? . . . I am writing not about objective reality, which is photographic, but as people see and *feel* reality, *their* reality."[41] Similarly, Kafka's writing about law is often phantasmagoric, because he is describing how people feel when caught in our legal system, which is often a hallucinatory sense of bewilderment, desperation, and absurdity, and in that sense he is a realist no matter how strange his fiction seems.

In *The Concept of Law*, often hailed as the preeminent work of legal philosophy in the twentieth century, H. L. A. Hart tried to isolate the necessary and sufficient conditions for a legal system to exist, and he posed the question of whether the term "legal system" could properly be applied to a situation where a tiny contingent of insiders understands the law and sees it as legitimate while the vast majority see it is illegitimate and hostile, a kind of colonial situation but within a single country. He acknowledges that such a system would be undesirable and unstable because the people who are subject to the law do not share the internal perspective toward it, and they see the law as if it were a colonial imposition; in other words, they do not share the sense of legitimacy, self-rule, and autonomy that the insiders feel. But he concludes lugubriously that such a two-tiered system nevertheless satisfies his minimum standard of a "legal system"—namely that there is some group of insiders, however small, who believe in the system and have the power to enforce it. But then he adds an important proviso often ignored by legal scholars who have pored over his work—namely that such a "legal system" is fit only for a nation of sheep.[42]

I would submit that this is pretty close to the situation we have in America: a small handful of persons and entities control the legal apparatus through money and political power, and they tell us how wonderful it is, and most people believe this rhetoric until they put it to the test, at which point they find out that the system is hostile, alien, and illegitimate.

And this is precisely what Kafka depicts. Kafka's protagonists believe that the law should be legitimate, that is, grounded in basic notions of justice and due process. They seem to be functioning fine until they are thrust into contact with the legal system and decide to push the system to justify itself, to force the judges to appear, to force the lawyers and gatekeepers to explain the legal procedures, to explain the reasons for the bureaucratic foul-ups and scheduling errors. The protagonists soon find that the system cannot justify itself; it can only use raw power to overcome the questioner.

The system that promises to invoke power only after the application of reason and procedure is ultimately ungrounded and reduced to the arbitrary power that it purports to replace.

Here we are reminded of Job, who was punished by God on a dare from Satan, and who pleaded with God to show himself and explain the imposition of such misfortune on a virtuous and innocent man. When God finally appears in response to Job's pleadings (the only time this happens in the entire Bible), God tells Job that the entire matter is beyond Job's limited comprehension and that he should be chastened for having the temerity to even request a reason. That is, Job's question "Why?" is answered by God, "Because I have the power, and I don't have to tell you whether I have a reason." Some critics have seen in this parable a victory for Job, in that he at least provoked a response from God; others, myself included, don't see how this is an improvement for Job, for now not only is he afflicted, but he learns that the reason for the affliction is arbitrary and unknowable.[43]

The truth of modern law—that it is empty—always comes too late. Kafka's protagonists often die at the point of realization. In "Before the Law," a man dies of old age while waiting for permission to enter the law from a gatekeeper who is held in check by other gatekeepers; in *The Trial*, the defendant is executed without a trial "like a dog"; in "In The Penal Colony," the penal apparatus allows a criminal to learn of his crime only after the sentence is inscribed on his body with needles; in "The Problem of Our Laws," the common people are not even sure whether there is a legal system; and in *The Castle*, the protagonist is forever trying to get official recognition of his rights but can never obtain a meeting with the authorities. The breaking point in all of these stories is the juncture where justifications break down. The system runs on fictions and false promises and complicities, and so any individual who asks for justification is punished ruthlessly. And despite this disappointment in the reality of modern law, we still carry the expectations of the Enlightenment that we are a government of laws instead of men, and that behind the law is reason and justice. Perhaps this illusion is what allows us to function. Modern law is a dream we all have to dream together.

PART I

Exegesis

I

Kafka's Life in the Law

Kafka was born in 1883 and died of complications from tuberculosis in 1924, shortly before his forty-first birthday, but he was connected to law for the entirety of his adult life. Kafka majored in law during his university years from 1901 to 1906, he was a law clerk in 1907 and worked briefly at an insurance agency in the same year, and then in 1908 he settled into a position as an attorney for the Workers' Accident Insurance Institute for the Kingdom of Bohemia in Prague, a job he held from 1908 to 1922, when he took a final medical leave.

Kafka's diaries and letters express profound boredom with legal education and the practice of law. But despite these outward protestations, or perhaps because of them, he often wrote about the law, not only in his best-known novel *The Trial* and the short story "Before the Law," but also in many published and unpublished manuscripts that we will shortly examine. By most accounts, Kafka was a rather undistinguished law student, but in practice he was a diligent and accomplished lawyer who was repeatedly promoted. He kept to a schedule of working at the office from 8 AM to 2 PM, so his writing was done mostly at night or during medical leaves. As we shall see, one of Kafka's greatest achievements was to function as a legal insider during the day and then write about the legal system from the perspective of outsiders at night.

Kafka studied law at the Karl-Ferdinand University in Prague (more generally referred to as Charles University in Prague), obtaining a doctorate in law. Being a "doctor of jurisprudence" meant that others referred to him as "Dr. Kafka," a term that garnered respect and is inscribed on his gravestone. The university at that time was divided into German and Czech divisions, although the German unit that Kafka attended was more prestigious, since at that time, prior to Czech independence following World War I, German was the official language of government and business.

Kafka's program of study and transcript have been preserved, and they clearly indicates that he studied Roman law and legal history, economics, and canon law, as well as typical courses in criminal law, commercial law, administrative law, and international law.[1] To earn the degree, Kafka had to pass three state examinations administered by professors at the university, and he wrote a thesis entitled "German and Austrian State Law, Common Law, and Political Economy."[2]

Kafka made no secret of his dislike for law. In his letters and diaries, he referred to Roman law as "disgusting" and meaningless,[3] and he said that the study of law involved chewing sawdust that countless students had already chewed.[4] The study of law was not Kafka's first choice; he originally picked chemistry but was deterred by the laboratory work, and then furtively explored the idea of studying philosophy and German language and literature, before finally settling on law. In explaining this move, he professed an indifference to all of the subjects taught at the university, or as he would later describe the decision, "It was a matter of finding a profession that would be most likely to allow me to indulge this indifference without injuring my vanity too much. Law was the obvious choice."[5] Yet despite Kafka's professed boredom with and disinterest in law, he ended up writing a great deal about law, and there is a sense in which his writing—certainly in comparison to other writers of legal fiction—mirrors the density, terseness, and formality of legalese. His stories and letters are peppered with legal terms, at times referring to his childhood as a trial, admitting that his lengthy letter to his father was full of lawyer's tricks, and referring to his broken engagement as a court proceeding.[6] Much of his novel *The Castle* reads as contrasting passages where each side makes arguments in favor of their interpretation of events or documents, very much in the manner of legal briefs. Even if Kafka professed indifference toward law, or claimed that it was solely a meal ticket for him, his writing reveals a deep fascination with law and legal systems.

After obtaining the doctorate, passing the state exams, and completing his clerkship, Kafka was ready for employment. With the help of an uncle, Kafka found a position at an insurance agency, the Assicurazioni Generali, where he worked long hours. His job application has been preserved to this day, and it includes a curious statement that he had no intention of remaining in the legal profession; it is not clear whether he meant this earnestly or merely said it as a strategy to get the job, that is, to demonstrate a commitment to insurance rather than law.[7] But in any event, Kafka disliked the insurance position in large part because of the long hours, which prevented him from writing at night, though he did express to friends an interest in insurance law, and he would soon end up spending his career in the field of workers' compensation, which is a type of insurance.

At this juncture in his life, Kafka had been writing for his own enjoyment and for a small circle of friends, most notably Max Brod, a classmate Kafka met at the university after a lecture where Brod spoke on Schopenhauer and was critical of Nietzsche, whom Kafka defended. The two became best friends for the remainder of Kafka's life. Brod was a tireless promoter of Kafka's fiction, and after Kafka's death, Brod assumed the role of literary executor, editor, archivist, and biographer. Largely through Brod (who had a successful literary career well before Kafka's), Kafka was exposed to literary circles in Prague and became increasingly serious about writing for a public audience, and it was also through Brod's connections that Kafka came to the attention of publishers and received positive reviews and a prestigious award for his writing. Both Kafka and Brod had law degrees and held daytime jobs (Brod worked for the post office) and wrote at night and on holidays.

When it became clear that the insurance job left Kafka very little time for writing, he immediately plotted an alternative route by taking courses at the Prague Commercial College in the newly emerging field of workers' compensation insurance. One course was taught by a man who would soon be Kafka's boss as managing director at the Workers' Accident Insurance Institute for the Kingdom of Bohemia in Prague (the "Institute"), the local branch of the newly formed governmental agency that administered workers' compensation schemes throughout Austro-Hungary. Although Jews were not generally hired by the Institute (there was only one other), Kafka had a connection that he likely exploited: the Institute's head was the father of a childhood friend. Presumably, this led to Kafka being hired at the Institute in 1908. He would earn steady promotion until his retirement in 1922, when he was permanently disabled from tuberculosis. All told, Kafka was employed at the Institute in a legal capacity for fourteen years.

The Institute

The Institute was a newly created bureaucratic arm of the Austro-Hungarian Empire, formed at the turn of the century to administer a nascent workers' compensation scheme. The Institute was *semi*governmental in the sense that the government chartered it, yet it was funded as a private concern based on contributions from private employers. In its formative years (before Kafka's arrival), the Institute ran at a severe deficit because employers' contributions were based solely on the number of employees, a figure that employers would drastically underestimate; later, the employers' mandatory contributions were keyed to classification of businesses according to risk factors in addition to the number of employees, resulting in a higher rate of contributions (in other words, the Institute became increasingly viable during Kafka's tenure). Kafka's duties at the Institute included tasks that we would normally associate with a lawyer who works for a state workers' compensation agency, including "classifying businesses according to their risk quotient," "organizing inspections," "[drafting] appeals against the companies' objections," and "represent[ing] the Institute in court."[8] The court system that governed workplace accidents and insurance assessments was a highly decentralized network of local administrative offices, panels, and tribunals. In addition to his work in the Institute's central office in Prague, Kafka was assigned a territory of Northern Bohemia where he inspected factories and determined the risk quotient for workers. On these trips, much of his time was spent wandering around the industrial towns and observing how the workers lived, gathering material that would later surface in his fiction.[9] At one point, Kafka wrote to his best friend, Max Brod, about the endless industrial accidents:

> In my four districts—apart from all my other jobs—people fall off the scaffolds as if they were drunk, or fall into the machines, all the beams topple, all embankments give way, all ladders slide, whatever people carry up falls down, whatever they hand down they stumble over. And I have a headache from all these girls in porcelain factories who incessantly throw themselves down the stairs with mounds of dishware.[10]

Many commentators have made the obvious point that this line of work affected Kafka's fiction, both in his depiction of alienated outsiders and in the formal legal style of his fiction. Interestingly, Kafka's writings from the Institute have been preserved, and some of them (a rather small number, actually) show a marked similarity to his fiction. One oft-cited example is the similarity between his passage from an Institute report (appearing first below) and a passage from his story "In the Penal Colony":

> Not only all precautionary measures but all safety devices as well have failed in the face of this danger, either because they have proved to

> be totally insufficient, or because they have on the one hand lessened the danger (by securing the blade-slot with automatic blade-guards or by a diminution in the size of the blade-slot itself) but on the other hand actually increasing it by not leaving enough space for the wood shavings to fall through, so that the blade-slot becomes clogged and the plane operator frequently incurs an injury to his fingers when he attempts to free the slot of the shavings.[11]

> It was a huge affair. The Bed and the Designer were of the same size and looked like two dark wooden chests. The Designer hung about two meters a bove the Bed; each of them was bound at the corners with four rods of brass that almost flashed out rays in the sunlight. Between the chests shuttled the Harrow. . . . Both the Bed and the Designer have an electric battery each. . . . As soon as the man is strapped down, the Bed is set in motion. It quivers in minute, very rapid vibrations, both from side to side and up and down.[12]

Both of these passages are extremely dense and flat, as if refusing to rise above the descriptive mode for some type of normative assessment; that is, the morality has been carved out.

At other times, Kafka could be a staunch defender of insurance and workers' rights. Consider also the following passage in the Institute's Annual Report for 1908 where Kafka summarizes the changes that the Institute wanted to make to the existing "inadequate" law: "[Once the law is changed], the Institute will no longer be met with open and covert hostility from both sides, as unfortunately so often happens today, since people have become accustomed to viewing the Institute as the originator of all shortcomings in accident insurance, while it is only the guiltless representative of a law that is perhaps inadequate, and in this case, inadequately interpreted as well."[13] At the same time, Kafka's black humor seeps through his official writings, such as when he wrote in the annual report that during the years before it obtained adequate funding from employers, "the Institute seemed to simply be a corpse, whose only living element was its growing deficit."[14]

Perhaps the Institute most affected Kafka in terms of how the injured workers accepted their injuries as inevitable, something that Kafka conveyed to friend Max Brod: "How modest these men are; instead of storming the Institute and smashing it to little pieces, they come and beg."[15] In addition, the records of the Institute reflect that there were situations where employers sought to subvert or outright cheat the Institute, and there was at least one occasion where Kafka had to bring a criminal action against a business that fraudulently classified itself in a manner to pay an inadequate amount of workers' insurance. In any event, Kafka spent his entire adult life working at the Institute, his only other work experience being the previous position in an insurance company and brief tenures at his father's "fancy goods" store (e.g., accessories), not to mention a brief stint managing an asbestos factory in an ill-fated family venture, which will be discussed later in this chapter. The crucial point with respect to Kafka's experience as an attorney is that the Institute shaped his view of the law by exposing him to injured workers caught up in a bureaucratic maze, but however much he complained about this job (and he complained disproportionally in comparison to the demands of the job), he kept the job, and there is no indication that he sought other employment.

Indeed, despite Kafka's oft-repeated complaints that the office is a "horror," and that "writing and office cannot be reconciled," the truth of the matter was that Kafka had a good job and was well treated and well compensated.[16] He was steadily promoted, from deputy clerk in 1908, to trainee in 1909, to law clerk in 1910, to vice secretary in 1913, to secretary in 1919, to chief secretary in 1922. After only two years at the Institute, he was already writing large sections of its annual report, and he was made head of the Appeals Department, which handled objections by employers about the risk assessment placed on their companies. In his third year, he was authorized as an accredited representative of the Institute. By all accounts, Kafka was well liked at the Institute, particularly by his mentor, with whom he could discuss literature. It is true that Kafka was only one of two Jews at the Institute, and he told Max Brod (who was inquiring about a possible position at the Institute for another Jew) that the Institute would simply not consider any more Jews. But toward Kafka, there did not appear to be any measurable anti-Semitism, and the Institute gave Kafka repeated raises and plentiful time to recuperate from his illness. By one contemporary estimate, he earned the modern-day equivalent of $90,000 for a thirty-six-hour, six-day workweek in a public sector job. And by working for an agency that was affiliated with the government (though funded by contributions from private employers) he was deemed an indispensable state employee and was therefore exempt from being drafted to fight in World War I.[17] Considering that he had few personal expenses (he was able to live at home or in his sisters' apartments for extended periods and able to eat at home for long stretches of his adult life), we can even say that he lived a lifestyle that was middle to upper-middle class.

Kafka's writings for the Institute reveal a professed intention to expand legal protection to as many workers as possible, but always from within the framework of the existing legal system, well short of calling for widespread revision or revolution. In fact, to get the law license and the government job, Kafka had to undergo a state examination into his character, which did not find any radical political associations. So whatever his private political beliefs happened to be, he did not venture very far into social activism.

Kafka's work comports with the obligation of an attorney to advance the interests of his client. In the Institute's Annual Report for 1908, a freshly hired Kafka put forth a technical series of arguments that were critical of the Administrative Court's refusal to extend workers' compensation protection to all employees across a variety of industries, referring to the current law and its interpretation by the court as inadequate; several years later, the legislature agreed with Kafka's position and extended coverage in the manner sought by the Institute. In subsequent years, Kafka would contribute articles on the need for mandatory insurance in motor vehicles, as well as occupational safety standards to prevent workplace injuries. These were cutting-edge legal reforms in his day, but they were hardly radical when compared to the Marxist and anarchist agendas to which Kafka was exposed in intellectual circles. Kafka's willingness to work within the existing legal system was made clear in his inaugural address for the new leader of the Institute, Dr. Marschner, a man whom Kafka very much admired. In this public address, Kafka praises him for his "strong and lively sympathy for the working class," yet "respects the limits set to his endeavors in this direction by the law and the present-day economic situation."[18] Kafka ends the speech by lauding the Institute for its reforms of the law: "One thing is now certain: good work will be done, and whatever is possible in the way of desirable and useful reforms, *within the framework of our present laws*, will be done."[19]

Kafka also proposed the creation of a hospital for persons suffering from nervous disorders, to be used first for returning soldiers who were suffering from psychological injury, and here his language was more colorful, addressing his audience as "Compatriots!" and asserting that the creation of a hospital "would be our undoubted human, patriotic, and national duty."[20] His proposal was signed by over a hundred notable persons. Here, again, as in the Institute writings, Kafka was capable of invoking the fundamental moral tenets of modern law. Why this type of argument never made it into his fiction is a topic that we must explore.

Kafka's view of law was also shaped to some degree by his immersion in a civil law tradition, which emphasizes codes instead of case decisions, and which traditionally has a heavier emphasis on Roman and canon law. It was also influenced by the constant changing of the law, which happened at a pace that is impossible for Americans to fully comprehend. A recent book on the history of Czech law, published by the same university where Kafka earned his law degree, narrates a concise account of the legal innovations and changes in the nineteenth century, and it is virtually impossible to follow. The law was undergoing a rapid period of codification, the most notable of which was the Austrian Civil Code of 1811, but there was a constant stream of new constitutions, imperial acts, and amendments. For example, there was a new Criminal Code in 1852, which was amended in 1854 to outlaw physical beating as a punishment, and then a new Code of Criminal Procedure in 1873. The law was a constitutional monarchy, but according to the 1867 Constitution and prior versions, the emperor was declared "sacrosanct, inviolable, and not answerable."[21] New legal systems were being created—new courts, new administrative agencies—all within a new country (Austro-Hungary). As modern as the law may have seemed at the point when Kafka graduated law school in 1906, we should remember that universal suffrage for men did not come until 1907, and women were in a very disadvantaged state by comparison to men, and there were no women lawyers. Feudal subjugation was not outlawed until halfway through the nineteenth century. So Kafka bore witness to the emerging modernization of law, with premodern notions of an "emperor" juxtaposed with an increasingly complex bureaucracy, making for a bizarre mixture of the old and the new.

In outward form, the legal apparatus was a separation of powers between the hereditary emperor constituting the executive branch, an elected legislature, and an independent judiciary, with a constitution that guaranteed basic rights. Here is how a legal expert from Charles University described the legal system in operation just prior to Kafka's birth:

> The Fundamental Law guaranteed a wide range of civil rights and freedoms, such as the right of free association and assembly, the right of inviolability of domestic rights, the right to acquire property, the right to petition, postal secrecy, the liberty of instruction and teaching, the freedom of speech and scientific research, the freedom of religion, etc. . . . The Supreme Administrative Court was established in 1873. It was regarded as an important safeguard of civil rights; it could decide that the individual decision of an administrative body was issued contrary to law, and therefore, provide an effective remedy. On the other hand, in 1869 special imperial law number 60 allowed the imperial government . . . to declare a state of emergency and suspend in whole or in part political rights guaranteed by the Constitution.

> This law was quite frequently used by the government in the 1880s and 1890s. . . . [A] Constitutional Court was entrusted with constitutional review as well as resolving conflicts of competences. The Fundamental Law of the State on the judicial branch [authorized] independence of the judiciary and fundamental principles of court proceedings, including public and oral hearings, the accusatorial principle in criminal proceedings, and a jury system for certain categories of crime. . . . Preliminary (pre-trial) proceedings were held by an investigative (examining) judge.[22]

On paper at least, the law of Kafka's time was not a free-for-all. To the contrary, it was ordered, logical, and coherent, even if it was nascent and still working out some kinks. And even after World War I, the new Czech government continued to apply much of the same legal form by enacting a Reception Statute that continued the legal structures of the Austro-Hungarian Empire.

Prior to Czech independence, the law was administered in German, which was the official language of the courts and the administrative state, despite the fact that only a small minority of Czechs spoke German. Perhaps this explains why Kafka's writing on law is flavored with colonialism, since the native Czechs were subject to a German law imposed from Vienna, meaning that the law was a secret code in the eyes of the Czechs without training in German.[23] Some critics have claimed that Kafka's work is actually an ironic parody of the formal German-ese of the bureaucracy, holding that Kafka exaggerated this language to the point of absurdity, creating a subversive "minor" literature in opposition to the "major" literary world of German arts and letters.[24] In any event, the civil law tradition is reflected in his stories that refer to the law as a "secret *code*"[25] (as opposed to case decisions or precedents), and he affords an active role to examining magistrates.[26] The influence of canon law can be found in the reverential, almost mystical, status afforded to the law, which is described as "radiant" in "Before the Law" and is ministered by a chaplain in *The Trial*.

Kafka's work at the Institute also reflected the shifting political landscape of his day. Jews tended to move in German circles, but the majority population in Prague was Czech, and they bristled at the control and authority exerted from Germany and from local Germans. This led to anti-German and anti-Semitic sentiments in the general population. Kafka himself moved in both circles (German and Czech), and he famously asked, "What have I in common with the Jews?"—suggesting that he was not highly identified with any particular nationality or religion. But in the eyes of nationalists, he was unquestionably a person of German-Jewish identity, and on several occasions, Kafka watched as the capital sent troops to Prague to quell anti-Semitic riots spurred by Czech nationalists, once complaining that staying in Prague was tantamount to acting like a cockroach that refuses to be driven from the bathroom. Most Jews (like Kafka) spoke the official German, plus some Czech, and some Yiddish. The key fact here is that when the Czech state won independence after World War I, the Institute became a part of the new Czech state, Kafka continued to work there, and by all accounts the transition was smooth.[27]

While Kafka's writings on law reflect the civil law tradition native to Europe, and his legal practice indicates a willingness to work within existing law in a professional capacity, none of this diminishes Kafka's relevance for those of us in the common law tradition. Despite the differences between Kafka's legal system and our own, his popularity in the English-speaking world is a sufficient indication that his message about law is not restricted to the civil law tradition, but is equally relevant to our own common law system because, as I will show, both are based on the same philosophical assumptions. The bottom line is that Kafka was raised under modern legal systems not dissimilar to our own.

The Asbestos Factory

While scholars have made much of Kafka's work as a lawyer, far less attention has been paid to his role as a partner in a family-owned asbestos factory. The interesting point here is that Kafka's job at the Institute was to protect *workers*, yet in the asbestos business he was a *manager* charged with getting the most out of his workers. Tellingly, Kafka's writings on the factory show more interest in the workers than in the management of the business.

The idea for an asbestos factory was apparently first floated by Kafka's brother-in-law, Karl Hermann. Such factories were gaining popularity outside of Prague in the area where Karl Hermann was from, but there were comparatively fewer companies in the Prague area, so the idea naturally presented itself to establish a factory near Prague. Karl did not have sufficient funds to establish the factory, so he turned to the Kafka family. Kafka's father did not want to structure the investment as a straight loan, so they hit upon the idea of structuring it as a co-ownership between Karl and the Kafka family, with Franz as the nominal representative of the Kafka side. Franz became a silent partner, as it were, and there is speculation that Kafka's own money and that of one or more distant relatives was also tied up in the factory, or at least that Kafka appealed to them for investment.[28] The company was formed in 1911 with the name Prague Asbestwerke Hermann & Co., and it grew to dozens of workers, operating out of a factory in the suburbs of Prague. Presumably, Karl Hermann, as well as the entire Kafka family, felt that Franz would contribute time and energy to the asbestos business since he was a lawyer and was in the business of inspecting factories. And indeed there are some indications that Franz was originally enthusiastic about the project and may even have been a force of persuasion for the family to invest. Yet almost from the beginning, Kafka revealed an indifference to the business. He told his father that he was willing to be a partner if it meant taking a passive role of withdrawing profits, but not if it required active involvement after his workday at the Institute. Kafka's father assumed that he would take a larger role in the day-to-day operations of the factory, especially since Karl had to be away from the factory to handle sales, promotions, and other business meetings. Kafka's diary shows that his father reproached him for neglecting the factory, at one point depicting his father as saying, "You danced me into this [the factory]."[29] And in a letter to Max Brod he talked about the family's belief that Kafka was the driving force behind the factory ("in everybody's opinion, I bear the chief blame for the establishment of the factory"), which he says that he must have done in a dream.[30] He characterized his father's view as, "I [Franz] saddled you with the factory and then left you to it."[31]

Kafka found the "miserable factory" to be an unwanted—and unprofitable—distraction from his free time after work, admitting that he did not take the time to really understand the factory's details.[32] There were a few brief interludes in the first couple of years when Kafka spent afternoons there, which limited his time for other activities, especially writing. All around, then, the factory was a failure that affected everyone in the family, but Kafka bore the brunt of the blame in the eyes of the family. Eventually, as a kind of substitute, Karl Hermann brought in his brother Paul as a partner, and the shop was managed by a foreman brought in from Germany. Despite these efforts, the prospects of the factory were dashed when the Hermann brothers were called up to serve in World War I, and the factory all but ceased operations in early 1917, finally liquidating and deregistering in summer 1918.

The entire incident has some bearing on the question of modern law, in the sense that modern law (that is, corporate law) is the framework by which the business was formed and by which the players assumed their roles (investor, manager, employee). Kafka's diary reveals that he was not paying attention to the corporate lawyer who set up the structure of the company, and in fact asked some questions that revealed his inattention, and thus he was distancing himself mentally from the project at the beginning, even as (according to his family) he was a participant. The whole project, then, was marked by a deep ambivalence.

Kafka's writings on the factory do not reveal business-related comments, suggestions, or ideas for improving the product or increasing sales. It seems that he was a very passive manager, unwilling and uncomfortable. His observations were mainly about the modern factory system:

> Yesterday in the factory. The girls, in their unbearably dirty and untidy clothes, their hair disheveled as if they just got up, the expressions on their faces fixed by the incessant noise of the transmission belts, and by the individual machines, automatic ones, of course, but unpredictably breaking down, they aren't people, you don't greet them, you don't apologize when you bump into them, if you call them over to do something, they do it but return to their machine at once.[33]

Clearly, Kafka was more comfortable working as an observer and advocate for workers than as one of their managers. On a deeper level, there was a conflict with his father. As a youngster, Kafka worked in his father's store and was appalled at the way that his father browbeat the workers. Calling the situation "insufferable," Kafka said that he "could not but side with the staff," which his father took as an indication that Kafka lacked business sense; for his part, Kafka said that "I cannot understand how anyone could be so abusive to a stranger," and he said that witnessing the relationship between his father and the workers affected him deeply.[34] Indeed, if we are to believe Kafka's diary, the entire staff at his father's store gave notice at the same time (in other words, a strike) and had to be persuaded by Kafka to return to work; at another point, Kafka was called upon by his father to get an employee to state that he was not legally an employee but simply a clerk, in order to reduce the workers' compensation insurance premium due from his father. All of the mixed emotions in Kafka's notoriously complicated relationship with his father—a pragmatic man who didn't understand his son—clearly carried over into the asbestos project.

Legal scholars have spent little time discussing Kafka's role in the family asbestos factory. In part, this is because little is known about the factory other than what Kafka revealed in his diary and letters, and the official records tell us nothing about the family drama surrounding the factory. However, it was a sufficient source of misery for Kafka that he wrote his friend Max Brod that he was contemplating suicide after the family scolded him for paying too little attention to the factory (this caused Brod to show the letter to Kafka's mother in an effort to have her arrange for a different person to monitor the factory). Still, the incident bears discussion since it was one of the few times that Kafka was involved in a legal structure. Kafka's work experience at his father's store, at the demanding insurance company, and at the asbestos company seems to have convinced him that modern business entities have an inherent capacity for abuse. For Kafka, this manager-employee relationship was simply too evocative of the father-son relationship in which he felt neglected, unrecognized, and belittled—very much like the characters in his novels who struggle with authority figures.

There are two great ironies in the asbestos project. The first is that despite his disavowals, Kafka probably showed early enthusiasm for the project in an effort to impress on his father that he could accomplish something worldly instead of constantly withdrawing into his literary dreams. In the process, through hostility or indifference, he ended up disappointing the very person whom he sought to impress. We know that his father had a low opinion of Kafka's position at the Institute (perhaps because the Institute was operating at a loss when Kafka joined it), and a low opinion of Kafka's best friend, Max Brod (whom his father referred to as "meshugge," the Yiddish word for "crazy"). Yet this futile effort to please his father, bound up with an equal measure of hostility and disdain for the cruelty that he saw his father commit as a manager, was simply too much for Kafka. In the end, he once again withdrew into his writing, assiduously avoided discussing the factory with his family, and put in half-hearted efforts to run the business.

The second irony is that Kafka, whose fiction is often considered dark, claustrophobic, and horrific, was involved in producing a product that is now known to be deadly for releasing toxins in the air. Kafka's diary reports him breathing dirty air in the engine room at work. He would later die of pulmonary tuberculosis, a lung disease that can be triggered by exposure to asbestos.

And yet what I find most revealing about the asbestos factory was an unusual exchange of letters between Kafka and the Revenue Department in Prague. In the fall of 1922, less than two years before his death, Kafka received a notice from the Revenue Department about the asbestos factory. The factory had closed five years earlier, but the Revenue Department was still sending inquiries:

> November 3, 1922
> Herr Dr. Franz Kafka:
>
> You are required to answer the communication from this office dated September 25, 1922, Rp 38/21, within eight days. In the event

of your failure to do so the matter will be referred to the District Finance Headquarters, Prague, and you will become liable for payment of a fine.[35]

Kafka's draft response, written on the back of the official letter, is opaque and dizzying:

> Your inquiry has already been answered by me, not verbally, because I am seriously ill, but on a postcard and immediately. The card was certainly delivered, for sometime later I received from your Department an inquiry as to what I was referring to on that card, there being no record at your office of any summons dated September 25, 1922. In order to avoid complicating this matter, as completely unimportant to the Revenue Department as to myself, I did not answer this second inquiry, incidentally wishing to save postage; if the original letter was no longer in your files, I was quite justified in letting it go at that. But since the matter has now been revived by your communication of November 3rd and I am now, in spite of having long ago answered in a correct manner, even being threatened with a fine, I should like to inform you once again that [since 1914] no further investments have been made by the partners and that the firm ceased to exist in March 1917. I hope that this time my answer will reach the department concerned.[36]

This letter becomes increasingly curious upon repeated readings. There is a tangled web of accusations, tensions, contradictions, and ambiguities lurking just beneath the practiced formality of the surface. Interestingly, this letter has attracted virtually no attention from Kafka scholars, as far as I can tell, but I think that it contains a crystallized version of Kafka's larger critique of modern law.

First, the letter is passive-aggressive and heavily defended, to the point where the reader must wonder whether Kafka's tortuous response is actually intended to convey information that could clear up the matter, or whether Kafka is mocking the Revenue Department's bureaucratic bumbling by giving them a taste of their own confusion. Second, what does he mean in the final sentence by expressing "hope" that his answer will reach the right department? This could be a gracious sentiment that the matter will soon be resolved, or it could be a veiled accusation that the Revenue Department is so incompetent that one is left with no remedy other than blind hope.

And given that Kafka's most recent communication was apparently not received because it was delivered to the wrong internal department, he is surely flirting with danger by sending another letter, which, if lost in the bureaucracy like the first letter, could result in an administrative or criminal penalty, with all the concomitant headaches and consequences that would involve for a government lawyer such as Kafka. It is almost as if he is daring them to lose this letter, too.

And what are we to make of the exculpatory references to his illness, to the insignificant nature of the inquiry, and to his implication that communication with the Revenue Department is a waste of postage? These can be read as accusations against himself and/or against the Revenue Department, but he is clearly inserting a sideways comment that the Revenue Department has brought unnecessary inconvenience and expense to a sick man.

What this letter is really about is the relationship between the individual and the state apparatus. That relationship is heavily weighted against the individual. Kafka's letter is an attempt to walk a thin line between compliance with authority and critique of that same authority. Kafka knew that, as a nameless and faceless subject of the bureaucracy, he was in no position to flatly accuse the Revenue Department of stupidity and incompetence for inquiring about a minuscule matter that occurred five years previously, a tiny matter that they had managed to bungle by losing the paperwork. Kafka knew that the authorities (including state institutions) always have a patina of respectability and a presumption of rationality that automatically makes the victim appear unhinged. A direct attack on the Revenue Department could bring down the suspicion of the intelligence agencies and the police apparatus. On the other hand, Kafka could not keep silent in the face of the absurd injustice of an impersonal institution threatening him with punishment for its own mistake. The letter reveals a hidden struggle for power and recognition that must remain below the surface, a struggle that gets repeated in all of Kafka's legal fiction, which always takes the form of an individual who is trying to obtain recognition from distant and punitive authorities. It is the literary equivalent of the frustrated taxpayer who brings millions of pennies to the county register in order to pay his property tax, thereby complying with the government regulation but doing so in a mocking and ironic manner.

We don't know whether Kafka ever mailed this letter. But the draft was saved by Brod, who was Kafka's closest friend, literary executor, and biographer; Brod was early convinced of Kafka's genius and therefore assiduously kept every scrap and doodle from him. After Kafka's death, Brod published the draft letter, along with other fragments, saying only that he saved the letter because it gave a sense of the issues that Kafka was dealing with in the unpublished novel *The Castle*, which he had been writing that year. And indeed, as we shall see, there is a scene in *The Castle* where the protagonist K. listens to a long speech by the village mayor about how a letter can be issued by the authorities in error, due to the complicated inner workings of the Castle bureaucracy, to which K. responds, once again passive-aggressively, that the explanation "gives me some insight into the ridiculous tangle that may under certain circumstances determine a person's life."[37]

I would go even further than Brod's assertion that this draft letter reflects merely *The Castle*; rather, it strikes me as a real-life coda to all of Kafka's legal fiction. Surely it brings to mind "An Imperial Message," the short story where an emperor writes a letter to a humble subject and places the letter with the royal messenger for delivery, but the journey is so long that the message can never arrive. It also brings to mind the ironically titled story "A Common Confusion," where a man named A travels to location H to conduct a transaction with a man named B, but A gets waylaid, and then B comes looking for A at A's home, and meanwhile A has returned home but injures himself to the extent that he can only sit silently while B leaves A's place enraged. And it brings to mind Kafka's *Letter to His Father*, a stinging indictment that Kafka wrote in his midthirties as an ostensible avenue for repairing their relationship; Kafka addressed the letter to his father but gave it to his *mother* for delivery, perhaps suspecting that she would return it to him without delivery to the father, which she did.

Such mishaps are the stuff of Kafka's writing: letters that aren't sent or delivered, miscommunications with authorities, documents whose surface rationality crumbles upon inspection, arbitrary regulatory procedures, the threat of penalties hanging over innocent people, and the black humor of a hapless victim who asserts his right to obtain recognition from an authority figure, which is always denied. These Kafkaesque themes sound familiar to us. The reason for this is simple: despite the undeniable differences between Kafka's world and our own, both worlds are built upon modern law and modern administrative systems.

There is a legend surrounding Kafka, one might call it a kind of mythology, that he died without recognition after living a saintly and sensitive life in which the world could never live up to his ascetic demands for purity and grace. This view was propagated by Max Brod (who took liberties to remove, for example, sexual matters from Kafka's letters and diaries) and by the religiously inclined initial translators of Kafka's writings, namely Willa and Edwin Muir. The truth is that Kafka led a rather normal bourgeois life and was not unknown. While it is true that his work was not widely read, and his publications sold only several thousand units during his lifetime, he was highly appreciated by other writers and by critics. During his lifetime, his work was recognized and published alongside leading intellectuals like Martin Buber, Robert Musil, and Thomas Mann. Hundreds attended his funeral service, which is remarkable given his early death. Kafka spent much time in what has become known as the "Prague Circle" of writers and artists, and he had little trouble finding avenues of publication for his stories. Overall, he was well compensated, held a very good government job, had a strong circle of friends, and spent fun evenings with friends and courtesans (mostly waitresses/girlfriends), and he enjoyed an enviable measure of literary success in his lifetime. Despite his complaints about his family, which were mostly legitimate in the sense that his parents clearly did not understand their son, he was able to live at home and take his meals there for most of his adult life, and he was able to travel for both work and leisure. There is no denying that Kafka dealt with a complex home situation and that his relationships with women were strained, but in terms of being a functioning member of society, he lived a rather middle-class and untroubled life. Of course, as we will see, this was not true for the characters in his stories.

2

Isolating the Relevant Texts

This chapter seeks to identify the particular works where Kafka dealt with the topic of law and legal systems, so that we can isolate these key texts for our discussion. This may sound like a straightforward task, but it isn't. Rather, it requires that we make a series of interpretive decisions about which texts to include and which to exclude.

For one thing, there is a preliminary question about how to define the topic of "law" so that we can identify a story as dealing with "law." For example, should we include Kafka's stories that deal with *political* systems but do not mention *law* specifically? In one sense, such stories might be excluded from the subject of law since they are not specifically about law or legal proceedings per se, but in another sense they involve law more generally in the sense that the legal apparatus sustains the framework for the political structure—for example, by establishing a constitution and a court system. On this issue, and similar ones, I have decided to err on the side of inclusion by addressing all of Kafka's writings that deal with law in the broadest sense (including politics, administrative proceedings, informal hearings, protocols, and judgments), with the proviso that we should give precedence and added gravity to the stories that focus specifically on law.

A second question is whether to limit our inquiry to stories that were published at Kafka's insistence, or alternatively, to include the unpublished works. There is an immediate obstacle to limiting ourselves to his published works, which is that during his lifetime, he published no novels about law and only three stories that dealt specifically with law, namely "The New Advocate,"

"Before the Law," and "In the Penal Colony" (strictly speaking the latter is more concerned with punishment than with law, and "The Stoker," also published in his lifetime, deals with an administrative inquiry on a private ship, not a legal proceeding). Therefore, if we adopt a highly restrictive criteria for inclusion, Kafka's entire published output on "law" consists of two stories that run about four pages in the aggregate.

This reflects a more general dilemma. The bulk of Kafka's writing remained unpublished at the time of his death, including the novels *The Trial* and *The Castle*, and many other stories that are discussed in this book. A further complication is that some of his stories were more "unpublished" than others, so to speak. That is, some of these works were sufficiently completed to the point where Kafka could read aloud from them (for example, *The Trial*), whereas others were apparently never read aloud and were drawn from fragments in his notebooks. An even further question is whether the unpublished works were deliberately unpublished. In other words, perhaps those stories remained unpublished not because they were inferior in Kafka's eyes or in the eyes of publishers but rather because Kafka died so young and lived through upheavals that slowed the publishing industry during World War I. Further, there are conflicting opinions in the secondary literature about Kafka's willingness to publish his work, ranging from Brod's depictions of Kafka as hypersensitive about publication, to more recent views that Kafka willingly sought publication. Kafka's letters show that he corresponded freely with publishers and had little trouble finding avenues of publication for stories that he wanted to publish. Again, my goal is to be inclusive and charitable, so I have decided to include both published and unpublished stories, but to give pride of place to the published works.

A third question is to what extent we should draw insights from his private diaries and letters, which contain vignettes about law and various comments about his legal education and practice. On the one hand, these might appear out of bounds because they were never meant for public consumption, but perhaps this is precisely what makes them important—perhaps they afford an unprecedented and honest look at Kafka's real feelings about law. Again, in the interests of inclusion, I have decided to allow these sources as complements to his fiction.

Finally, there is the question of his office writings, which have recently appeared in English translation. On the one hand, these are legal documents that Kafka wrote, so they should be highly relevant to his view of the law: after all, they are Kafka's contribution to the legal system in reality. On the other hand, they were not written in his individual capacity but rather on behalf of a state agency, so they might not reflect his personal feelings about law, any more than a legal memorandum prepared by an associate at a law firm reflects that person's particular view of law.

The two editors of the English version of Kafka's office writings are unquestioned authorities of Kafka, and they take the view that "Kafka's office writings are an integral part of his literary *oeuvre*."[1] They see a family resemblance between Kafka's literary work and his office writings at the Institute, even suggesting that some of the themes in the fiction have their roots in his office work; for example, Kafka may have drawn from a legal case at the Institute to get the idea to use a land surveyor as the primary character of *The Castle*, and some of the characters in his stories have names (and situations) that are similar to those he encountered at work. This view has some support from Kafka's best friend and executor, Max Brod, who claims that entire chapters of Kafka's novels can be traced to his work experience.

However, when I finally got a chance to read the office writings, I found that they didn't tell me very much about Kafka's view of law. There were certainly a few unmistakable Kafkaesque flourishes, but overall it was hard to tell that Kafka was the author of the materials that I read. As a practicing lawyer, I can attest that there is a certain legal style that is common to the genre and constrains how lawyers communicate. To read a lawyer's professional writing tells us less about the individual lawyer than it does about the limits of expression imposed by the profession, or about the type of client that the lawyer happens to be representing. Kafka had to take the law seriously on its own terms from 8 AM to 2 PM six days a week in order to earn a living, and therefore his office writing is bound to be infused with greater respect for the legal system than he might express privately (this indeed is a problem of mounting an "internal" critique of law, because to play the "game" of law as an attorney, one must assume its basic legitimacy). In my opinion, it would be a mistake to see Kafka's office writings as a major statement of his view on modern law, but we can acknowledge that his work and his job of producing these documents affected his vision of modern law.

These interpretive questions about how much weight to assign various sources have kept legions of Kafka scholars busy for decades. In my view, there is no magic formula for determining which sources to include and which to exclude. In the legal scholarship surrounding Kafka, I have seen some scholars struggle mightily with a single work (overconcentration, if you will) and others who focus outside the legal fiction to the point where almost everything that he scribbled or said is granted equal relevance (dilution, if you will). I wish to steer between these extremes and stick to a clear list of stories that deal with law and legal systems, broadly defined, as a way of at least framing a common universe of Kafka's stories for discussion.

To accomplish this, I have adopted what might be understood as a "core and periphery" approach to Kafka's writings on law; this approach seeks to identify a core group of stories that contain Kafka's essential vision of modern law, while recognizing other sources at the periphery without allowing them to displace the central works.

Core and Peripheral Texts

Kafka's entire published works run a couple of hundred pages, a paltry output for a writer of his reputation. He wrote three novels that were left unpublished (*Amerika*, *The Trial*, and *The Castle*), and his longest published work is probably "The Metamorphosis," weighing in at a mere fifty pages. His published "books" consist mainly of stories that had previously appeared individually in various journals.

More specifically, the volumes published by Kafka during his lifetime were as follows: the short stories in a volume entitled *Meditations* (originally published in 1912), the story "The Stoker" (1913), the story "The Metamorphosis" (1915), the story "The Judgment" (1916), the story "In the Penal Colony" (1919), the short stories in a volume entitled *A Country Doctor* (1920), and the short stories appearing in a volume entitled *A Hunger Artist* (1924), which was approved, edited, and proofread by Kafka but posthumously released.[2]

As we will discuss later in more detail, after Kafka's death in 1924, Max Brod gathered, reconstructed, and eventually prepared for publication all of Kafka's unpublished texts—including the novels, the unpublished stories, the diaries, and certain letters—in strict violation of Kafka's written injunction that his unpublished work should be burned.[3]

Brod used Kafka's instructions as leverage to obtain control over the great majority of Kafka's unpublished writings from third parties, except for certain letters and sketches that were in possession of other friends or the women whom Kafka courted, most of which eventually made their way to the public. Interestingly, as we shall see later, there were certain other papers and manuscripts that have never been made public because their fate was the subject of a bitter controversy in the wake of Brod's death. This dispute, which has only recently been resolved by the Israeli courts in favor of public ownership of the documents, is a kind of proof from beyond the grave that modern legal systems do not offer the clear answers and measured justice that they promise.[4]

Brod was taken with Kafka's talent from the start of their friendship, and he considered most everything that Kafka wrote or said or drew to be worthy of safekeeping. Brod himself, in his influential biography of Kafka, does not make a serious distinction between the published and unpublished works, and he even claims to have rescued some material that Kafka had discarded in the trash. Using Brod's logic, many (perhaps most) readers of Kafka do not make a serious distinction between the published and unpublished works.

And yet if we follow Brod and make no distinction whatsoever, we ignore the plain fact that Kafka himself chose certain stories for publication, setting their sequence, and we must respect that choice to some extent. Therefore in what follows, I focus first on the published texts and then on the unpublished ones, but I judge both to be relevant to the extent they deal with law. In any event, I think that it makes sense to focus first on the works that were published and deal with law and then move outward in concentric circles to the works that were unpublished and are tangentially related to law. I think that this approach gives consideration to all of Kafka's relevant work (that is, it doesn't overlook any important legal fiction), while also respecting the difference between published and unpublished texts.

With this in mind, here is how my core and periphery approach works.

At the central core, I place the stories about law that were published at Kafka's insistence during his lifetime, namely "The New Advocate," "Before the Law," and "In the Penal Colony." These are Kafka's official, published statements about law. Of the three, "In the Penal Colony" does not deal with law per se (it takes place in a remote location and deals with an old method of punishment), so I place it third in importance of the published texts.

Outside the central core, but close to the center, I place those works that deal with law but that were unpublished. These include *The Trial* and "The Problem of Our Laws."

At a wider periphery, I include unpublished stories that deal more with politics than with law. These include "The Refusal" and "The Great Wall of China."

At an even wider periphery, I find relevance in the unpublished novel *The Castle*, which deals with the law-related theme of a person trying to obtain recognition from a governmental authority concerning his status; furthermore, it is Kafka's clearest statement about how life is actually lived in a community where modern law has failed.

Finally, there are various stories that deal tangentially with themes that have some rather obtuse relation to law but have bearing on the psychological states of persons who feel unjustly accused, such as the early (and not very Kafkaesque) story "The Stoker," the masterful "The Judgment" (often taken to be Kafka's breakthrough story), and the nightmarish "Knock at the Manor Gate."

And at a final remove, I take the letters and diaries, the office writings; at the farthest remove, I see secondhand accounts from friends and acquaintances as the least influential.

Putting all of this together in a scheme, the important works of fiction by Kafka on law are as follows:

"The New Advocate" (published story)
"Before the Law" (published story)
"In the Penal Colony" (published story)
The Trial (unpublished novel)
"The Problem of Our Laws" (unpublished story)
"The Refusal" (unpublished story)
"The Great Wall of China" (unpublished story)
The Castle (unpublished novel)
"The Stoker" (published story)
"The Judgment" (published story)
"The Knock at the Manor Gate" (unpublished story)

Notice what is *not* included. I have bracketed "The Metamorphosis," "The Hunger Artist," "The Burrow," and the novel *Amerika,* just to name a few.

In excluding certain stories, I do not deny that they contain elements that illuminate the more overtly legal and political texts. It is possible to read these texts, which seem to deal with personal matters, as reflections of broader social forces. For example, in a wonderful article, Richard Heinemann convincingly reads "The Burrow" as an example of what Kafka often referred to as the "bureaucratic mind," arguing that the modern predicament is to endure a dialectic of desiring the stability of bureaucracy while suffering from how it separates oneself from others by mediating all relationships in strictly formal terms.[5] This imaginative way of reading Kafka draws in large measure from Stanley Corngold's influential work on Kafka, where he convincingly argues that the imposition of artificial interpretive boundaries (that is, the tendency of critics to separate Kafka's texts into discrete areas such as his office writings, political fiction, stories about writing, religious works, and so forth) can lead critics to overlook how a story that is nominally about one subject may in fact indicate Kafka's thoughts on a seemingly unrelated subject.[6] While I certainly agree with this and admit that I have artificially narrowed the inquiry in this book by isolating "Kafka's legal fiction," I would say by way of justification that this isolation is *preliminary*: I want to start first with the legal fiction in isolation to get a handle on it, and then at a later time reintroduce the aspects of the nonlegal texts that illuminate the legal fiction. There is already so much scattered writing on various aspects of Kafka's legal fiction that the time is ripe for a temporary narrowing of focus, lest we miss the big question of whether Kafka has a global message about law as a social institution.

The Drawings

In addition to what Kafka wrote about the law, there is a further question about whether his artwork bears on the question of modern law.

Kafka was a lifelong doodler, and some of his drawings have been placed in his books by publishers, presumably at the suggestion of Brod. Most notably, these sketches appear in certain versions of *The Trial*, and I think that this makes sense. That is, I think we need to take seriously that Kafka had something to say about modern law in his artwork, and that we should consider them as part of his take on the law.

Kafka had a habit of drawing in the margins of pages, which is clearly visible from facsimiles of his manuscripts; Kafka threw out many of these drawings, but Brod reclaimed a few, either by request or by rescuing them from Kafka's wastebasket. Some of these drawings reappear in Brod's books on Kafka, and others were reproduced with his diary and letters, while still others are the subject of ongoing court battles and have never been published. Virtually all of these drawings were done in simple pen and ink. Kafka scholars have paid little attention to the drawings, perhaps because Kafka did not place much emphasis on them and even dismissed them when the topic was mentioned, although he did tell his fiancée, Felice Bauer, perhaps jokingly, that he could have been a great artist except that his method was ruined by a bad teacher. Brod clearly thought that Kafka could have been a major artist, and he avidly retained Kafka's drawings at every opportunity. In any event, there is now a collection of Kafka's drawings, available with an English text.[7]

For our purposes, I want to focus on a series of drawings that can be dated approximately 1911–1914, at a time when he was working through his major writings on law, especially *The Trial,* "Before the Law," and "The New Advocate." Therefore, at least in terms of timing, they constitute a kind of pictorial depiction of the stories about law, and in support of this, the drawings were included beneath the chapter headings in certain editions of *The Trial*. This series is labeled by Brod as "Six Marionettes on Invisible Strings" (a name of Brod's choosing), also referred to by some Kafka scholars as the "Six Black Figures"[8] (see Figure 1).

For Brod, the figures were reminiscent of *Hamlet*, since there are scenes of fencing, mourning, and death, and indeed there is some textual support in Kafka's diaries for an interest in that play. However, Kafka himself did not identify the figures with Hamlet, nor is it clear to me (or many others) that they are marionettes. And frankly, Brod's interpretations of Kafka's work is often way off the mark (in general, he interprets Kafka religiously, despite lack of textual support), giving rise to what some critics (such as fellow Czech Milan Kundera) have called the "puzzle" of how Kafka could have been so close to, and entrusted his work to, a man who so misunderstood him.

A more astute analysis is offered by Claude Gandelman, who convincingly classifies the drawings as expressionist and cleverly points out the similarity between the small black figures and insects (a theme obviously explored in "The Metamorphosis"), and also how the figures seem to form the letter "K," the first letter of Kafka's name and also the name of the protagonist in *The Trial* and *The Castle*. Gandelman sees the influence of the expressionist artist Alfred Kubin (whom Kafka admired and met) as well as the work of Paul Klee.[9] Other critics have likened these and other drawings to the work of expressionist George Grosz, who also composed a number of deeply disturbing black and white drawings that depicted class struggle, bourgeois excess, and mindless patriotism in Germany after World War I.

Each of these comparisons is plausible, but there is a crucial distinction that makes Kafka's work different, and that is that Kafka's figures are utterly alone. A better comparison would be to the sculptures of Alberto Giacometti, especially *Walking Man II*[10] (see Figure 2).

As in Kafka's work, Giacometti presents an isolated man who is in motion, but not from any particular place and not toward any particular destination. There is defiance to his walk, a kind of anger at the realization that he is nowhere and that whatever he gets out of the world will be a function of his own creation.

Another interesting parallel is the extent to which the sketches look like safety warnings that one would find on elevators, electrical equipment, ladders, and fuse boxes in any language (see Figure 3).

Note the similarity: nameless, faceless figures, on the brink of an accident or trauma, emaciated, without features or personality, stuck in a dangerous situation.

In turning to Kafka's figures, a couple of observations present themselves immediately. Note that the individual is always isolated, but there is no active

Figure 1. "Six Black Figures." Illustrations from *Franz Kafka: A Biography* by Max Brod ©1947, 1960 and renewed 1975, 1988 by Schocken Books. Used by permission of Schocken Books, an imprint of the Knopf Doubleday Publishing Group, a division of Penguin Random House LLC.

force creating this isolation; it is contextless. Notice also that there is no depiction of a face, which suggests that we are dealing with situations instead of persons, a point that W. H. Auden made when he pointed out that there are Kafkaesque *situations* but not Kafkaesque *people*, or as Joyce Carol Oates puts it, "In Kafka, we never encounter persons . . . we become mere figures, abbreviations, ciphers."[11] The blackness of the figures, on the stark white background, depicts alienation from whatever background might exist—family, workplace, town, shop, café, or even physical location and country.

The most remarkable drawing is the one where the individual is in a dock, or prison. Note here that there is no full enclosure; the individual is seemingly free to go. And yet he stays, as if submitting to the very ordeal. Another figure shows a man fencing against an unknown opponent, as if tilting at windmills. Another shows a man in front of either a blackboard or a mirror with what appear to be wooden crosses holding it up, as if to assess or defend himself. Other figures show exhaustion, melancholy, and submission.

Put together, these form a kind of story. A man fights against an unseen enemy. He loses the struggle and is placed in confinement. He is complicit in the detainment, waiting to prove his innocence. He is bent over and resigned but still appears at a table, indicating that he is at least somewhere with rudimentary furniture; he makes a presentation of an empty board (or stands in front of a mirror with no reflection). He is beaten and resigned. He finally walks away, enfeebled, with the aid of a cane, emaciated and frowning.

These drawings are germane to an analysis of Kafka's legal fiction because they involve many of the same themes. While more work still needs to be done with respect to analyzing Kafka's drawings, they provide a visual depiction of the crippling effects of modern law. His work is diametrically opposed to the classical courtroom sketch, as often shown on television to depict courtrooms when cameras are not allowed. If we could imagine a painting depicting the law in Dickens's *Bleak House* (a novel about an interminable probate dispute that cripples everyone involved in it), the depiction of *Bleak House* would never be so sparse and brutal. Kafka's art gives us ambiguity, dehumanization, punishment, submission, exhaustion, and crippling disappointment. Therefore, I would include Kafka's art as a component of his critique of modern law.

Kafka's Wills: Legal or Artistic Performances?

The list above is based on material available as of the date of publication. As of 2016, the Israel appellate court has ordered the disclosure of some long-hidden material that may shed additional light on Kafka's legal

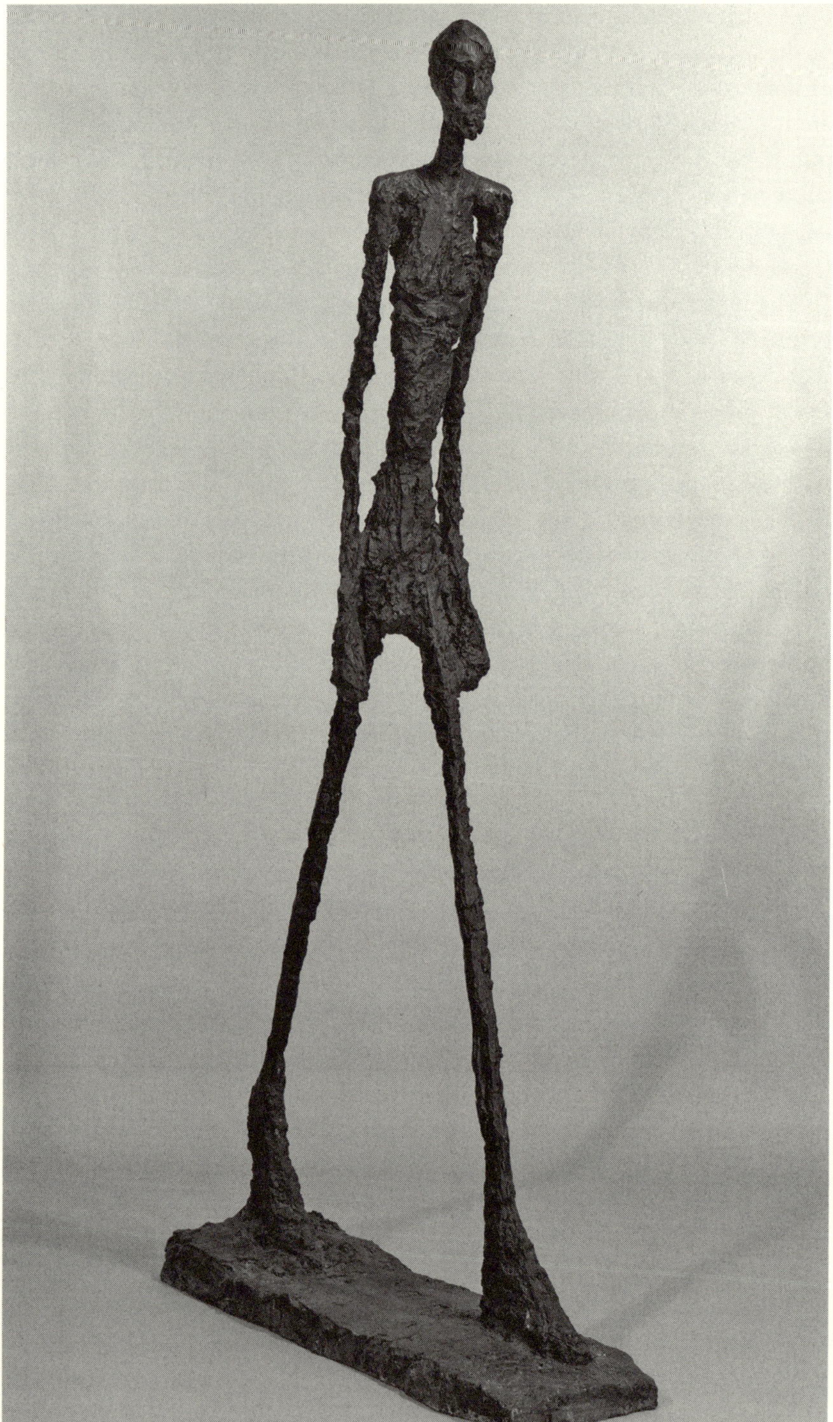

Figure 2. Alberto Giacometti, *Walking Man II*. Courtesy of the Art Institute of Chicago/Art Resource, NY.

Figure 3. Safety warnings on an elevator. Author photo.

fiction. As noted earlier, there is a cache of manuscripts heretofore unpublished, consisting of some long-secreted material from Kafka and from Max Brod's journal entries about Kafka. Since Brod had emigrated from Prague to Israel to escape the Nazis, the matter was handled in Israel, and the Israeli court has ruled that the documents must be turned over to a public institution in Israel. This decision rejected the claims of ownership asserted by the alleged heir of Max Brod's estate, as well as by the pleas of other institutions (in Germany and elsewhere), which already hold some of Kafka's manuscripts. As one might expect, the Israeli courts have said that the 100-year delay and contestation regarding these papers is itself Kafkaesque.

We must address these manuscripts for two reasons. First, because as stated above, my conclusions can be qualified by what is ultimately discovered in the documents. Second, and more importantly, the history of these documents is a kind of proof of Kafka's point about modern law. That is, the fight over his manuscripts is a kind of performance art that Kafka set in motion, perhaps knowing that it would cause confusion. In any event, the facts of the dispute can be roughly stated as follows:

- During Kafka's lifetime, he had a tendency to destroy, discard, and burn his writings. Some claim that he destroyed the majority of his writing, but an accurate percentage is difficult to gauge. Certainly, Brod reported that he rescued some of Kafka's work from the trash and that after Kafka's death he found burned notebooks among Kafka's things. Thus, there is some reason to believe that Kafka was long inclined to have his work burned after his death.
- Brod spent his entire relationship with Kafka coaxing and saving all items of Kafka's writing, from large manuscripts to small postcards and drawings, making it his mission to preserve Kafka's corpus of work and to present him as a literary figure of major importance. Kafka was certainly aware of this diligence on Brod's part. In this sense, Kafka was aware that Brod would be averse to destroying anything remaining after Kafka's death.
- In 1921, Kafka showed Brod a letter instructing Brod that upon Kafka's death, he should gather and burn all of Kafka's materials without reading them. Brod informed Kafka that he would not follow these instructions.
- At some point in the subsequent years, Kafka wrote an additional letter to Brod, similar in content to the first letter, though slightly more permissive about which books should be allowed to stand.
- In 1924, Kafka died without a formal will and with few possessions; his family did not seek to publish his literary materials.
- As a matter of courtesy and respect, Kafka's family permitted Brod to take possession of Kafka's papers, at which time he found the two "wills" mentioned above (one of which was previously shown to him).
- Brod decided to ignore Kafka's first and second written requests to burn his materials.
- In short order, Brod arranged for publication of Kafka's short stories, novels, and other materials (including materials previously published and unpublished) in German, and then in English. Brod acted as editor for the material and made decisions as to the order of chapters

in the novels and the titles of short stories. Brod also began a lifelong process of contacting Kafka's friends, relatives, fiancées, and other correspondents, asking for a return of all papers so that they could be published. He also wrote an influential biography of Kafka.

- In 1939, Brod took the last train out of Prague before the Nazis closed the border, and he was carrying a suitcase of Kafka's writings. He eventually settled in Palestine (prior to it being "Israel").
- Brod's relocation to Palestine was in keeping with his Zionism, although Kafka's Zionism was ambiguous at best; he studied Hebrew toward the end of his life, and he talked with his last girlfriend about moving to Palestine and running a restaurant. It is impossible to say how serious Kafka was about making a home in Palestine.
- Kafka's sisters were deported to concentration camps, leaving only nieces and distant relatives who might possibly have a colorable claim to the manuscripts.
- In Palestine, Brod continued to oversee the placement of Kafka's manuscripts for publication, telling a newspaper that his mission in Palestine was to preserve and promote Kafka's legacy.
- After Brod's wife died, he carried on a relationship with a married woman, Esther Hoffe, who acted as a secretary in the organization of Brod's own work and in his critical assembly of Kafka's materials and, some suspect, as his love interest.
- In 1947, Brod gave certain materials to Hoffe, and in 1948 he prepared a gift letter that provided that Esther was to receive Brod's literary materials (presumably including the Kafka materials) to do with as she pleased during her lifetime, but then to turn everything over to a public archive in Israel.
- As trouble struck the Middle East, Brod deposited some manuscripts in Swiss vaults with joint ownership with Kafka's nieces.
- Brod wrote a definitive will in 1961 or 1962 that left the literary estate to Hoffe for life, but contemplated that the material would be turned over to a public archive, and he listed four examples. According to Martin Buber's wife, who is curator of the Buber papers in Israel, Brod and Hoffe visited the archive to explore the idea of placing all three men's work in one location (i.e. Kafka, Buber, and Brod).
- Kafka's niece had a son who attended Oxford University and befriended the renowned Kafka expert Malcolm Pasley. Subsequently, all four of Kafka's nieces turned over Kafka's

manuscripts and other materials to Oxford University, making it the largest holder of Kafka's manuscripts.

- In 1968, Brod died, leaving Esther Hoffe as custodian or beneficiary of the Kafka papers, which at that point were spread around her apartment and in various safe-deposit boxes in Israel and Switzerland.
- In 1974, as part of Brod's probate, the state of Israel asserted a right to Kafka's papers bequeathed by Brod to Hoffe, but this was rebuked by a court decision saying that Hoffe had the right to handle them during her life.
- In 1975, Hoffe was arrested at Tel Aviv airport on suspicion of removing cultural papers from Israel without first copying them with the Israel National Archive (a crime), and a search revealed copies of Kafka's letters and original documents from Brod, ostensibly to be offered for sale.
- In the late 1980s, Esther Hoffe sold some of Kafka's letters and materials to a private buyer in Germany, and in 1988, Esther auctioned the original manuscript for *The Trial* to a German buyer, and it ended up at the German National Archive in Marbach.
- Esther died in 2007, leaving her estate to her two daughters, who claimed the right to any remaining Kafka manuscripts under Esther's estate.
- The daughters proposed to sell the manuscripts at auction, perhaps by weight.
- A lawsuit was filed in family court in Tel Aviv to determine where the Kafka papers should go. The following parties were represented: Brod, the Hoffe family, and the Israeli and German national archives.
- In 2012, the family court judge issued a ruling (in Hebrew) that the materials must be turned over to the Hebrew National Archive. Citing Ottoman law predating the establishment of Israel law, the judge found that Brod never made a completed gift of the Kafka materials to Esther, and therefore she (and her daughters) were holding the Kafka materials as an executor for Brod and not as a beneficial owner in their own right.
- An appeal was filed with the district court, which in 2015 issued a decision (again in Hebrew) that the manuscripts must be turned over to Hebrew University.
- By the time the matter was resolved, Kafka had been dead nearly 100 years. Brod had been dead nearly 50 years. Hoffe was dead, and so was one of her daughters.[12]

There is a lot to unpack here, and much of what I have learned has been translated from Hebrew (and learned from conversations with the reporters from the newspapers covering the trial and the appeal), so there is an extra layer of complexity, especially since the judicial opinions are not currently available in English.

Two questions are raised by this tangle: (1) what does it say about modern law? and (2) did Kafka purposely create this tangle as a kind of performance art?

As a lawyer, my first sense was that the entire matter was botched from the start, perhaps intentionally. Legally speaking, under Czech law at the time of Kafka's death, neither of his "wills" was binding since they were not witnessed by independent parties, they did not contain the key clauses setting out the terms of passage of the property, and they were not filed with the proper authorities. This means he died intestate (without a will), and the owner of the papers would actually be the Czech government. I have confirmed this with lawyers and law professors in Prague, and they agree that this would have been the result under Czech law, had it been followed.

But even assuming that Kafka's "wills" were valid, there is a further question of whether Brod violated his duty as executor by ignoring the plain meaning of Kafka's instructions to burn the materials. Courts generally look to the plain meaning of a will, and when Kafka said that he wanted his work burned, most courts would not admit parole evidence in direct opposition to this request.

But let's say that the documents are valid, and that Brod was the duly appointed executor, and let's also say that he was empowered to override Kafka's instructions. Now we face a further question of whether the papers should have been taken to Palestine and placed under Brod's will for submission to the Hebrew museum. By what right did Brod grant himself the sole arbiter of what material to withhold from publication (a position clearly inconsistent with his claim that the world needed to see everything that Kafka wrote) and then gift them to a stranger who had never met Kafka?

As for Hoffe, by what right did she violate Brod's will (and by extension, Kafka's will), neither of which contained any hint of selling the manuscripts for money? And how can her daughters further dehumanize Kafka's legacy by measuring the worth of his papers by their weight or by an auction?

Finally, how does the state of Israel, which was not in existence during Kafka's life, get a claim on Kafka's papers, especially when he was Czech, wrote in German, and never went to Palestine? Is there not something very strange about saying that a writer who stressed nonarrival and nonbelonging should somehow belong in a place to which he had no connection? But should his work belong in Germany, where much of his family was killed? Or England, where a large collection of his papers ended up merely by a stroke of fate after his death? And finally, what can we say about the morality of Brod's decision to ignore Kafka's instructions and to make public tiny scraps of his life while acting as a godlike figure who had the sole ability to determine what the world was entitled to see?

The whole matter is a tangled ball of confusion, and this may have been Kafka's intention. Milan Kundera asserts that Kafka's instruction to burn his work was because he simply felt that it was not very good, and he was ashamed of it. But I think it is more than this: after all, Brod was instructed to burn all of Kafka's materials sight unseen, and the only way to find this instruction was to violate the injunction. So it can be claimed that Kafka was making a mockery of rules and by extension the rules of modern law. I think we must take seriously the notion that Kafka's "will" was a kind of performance art that revealed the weaknesses of modern law. After all, he was a lawyer and could have easily drafted a simple and binding will.

My reading of Kafka's "wills" as performance art is bolstered by Brod's own admission that "I am far from grateful to him for having precipitated me into this difficult conflict of conscience [over whether to burn or publish the manuscripts], *which he must have foreseen*, for he knew with what fanatical veneration I listened to his every word."[13] In fact, Brod admits flatly that these documents are not wills in any meaningful sense: "No will was found among Kafka's literary remains," and he refers to the letters as "categorical instructions" even though they were never delivered to him, the two instructions contradict each other, and the instructions came up only in conversation over Brod's will, at which time Kafka allegedly pointed to a closed letter and specified what his last testament "will be," while the whole conversation was in a "jesting tone" with an "underlying seriousness."[14] If we take Brod at his word that Kafka *must have foreseen* the *personal* conflict into which he was throwing Brod, we should also recognize that both men were lawyers and that they could not have failed to see the *legal* conflict raised by Brod's taking possession of all documents and demanding the return of all documents from others under the banner of Kafka's "executor"—a term that doesn't even make sense if there is no will in the first place. Thus we are left with the distinct possibility that Kafka's "wills" were meant as a work of art, much in the same sense that Joyce Carol Oates spoke of the suicidal person whose final act is a work of art.[15] Intentionally or not, Kafka left a legal mess that made of mockery of modern law and showed that despite a hundred years of "progress," it could not provide a clear answer as to where the texts belong.[16]

I am not alone in suggesting that Kafka's "wills" ought to be considered as worthy of study for those interested in Kafka's view of law. Given the paradox that Kafka was a lawyer whose wills failed in the *legal* sense (because they lacked the proper formalities), we must wonder whether their true purpose was not so much to effectuate a legally binding obligation, but rather to express what are now known as the "moral rights" of an author to determine what happens to his texts. A more extreme position might be that the letters were purely literary exercises (that is, nonlegal documents but simply autobiographical stories), since they were never delivered. In a thoughtful paper on the initial court proceedings, Israeli law professor Nili Cohen suggests that the wills reflect Kafka's distrust of modern law in that they were not written to withstand judicial scrutiny, precisely because Kafka wanted to avoid having his work (or his legacy) subject to the vagaries of judicial interpretation. Brod, by contrast, clearly did not share Kafka's distrust of modern law, and thus he was game to entrust the fate of Kafka's manuscripts to the courts. As Cohen says, "Brod [if he had lived] may have been surprised by the court's rulings . . . not Kafka."[17] This book is not the time or place to go into the labyrinth of events and the court proceedings in Israel, but we can make note of the situation and assert with confidence that the wills deserve a place alongside Kafka's other writings on the law and that the reader ought to be at least acquainted with these proceedings surrounding Kafka's manuscripts.

The eventual publication of these manuscripts is currently captivating the imaginations of Kafka scholars, but in the end, however, I am not too concerned about what we find in the lost manuscripts. The key to Kafka's legal fiction does not lie in some dusty set of personal documents kept under lock and key, nor in some obscure facts about Kafka's life, nor in some new way to translate German to English. There is no touchstone; everything we need is already clear from the published works. The magic of Kafka's legal fiction—the chord that he has struck in readers for a century—is rooted in the disappointment that modern persons like us still feel in the disconnect between how modern legal systems are supposed to be versus the reality of how modern systems actually function. In each story, the protagonist asserts a claim based on what he thinks he deserves from the legal system, only to be thrown into an actual system that is plagued by failure, contradiction, and absurdity. Toward this end, Kafka scholar Walter Sokel captured something important when he said that "the irony of Kafka's texts resides in the discrepancy between the ostensible and the actual. Ostensibly, the protagonists' claims appear to be justified, but actually it is absurd."[18] To make a fetish of the new material is to fall into the trap of

Kafka's characters who delude themselves that redemption, clarity, and deliverance are waiting just around the corner. We have his stories, his office writings, his drawings, his experience at the asbestos factory, and we know that he left a mess with his "wills"—that is more than enough material on which to focus.

3

Narrative Summaries

We have isolated Kafka's key works dealing with modern law, which I have labeled as "Kafka's legal fiction." It is now time to summarize the narrative elements of these stories so that we are all on the same page, so to speak. These following summaries are deliberately succinct, as these works will be discussed in more detail in Part II of this book.[1]

"The New Advocate"

"The New Advocate" is a two-paragraph parable published during Kafka's lifetime. Kafka obviously felt strongly about it, since he insisted that it be the lead story in his anthology of stories called *A Country Doctor.*

It deals with the conversion of Alexander the Great's horse, Bucephalus, into a bar-licensed attorney. Bucephalus has received the approval of the organized bar and encountered a friendly reception in the legal community: the legendary battle-charger is now turning the pages of law books in the library. The narrator concludes that this is as it should be, since nowadays "there is no Alexander the Great." The text is deliberately ambiguous as to the precise form that Bucephalus assumes, that is, whether he is a horse, a human, or a hybrid.

"Before the Law"

This is perhaps Kafka's best-known very short story, and like "The New Advocate," it takes the form of a parable. It was published on a stand-alone basis in Kafka's lifetime, and it also appears in *The Trial* as a parable told by the court's chaplain (or "priest" depending on the translation) during a conversation with the accused Josef K. in the cathedral where he is supposed to meet a client. Kafka referred to the story privately as "the Legend" and wrote in his diaries that it was a source of pride.

In the parable, a man from the country seeks admission to the law, but encounters a doorkeeper who says that admission cannot be granted now. When the man asks about future admission, the doorkeeper says that it is possible, but cannot happen now. The man tries to peer through the door, but the doorkeeper informs him that the law is protected by a series of doorkeepers, each more powerful than the next, such that this lowly doorkeeper cannot even bear to look at the third doorkeeper. This news frustrates the man from the country who feels that the law should be accessible to everyone. So the man sits for years at the door to the law, engaging the doorkeeper in banal conversations and trying to offer bribes, which are accepted only to appease the man from the country. Eventually the man is ready to die, and he sees a radiance coming from the law. He has the strength to ask one more question, so he asks the doorkeeper why nobody else has sought admission through this door when everyone strives to find the law. The doorkeeper realizes that the man is dying, and he stoops to explain: "No one else could ever be admitted here, since this door was made only for you. I am now going to shut it."

"In the Penal Colony"

"In the Penal Colony" is the story of a man known only as the Explorer, who travels to a tropical penal colony at the invitation of a New Commandant to witness the execution of a man pursuant to a methodology invented by the Old Commandant. The execution device, referred to as the "apparatus," engraves the sentence on the body of the victim through the use of long needles, then lifts the impaled body and tosses it into a pit. The accused never knows the sentence in advance, but rather "learns it on his body." This punishment is administered by an Officer who acts as judge and executioner simultaneously, under a primitive rule: "My guiding principle is this: Guilt is never to be doubted." The twelve-hour procedure writes the punishment on the body of the condemned man, rotating the body, somehow enabling the man to discern the sentence (by feeling the impression of the letters) after six hours.

In this case, the condemned man is being inscribed with the words "Honor Thy Superiors," as he fell asleep on duty, neglecting his assigned task of standing outside the Captain's door and rising every hour to salute the door. The condemned man is submissive and passive despite not being informed of his sentence. The Officer and an assistant strap the condemned man to the bed of the apparatus and then insert a disgusting old mouthpiece, inducing vomit. The Officer can sense the Explorer's revulsion toward this procedure, and he rightly fears that the Explorer will send a negative review to the New Commandant, thereby leading to the abandonment of this procedure. To prevent this, the Officer removes the condemned man and places himself in the apparatus, changing the sentence to "Be Just." This appears to be some sort of suicide mission to impress the Explorer, but as the machine begins its work, something goes wrong: the machine does not write smoothly but simply stabs away at the body of the Officer, ultimately spiking him in the forehead and killing him. After this display, the Explorer leaves alone.

The Trial

The Trial is the story of the arrest, trial, and execution of Josef K., the chief clerk of a bank, who never learns the nature of the charges leveled against him nor the identity of the accusatory body. The story begins when K. is awakened on the morning of his thirtieth birthday by two guards who inform him that he is under arrest and prepare him for an impromptu interrogation that will take place in his apartment. The arrest comes without warning and without specific charges being brought. K. is shocked as the guards proceed to eat his breakfast and try to trick him into parting with his high-quality clothes, insinuating that K. is already guilty. At this point, K. can only guess as to the mysterious forces that command such guards: "What office did they represent? After all, K. lived in a state governed by law, there was universal peace, all statutes were in force; who dared assault him in his own premises?" Presently, a hearing is assembled in the room of another boarder as the neighbors watch through the windows. The guards instruct K. to wear black for what turns out to be a tense but uninformative interrogation by an examiner who merely tells K. that he is under arrest, but not in the typical sense: "You are under arrest, certainly, but that's not meant to keep you from carrying on your profession."

K. is soon informed by a phone call that his case will be heard on weekends, the first hearing being on a Sunday in a distant suburb. The address provided over the phone is for a large apartment complex, and K. cannot find the courtroom. Since he is too ashamed to ask for directions to the courtroom, he makes up a story that he is looking for a carpenter who lives there. The residents of this particular building can discern that K. is a defendant, and they point him toward the courtroom, in the top floor (the attic) of the dingy apartment complex. This theme recurs throughout the book, namely that defendants have a special "look" that others can discern, and that "the law is attracted by guilt." The hearing begins comically, as the prosecutor asks, "So you are a house painter?" to which K. replies, "No, I'm the chief financial officer of a large bank." This confusion propels K. into a long soliloquy on the incompetence of the court and its insidious role as an "extensive institution" for "arresting innocent people" and "instituting senseless proceedings," comments that cause half the people in the courtroom to cheer him repeatedly, while the other half stand idly. The proceeding is disrupted when a man begins to violently kiss a washerwoman in the back of the courtroom, and when K. runs over to break up their embrace, he notices that all the men in the crowd are wearing badges indicating their allegiance to the court, even those men who were seemingly cheering his attacks on the court. He is then informed by the prosecutor that his behavior has destroyed any advantage that he might have gained from an interrogation. K. leaves in a huff, only to return the following Sunday in the vague hope of furthering his case. On this day he finds the courtroom is empty, and when he examines the law books on the prosecutor's table he finds sexual drawings and comic book images. K. then has an intimate conversation with the court washerwoman whom he had earlier tried to protect, and he even entertains the thought of taking her away from her miserable life, when a law student comes up, physically removes her, and begins kissing her before taking her to his superior, the examining magistrate. K. cannot tell if she is being taken against her will or by consent, but her husband soon arrives and tells K. that the washerwoman is consensually involved with the court officials. As K. is led upward to the court catacombs he sees other victims waiting passively, and eventually he has a panic attack, loses his breath, and has to be forcibly removed from the premises.

At this point the novel becomes even more surreal. K. is working late one night at the bank and hears groans coming from behind a supply room door. When he opens the door, he finds that the two guards who arrested him are being whipped by a flogger for their callous behavior in connection with K.'s arrest. K. tries to bribe the flogger to prevent the beating: "I don't even consider them guilty; it's the organization that's guilty." The bribe is refused, and K. shuts the door to muffle the wailing. One week later the entire scene is repeated.

Soon afterward, K.'s uncle hears about the trial and finds a renowned lawyer named Huld to represent K. A meeting is called at Huld's house (he works from home, or rather from a bed in his home) between K., his uncle, Huld, and the Chief Clerk of the Court who happened to be visiting. K. is distracted by Huld's maid, and he leaves the meeting in order to begin a sexual affair with her. By the time he returns to the meeting, the Clerk has already left, causing embarrassment to Huld and to K.'s uncle, and hurting his case.

K. begins to realize that he is dealing with a strange court of ambiguous jurisdiction. Everything about the court is secret, including its records, its proceedings, and the identity of the judges. Further, the court does not read the petitions placed before it, nor does it require accused persons to defend themselves (though the court will tolerate a defense). Finally, the structure of the court is so complicated that nobody really understands its many levels, and nobody has a complete picture of the tortured life of a single case. Faced with this, litigants are initially obsessed with their cases, but over time they settle into passivity.

At the suggestion of a client from the bank, K. visits the court's official painter, Titorelli, who lives in a remote attic connected to a court building and informs K. that "the High Court is totally inaccessible to you and me and everyone else" and that K. faces one of three possible outcomes: actual acquittal (the best result, but never granted); apparent acquittal (occasionally granted, but allows the possibility of rearrest and retrial); and protraction (where the case lasts indefinitely).

In frustration that his case is not being resolved, K. meets with Huld for the purposes of dismissing him. At Huld's house, K. is introduced to Block, a formerly successful merchant who has lost his savings and now lives with Huld so that he can devote himself exclusively to preparing his case for trial. When K. insinuates that Huld is powerless within the court system, Huld responds by calling the merchant Block into the room and humiliating him with the news that despite the passage of five years his trial has not yet even begun, a revelation that crushes the old man.

In the penultimate scene of the novel, K. is given the task of entertaining a bank client by providing a tour of a cathedral, but when the client fails to arrive at the church, K. is left alone with an unnamed priest, who turns out to be the prison chaplain. The priest not only knows about K.'s case, but cryptically suggests that he arranged for K. to be brought to the chapel. When the priest informs K. that the trial is going badly, K. says that he trusts the priest, to which the priest responds with a parable about deception that is contained in the materials prefacing the law (the parable "Before the Law"). This parable is followed by a dialogue in which the priest and K. struggle with various interpretations that can be brought to bear on the parable.

The final chapter opens one year after the ordeal began: K. is taken from his apartment by two fat, pale men in top hats. K. understands why they have been sent, and he openly pokes fun at their appearance. They stand on either side of him as they walk him through the streets, letting K. direct their route. Three men locked together shoulder to shoulder make for an odd grouping, but when they pass a policeman, K. makes no effort to attract his attention. They arrive at a quarry, and the two men remove K.'s shirt and hold him down while passing a knife back and forth over his body, waiting for K. to grab the knife and kill himself. When K. refuses to act, one of the men sticks the knife through K.'s heart, and the book closes with the famous line: "'Like a dog!' he said; it was as if the shame of it must outlive him."

"The Problem of Our Laws"

Many of the themes played out in *The Trial* are also reflected in the short story "The Problem of Our Laws," which describes a scene where "the people" (including the narrator) are governed by secret laws entrusted to the nobility. Yet there is confusion over whether the laws exist at all. The people are waiting submissively for a day when the law will be clear and belong to everybody (not just to the nobles), but they are not sure whether this will occur. This lack of knowledge divides the people into two classes, each representing a coping mechanism. The popular tradition says that the law is a secret code hallowed over time, and that if they watch the nobles they can learn the law and one day make it accessible to all. In contrast to this view, a smaller group takes the nihilistic perspective that the "law" is whatever the nobles happen to do; they act according to whim (that is, arbitrarily) and then christen it as the "law."

Common to both views of the law is an attitude of near total submission: the people are united in the view that at present the law does not deserve to be entrusted to the people, so they take an attitude of submission toward the law. In a sense, the people are complete followers—no single person has the bravery to boldly repudiate the nobility for hiding the law (or for pretending that the law exists); however, they are all willing to follow any person who does so. The people are afraid to expose the law as groundless and repudiate the nobility because this would deprive them of their one remaining comfort and constant in life, namely that they are governed by laws, whether those laws happen to be real or imaginary.

"The Refusal"

"The Refusal," unpublished in Kafka's lifetime, is less graphic than "In the Penal Colony" and *The Trial*. It is closer to "The Problem of Our Laws" in tone and in the themes that it addresses, which include the inability of ordinary people to understand the laws by which they are governed, the vast distance separating insiders from outsiders, and the paralyzing submission of the powerless. The narrator in "The Refusal" is an unnamed "civilian" located in a small village far removed from both the frontier and the capital. In this village, the citizens are passively subservient to the lone government representative in their midst, a colonel who happens to be the chief tax collector. This man has not been elected to any post, nor is there any clue about how he was invested with power in the first place: "This colonel, then, commands the town. I don't think that he has ever produced a document entitling him to this position; very likely he does not possess such a thing." The colonel lives in a home overlooking the market square, where the citizens ritually assemble to present their requests, which (as the title indicates) are summarily refused. The colonel presides at such meetings by holding two bamboo poles, an ancient custom to imply that he supports the law and is supported by law. In front of this lowly but powerful representative from the capital, the citizens submit modest requests (such as for a tax exemption or a reduced price for timber). The colonel never addresses the citizens directly, and he grants only requests that are de minimis, always refusing the meaningful ones. Typically, he whispers into the ear of an official who announces, "The petition has been denied," which has the unexpected result of making the citizens feel relief instead of frustration: "The citizens can always count on a refusal. And now the strange fact is that without this refusal one simply can't get along." This process is not a mere formality, according to the narrator, who tells us that the people make requests in good faith only to be met with refusal every time. This arrangement is satisfactory to most of the citizens except the young people, who (according to the narrator) are foolish enough to entertain thoughts of rebellion while not being able to foresee the consequences of such action.

"The Great Wall of China"

The Great Wall of China is a longer, unpublished piece. The narrator and his community are cut off from access to the government, to the point where they do not know who is ruling the country: "We think only about the emperor. But not about the present one; or rather we would think about the present one if we knew who he was or knew anything definite about him." Operating under a lack of information, the local citizens can only speculate on why they have been ordered to build a Great Wall (which is being built in sections that now stand isolated and useless). The people, then, do not know who is ruling them nor the laws under which they are ruled, nor why they are building a Great Wall. Despite the lack of information, life is basically ordered along traditional lines. The narrator, however, recognizes that the people lack imagination and cannot govern themselves autonomously. The very thought of questioning the existing arrangement is too threatening for the narrator himself to contemplate, so he cuts off the inquiry: "To set about establishing a fundamental defect here would mean undermining not only our consciousness, but, what is far worse, our feet. And for that reason I shall not proceed any farther at this stage of my inquiries into these questions."

The similarity between this story and "The Refusal" is obvious—both stories involve citizens who are politically alienated yet who accept their subjugation and cannot entertain rebellious thoughts of setting up an alternative system. Much of the story contains parables that address the problem of distance between the rulers and the common people, who must find a way to live despite having no concept of the larger political systems. Pieces of this story were later broken down into smaller aphorisms and stories ("An Imperial Message"; "Couriers"), though it can stand on its own as an implication that our modern legal and political systems are equally befuddling as the premodern ones in ancient China.

The Castle

Kafka's last novel was unpublished in his lifetime. The plot—if one could call it that—is about a stranger named K. who shows up, perhaps uninvited, to a village. Crossing a bridge into the village, he enters the Bridge Inn, but no rooms are available so the landlord allows him to sleep on straw in a corner of the taproom. He is soon awakened by locals who inform him that the taproom—like all property in the village—is ultimately Castle property. K. wonders, "What village have I wandered into? So there is a Castle here?" When challenged for his lack of permission, K. claims that he is a land surveyor summoned by the Count and that his assistants will be arriving tomorrow. A young man in the crowd decides to call the Castle to check this story, and he reaches a steward who informs him that no land surveyor was summoned. The crowd is about to descend on K. as a common thief when the phone rings again, this time with a call from the Castle saying that the earlier phone message was a mistake, and that a surveyor may have been summoned. K. now thinks, "So the Castle has appointed him as land surveyor." With that, he falls asleep.

All of this takes place in the first couple of pages of the novel. The remainder of the story—hundreds of pages—recounts the subsequent week or so in K.'s life as he makes innumerable futile attempts to obtain recognition from the Castle. During this short time frame, K. falls in and out of romantic relationships, has endless conversations with bureaucrats, wastes time trying to get an audience with purported officials from the Castle, gets hired and then loses a job, receives ambiguous and bizarre letters praising him for work that he has not yet started, befriends outcasts, and moves through a series of tortured and complicated alliances that take him nowhere. Through the entire story, K. demands an official recognition of his role, and yet the more demands that he makes, the more he annoys everyone in the village. He never finds out if there is anyone in the Castle (which seems more like a series of run-down buildings on a hill), or whether the Castle is just an elaborate fantasy of the villagers. The novel ends in midsentence, as if there is no resolution.

"The Stoker"

"The Stoker" is an early short story that was published as a standalone piece but was also the first chapter in Kafka's first novel *Amerika* (sometimes referred to as *The Man Who Disappeared*), which was abandoned and unpublished. It culminates in a nonjudicial hearing held on board a German ship that has just docked in New York harbor. The complainant in the hearing is the Stoker, a German, who complains of harsh treatment at the hands of his superior, a Romanian; his case is pressed by the protagonist of the story, Karl Rossmann, a sixteen-year-old who has been exiled to America for impregnating an older servant woman. As the ship stands in port and the passengers disembark, Karl returns to the ship to recover an umbrella, and he takes a wrong turn on the ship, accidentally befriending the Stoker, who tells Karl of the abuse he has taken at the hands of the Romanian supervisor. After hearing the Stoker's tale, Karl leads the two of them to the ship's command center to press the case before the Captain and the other officers. The officers are sitting in a formation reminiscent of a tribunal. Karl summarizes the purpose of their visit and the Stoker's basic claim, and then the Stoker attempts to speak for himself. Unfortunately, he stutters and babbles incoherently, and grows enraged at Karl when he tries to help. The story ends in a contrived fashion when a man standing in the room turns out to be a Senator who is Karl's uncle and who whisks him away.

"The Judgment"

"The Judgment" has two characters, a father and son, who get into an argument, and it ends when the father sentences the son to death by drowning, and the son dutifully jumps off a bridge into a river. As the story begins, we learn that the son works in the family business, and that the father is a widower who lives with the son. The ostensible cause of the fight is a letter that the son intends to send to a friend in Russia who has fallen on hard times; the son seeks to inform this friend about his pending nuptials, and he feels a twinge of guilt due to the difference that fate has bestowed on the two friends. When he informs his father of the letter, his father accuses him of neglecting the friend, then implies that the friend is merely imaginary, and then tells the son that he (the father) has been writing to this friend surreptitiously and has won over this friend to the point where the friend crumples up the son's letters and reads the father's instead. The father mocks the son for getting married solely because his fiancée flipped around her dress, and then the father physically imposes himself on the son, ending his tirade with a death sentence, which the son executes, jumping over the bridge saying, "Dear parents, I have always loved you, all the same."

"Knock at the Manor Gate"

This is a surreal little story about a narrator and his sister who pass a manor on the way to a village. The sister takes some action that is never made clear: either she knocks at the door, pretends to knock at the door, or merely shakes her fist at it. Regardless, by the time the two have walked toward the nearby town, the villagers have a look of foreboding, but the narrator tells himself that his sister did not do anything that would be considered an offense under any system of justice. Nevertheless, the manor sends out some troops after them, and the narrator instructs the sister to go home and get properly dressed for whatever awaits. The troops arrive accompanied by a judge. Presently they enter the nearby structure, which turns into a prison cell, which is where the narrator finds himself, with the story ending on the question of whether he could endure any air other than prison air.

These, then, are Kafka's stories about the law. Let us put them together with his office writings, his artwork, and his own experience in the legal system. How do we make sense of this corpus as a whole? In my opinion, it is best understood as a critique of modern law. To make this claim, I now have to describe modern law in some detail, which is the subject of the next chapter.

4

Kafka's Target—Modern Law

What Is Modern Law?

Modern law, like modern science and modern medicine, is a specific manifestation of "modernity," understood as both a historical epoch and an intellectual orientation. In the broadest sense, modernity can be understood as a change in ideas and social practices brought about by rapid advances in industrialization and science from the mid-seventeenth century to the mid-twentieth century. The scientific successes of Galileo, Newton, and Leibniz were paralleled by a commitment among philosophers to apply the same rigorous method to morality, law, and governance. Philosophically speaking, this gives rise to the quest for what Stephen Toulmin has aptly characterized as a "Cosmopolis," meaning a society that is fully organized along rational principles. Looking at the matter from a more sociological viewpoint, Anthony Giddens sees modernity as a new mode of social organization emerging in Europe in the seventeenth century, based on industrialization, commodity production, wage-labor, urbanization, the rise of nation-states, and the decline of religion and tradition as foundational justifications for social institutions. Philosophically, this movement reached perhaps its most articulate philosophical justification in Immanuel Kant's famous work, "What Is Enlightenment?" which extols the use of reason to sweep away the irrationalities of tradition and religion and to finally place legal and political systems on a secure footing. The relationship between modernity and the Enlightenment is reflected in the often-used term "the Enlightenment Project" and entails the application of the scientific method to morality, law, and governance,[1] until every aspect of the social world was properly ordered. Or in more pejorative terms, to create a "gardening state" driven by an imperative of rational design.[2] There was a sense that more rationality would result in more freedom, autonomy, and security. And from Rousseau to Jefferson, there was a sense that men were born free and in possession of certain natural abilities to organize their own institutions, and that the power of such institutions sprung from the assent of those who built and ratified them.

When Kafka was trained as a lawyer, the prevailing rhetoric among German jurists was to consider law as a science and to codify this systemic knowledge into a giant rational system modeled on the natural sciences.[3] As legal historian John Merryman explains, the idea of law as a science was dominant in German legal theory:

> Legal science is primarily the creation of German legal scholars of the middle and late Nineteenth Century. . . . The concept of legal science rests on the assumption that the materials of the law (statutes, regulations, customary rules, etc.) can be seen as naturally occurring phenomena, or data, from whose study the legal scientist can discover inherent principles and relationships, just as the physical scientist discovers natural laws from the study of physical data.[4]

Modern law is supposed to be conceptually grounded in fixed principles of moral and political legitimacy, discernible by reason. The legal superstructure, as it were, sits atop morally acceptable commitments. This is similar to American law where (to simplify) the Declaration of Independence and the Constitution are built on principles of natural law and inalienable rights, which in turn provide a grounding for the legal system and for the content of law, which can be shaped by the "science of law." A given area of law—say, the law of trusts and estates—contains a particular rational structure for handling probate matters (e.g., the Illinois Probate Court System) and a particular content (e.g., the Illinois Probate Code) that reflects certain fundamental assumptions about personhood, property, and the role of government. This law has legitimacy to the extent that it reflects certain fundamental values held by the citizens who are subject to the law.

For example, so long as people believe that inheritance of private property is morally justified, it makes sense to have a probate code that sets forth a scheme for how a decedent's estate should be distributed, yet such rules make no sense in cultures that have abandoned the right of inheritance.

The idea of American law is that the legal system can be adjusted to reflect the fundamental values set forth in the Constitution, as amended from time to time. Under such an arrangement, the law would remain tethered to deep-seated and collectively held principles. Legal scholars and jurists can disagree about whether the law should reflect the original intent of the founders of the country, or alternatively, whether the Constitution is a living document that is open to interpretation or perhaps goes through minirevolutions in how we conceive of the relation between the state and the individual. In either case the underlying idea is that the law ought to reflect some set of shared fundamental values. As we shall see, there are two potential problems with this approach: (1) the law can become untethered to its foundational moral principles, and/or (2) the law can become substituted for the formerly held substantive principles, so that the law becomes the fundamental value, and justifies itself, as it were, with the deeper moral principles being ignored.

For the Europeans, who did not inherit a common law system to the same extent as England and America, the idea of a logical system took the form of a quest for a master code. In this spirit, Frederick the Great instructed his jurists to prepare a code based on pure reason, while Napoleon (one of Kafka's favorite historical figures) demanded a code that was so succinct that a peasant could read it by candlelight and become fully aware of his rights.[5]

This concept of modern law took hold on both sides of the Channel as well as both sides of the Atlantic Ocean. Modern thinkers from Bacon to Locke to Kant to Jefferson to Bentham extolled the virtues of a legal system grounded in first principles, logically arranged, and publicly available to citizens. Landmark treatises such as Blackstone's *Commentaries* (the cornerstone of early American law) contained long introductory paeans to the "science of law," attempting to provide a totalizing account of the entire legal system.[6] Legal historian Lawrence Friedman nicely captured the dominant thinking about the law during the modern period:

> Ultimately the age of reason became the age of legal codification. What society needed was a single, rational code. In it the lawmaker would set out, clearly and distinctly, principles of law flowing from human nature and the nature of life in society. Moreover, such a code would be uniform throughout the land. It can hardly be an accident that the codification movement went hand in hand with the rise of the unitary, powerful, absolutist nation-state.[7]

A formative figure in this project was Francis Bacon, who wrote at length about how the law ought to be rationally reconstructed into an ordered body of knowledge, with each subject broken down into subheadings, so that any citizen could look up a legal matter and obtain an immediate and clear answer.[8] This vision of a unified and complete body of law was articulated by Jeremy Bentham, who offered his services to codify the American common law legal system into a transparent system where both citizens and courts would have a common reference when determining the law and the legal process. Bentham, who also brought us the idea of a panopticon where prisoners could be perpetually observed, described the perfect system:

> In a system thus constructed upon this plan, a man need but open the book in order to inform himself what the aspect borne by the law bears to every imaginable act that can come within the possible sphere of human agency. . . . In the map of a law executed upon such a plan there are no *terra incognita*, no blank space: nothing is omitted, no thing unprovided for: the vast and hitherto shapeless expanse of jurisprudence is collected and condensed into a compact sphere which the eye at a moment's warning can traverse in all imaginable directions.[9]

Bentham and other thinkers of legal modernity set forth an idealized system consisting of a centralized, legitimate government with clear separation of powers, with a judicial apparatus that is administered by defined rules of procedure, guaranteeing substantive civil liberties. This goal—an encyclopedic law administered with machinelike efficiency, and growing increasingly rational—captures the spirit of the great codification projects in Kafka's day.[10] Indeed the most famous German legal philosopher in Kafka's era, Rudolf von Ihering, described the ideal of modern law as an attempt to approximate what would happen if justice itself descended from heaven with a pencil in hand to apply the law in a "mechanical routine."[11]

In common law countries such as the United Kingdom and the United States, which lacked centralized codes, lawyers still nourished a trope about the common law "working its way pure"—that is, the law undergoing a kind of Hegelian movement to higher levels of abstraction and logic, getting progressively better over time.[12] And this viewpoint continues to dominate to this day, with jurists, politicians, and laypersons extolling the virtues of our "rule of law" and the fundamental rights proclaimed and supported in our systems. In a highly acclaimed and award-winning book that contains a succinct and eloquent defense of the rule of law, Britain's former law lord, Tom Bingham, identifies the key components of a modern legal system that operates under the rule of law:

> The core of the existing principle is, I suggest, that all persons and authorities within the state, whether public or private, should be bound and entitled to the benefits of laws publicly made, take effect in the future, and publicly administered in the courts. . . . The hallmarks of a regime which flouts the rule of law are, alas all too familiar: the midnight knock at the door, the sudden disappearance, the show trial, the subjection of prisoners to genetic experiments, the confession extracted by torture, the gulag and the concentration camp.[13]

Notice how for Bingham it is an either/or situation: either one has rule of law or one has chaos.[14] This is something that Kafka will challenge by asserting that the rule of law can be lost amid the overgrowth of legal procedure.

The American way of seeing modern law was captured in a speech by President Obama:

> The Declaration of Independence, the Constitution, the Bill of Rights—these are not simply words written into aging parchment. They are the foundation of liberty and justice in this country, and a light that shines for all who seek freedom, fairness, equality, and dignity around the world. From Europe to the Pacific, we've been the nation that has shut down torture chambers and replaced tyranny with the rule of law. That is who we are. The Framers who drafted the Constitution could not have foreseen the challenges that have unfolded over the last 222 years. But our Constitution has endured through secession and civil rights, through World War and Cold War, because it provides a foundation of principles that can be applied pragmatically; it provides a compass that can help us find our way. . . . Ultimately we have held fast to the principles that have been the source of our strength and a beacon to the world.[15]

President Obama is famous for quoting civil rights leader Martin Luther King Jr. that "the arc of the moral universe is long, but it bends toward justice." This very point is echoed in a book called *The Moral Arc* by Michael Shermer, the editor of *Skeptic Magazine*, a fine publication that promotes the advancement of science and critical thinking. Shermer believes that there is an evolutionary improvement in legal thinking that parallels the advancements in the "hard sciences":

> Ever since the scientific revolution when scientists such as Bacon, Copernicus, Kepler, Galileo, Harvey, and Newton discovered that the universe is governed by natural laws and principles that can be revealed, understood, and used to make predictions and test hypotheses, thinkers in other fields during the Age of Reason and the Enlightenment sought to understand the laws and principles that govern political, economic, legal, social and moral systems, which they then used to make predictions and test hypotheses about how best we should live. Hobbes, Montesquieu, Beccaria, Locke, Bentham, Jefferson, Franklin, Paine, Kant, Quesnay, Hume and Adam Smith were all, in my reckoning, scientists who employed the best empirical and rational tools of their age . . . from which they discovered or derived such concepts as human natural rights, equal treatment under the law, individual autonomy, freedom of thought and expression, and other principles related to equality and freedom, on top of which they built a diverse, cosmopolitan worldview of Enlightenment Humanism.[16]

Likewise, Boaventura de Sousa Santos asserts that "the idea of creating a social order based on science . . . is paramount in the Eighteenth and Nineteenth Centuries."[17] However, thinkers who are optimistic about the arc of moral history tend to forget how quickly a legal system can disintegrate, or how easily one epoch can mistake its social constructions for eternal features of human nature. This is precisely the Marxist critique of modern law, namely that it enshrines the existing bourgeois system of relations as natural and derived from reason. As Engels said in parody of the emergence of modern law:

> Now for the first time appeared the light of day, the kingdom of reason: henceforth superstition, injustice, privilege, oppression, were to be superseded by eternal truth, enteral Right, equality based on Nature and the inalienable rights of man. We know today that the idealized kingdom was nothing more than the idealized kingdom of the bourgeoisie; that this eternal right found its realization in bourgeois justice; that this equality reduced itself to bourgeois equality before the law.[18]

That is, whatever the law says formally about us all being equal, the raw fact is that some of us are more equal than others.

But even Marx and Engels had a positive movement to counteract their skepticism of modern law. The Enlightenment proclamations of rights were merely an ideological reflection of the underlying inequalities built into the system of capitalism and wage-labor, and thus were just another mode of exploitation, barely an improvement over feudalism. Yet Marx and Engels clung to the notion that science (at least, "scientific socialism") can lead the way in discovering the best arrangement of the polity and the economy. This was concretized in the notion that once a revolution had occurred, and the narrow horizon of bourgeois rights had been crossed, there would emerge a world without law, or rather, beyond law, as the law would, as Lenin claimed, wither away.

Yet Kafka would have none of this. He did not follow the accepted notion of modern law as a bulwark against tyranny, nor did he see modern law as a stage toward a higher development of law. His pessimism was deeper.

Here is where Kafka will step in and claim that modern legal systems operate by a dangerous double gesture. They instill and then betray their own fundamental promises and values. Modern law is an ideological construct that dissolves when one tries to seize it: its solidity melts into air, and its clarity devolves into a series of contradictions; it will disappoint those who believe in its promise. Or to put the point differently, the condition of modernity is to stubbornly believe in the promise of modern law despite constant disappointment. Simply put, Kafka sketches a legal system that is delegitimated, bureaucratic, ambiguous, alienating, delaying, and endlessly deferring, a series of fiefdoms and blind alleys controlled by endless gatekeepers who are afraid to recognize their own insignificance. This is caused not by a lack of rules, but rather by the overabundance of rules, which is just as bad as having no rules at all; it is caused not by the lack of reason, but rather by the overabundance of a certain kind of malignant reason. We have reason, we have law, we have courts, we have procedures, and yet we still have massive injustice, alienation, and chaos.

The end result is tragicomedy: we are amused at Kafka's protagonists' stubborn insistence on their rights, but we also have a sense that the deeper they descend into the system, the more disappointed they will become. In not a single story does a character obtain any relief, solace, justice, or even a hearing before a judge. For Kafka, the modern legal system is so complex, and the division of labor so great, that no person can understand the entirety. And in any event, there is no center to the system, and its higher purposes are unknowable or perhaps even nonexistent.

In the final analysis there might as well be no law at all, since what appeared to be a highly rational apparatus is ultimately no more rational and no more just than the irrational decisions of a premodern legal system run by a priest or tribal elder. This is not what Jürgen Habermas called a "legitimacy crisis," that is, where the steering mechanisms of money and power in the "system" are divorced from the fundamental values of communicative ethics in the "lifeworld"; it is a not a "crisis" or a "disconnect," but rather a total and hopeless lapse of legitimacy. The imagined seat of power from which legitimacy might be derived (the king, the emperor, the judge, the Castle) is always an empty placeholder, since the actual power lies in the ability of agencies and functionaries to endlessly defer, delay, and mystify. So while the dominant view of the modern era saw lawlessness as the problem and modern law as the solution, Kafka argued that a pernicious kind of lawlessness could exist at the heart of modern law.

In this connection it is worth noting that roughly contemporaneous with Kafka's entry into the bureaucracy, the first German Society for Sociology was being formed, with Ferdinand Tonnies as director, Georg Simmel as a member, and Max Weber as treasurer.[19] All three men held strong misgivings about modernity, and their views give some sense of the trepidation that some Germans felt about modernity. These views were certainly in the air around the time that Kafka wrote his legal fiction and must have affected him.

Modernity was thought to betray a movement that historian Henry Maine described as moving "from status to contract," where social relations once cemented by traditional networks (the feudal system, relations within a guild) were slowly replaced by contractual relations between free men. This was decried by Marx in his diagnosis of capitalism having "put an end to all feudal, patriarchal, idyllic relations. It has pitilessly torn asunder the motley feudal ties that bound man to his 'natural superiors' and has left remaining no other bond between man and man than naked self-interest. . . . It has converted the physician, the lawyer, the priest, the poet, the man of science, into its paid wage laborers."[20] The movement from status to contract was echoed in the work of Durkheim as well, in his notion that society was increasingly characterized by "organic solidarity" based on supposedly free contracts and impersonal laws as opposed to the mechanical solidarity of earlier societies, and in Weber's notion that law was becoming inexorably formal and rational, moving away rapidly from its grounding in tradition, priests, oracles, and shared values.

In Kafka's novels, the victimized protagonist searches in vain for the Count in the Castle, for the judge in the courtroom, for the high official, for a meeting with a person who has the status to improve his situation; yet at the same time, he lacks the power to assert himself, that is, he lacks the ability to hire representatives who can solve his problems. Man is deprived of both legal status and the ability to assert his rights in a contractual setting, thereby left standing alone and facing a bureaucracy that is even more mysterious than the premodern situation. Kafka's protagonists are continually jockeying for an audience with the officials, and there is a suggestion that the rules are less important than the people who administer them. This becomes essentially a critique of the pretensions of modern society's self-image as governed by rules instead of persons.

Kafka's rough contemporary Tonnies saw the dominant feature of modernity as a shift in the social glue from the primacy of traditional authoritative relationships (so-called *Gemeinschaft*) to relationships based on voluntary choice and contracts (*Gesellschaft*), where self-interest, isolation, and alienation were paramount. In other words, each person in a modern society finds himself adrift among strangers, connected only by impersonal contracts and economic necessity, lacking in communal values that would provide a deeper connection between people.

Simmel characterized modernity as the first phase of history where "strangeness" among people became commonplace, where money took on the ultimate value in the place of both tradition and religion, and where routinized, seemingly meaningless work came to dominate daily life.

Max Weber—probably the most important thinker for Kafka because his brother was one of Kafka's law professors at a time when the two brothers were writing about similar themes—saw modernity as the working through of a Protestant ethic that was based on a theology that hard work and thrift would lead to providence in the afterlife. This attitude placed a premium on efficiency, instrumental rationality, and bureaucratization, but over time it eroded itself as untenable—the Protestant ethic having been undermined by the modern methods of logic and science, so that modern reason destroys the very glue that held people together, leaving only the law itself as a kind of substitute god, a kind of deified rulebook, creating a society of "specialists without spirit" trapped in an "iron cage" of rationalization, all running around and following procedures that seem rational but are lacking in deep connection to fundamental values.

Kafka's legal fiction is clearly on the side of these German thinkers rather than on the side of those who extolled the virtues of modern law. The collective picture emerging from these German thinkers is one of the tearing away of tradition and religion as focal points around which life revolves, and their replacement with an abstract and diffuse political and social arrangement where strangers are thrown together and united only by a common obedience to money and opportunism. The world sketched by

Tonnies, Simmel, and Weber is almost a blueprint for Kafka's novel *The Castle*, where a stranger comes into a village and spends a useless and interminable period of time futilely trying to find some point of connection with the locals and some recognition from the bureaucrats in the Castle who supposedly oversee the village.[21]

Here we must be careful not to lump Kafka's legal fiction with the negative utopias sketched by Aldous Huxley and George Orwell, who went into extreme detail on the machinery of manipulation by the powers that be. In *Brave New World* and *Nineteen Eighty-Four*, the abusive power structure is laid bare for the protagonist, the control is total, whether through narcotizing the population, genetic control, mind control, or torture—in any case, there is a clear state apparatus that is the enemy. Kafka's world is frightening for the opposite reason—there is a marked *lack* of a central authority to which one can appeal, which means that there is no enemy, just an endless series of people who are incapable of seeing beyond their appointed role in a highly rationalized yet empty regime that nobody understands. There is nothing and no one to fight against, yet one is persecuted all the same.

Capsule Summary of Kafka's Indictment

A useful way of expressing Kafka's critique of modern law is to view it as a series of indictments—a word that has double meaning, both used in the law to designate accusation of a criminal offense as well as the more broad sense of a problem or flaw. So in what follows, I will be looking at his indictments of modern law as set forth below.

Modern Law Has Come Unmoored from Normative Grounding and Is Self-Justifying.—In modern law, the underlying purposes and moral foundations of the law are lost in a haze of procedural and technical rule fetishism. The law becomes the justification for the law. A hermetic circle is formed. The members of the legal profession and the judiciary become technocrats who lose any concern with whether the law harmonizes with deeper principles of justice. The law is deified merely for its existence. There is nowhere outside the law to criticize the law, so it stands beyond criticism.

Modern Law Is Inherently Dystopian: It Creates a Permanent Class of Outsiders.—In modern law, the law is supposed to be public, clear, and accessible, so that everyone is "inside" the law. Yet Kafka points out that modern law is a solipsistic universe ruled by a few putative insiders who don't realize that they too are actually outsiders because the law and the legal apparatus are empty; they are guardians of an empty tomb. There are only outsiders who distrust and misconstrue the law, yet delude themselves into thinking that they are inside the law.

Modern Law Inverts Punishment So That It Predates the Crime.—Modern law is supposed to provide due process before an arrest, and punishment after a trial, but this becomes hideously inverted such that the presumption of guilt is dominant, and punishment is arbitrary yet inevitable.

Modern Law Fails to Accept the Ambiguity of Texts.—Modern law assumes a certain one-to-one mapping of language to the world, but in Kafka's fiction, as in the real world, texts involve interpretation all the way down, so that the ostensible clarity of law is based on a faulty concept of language. Modern law operates with a premodern and oversimplistic concept of interpretation.

Modern Law Falls Back on Laughable Rituals and Appeals to Authority.—Modern law devolves into a joke, a humorous charade that belies its sanctimonious rituals and self-congratulatory arrogance, which are an attempt to cover up its deficiencies. When a litigant finally gets to speak before some kind of tribunal, the incident is so surprising and destabilizing that the person falls apart with anxiety and chokes with speechlessness; one never gets one's day in court. The law is a cruel black comedy.

These indictments will be illustrated with references to Kafka's legal fiction as well as to recent case decisions by courts. These indictments can also be viewed in schematic form as a comparison between the promise of modern law and its abortive realization:

Ideal of Modern Law	*Reality of Modern Law*
Grounded in morals outside law	Self-grounded in existing laws
Transparent	Opaque
Plain meaning	Polyvalent and ambiguous
Power is centered	Power is decentered
Litigants move vertically	Litigants move horizontally
Solemn	Comic
Efficient	Endless delay
Humanizing	Dehumanizing
One can step *into* the legal system	No inside; only gatekeepers

Navigable	Impossible to navigate
Disputes resolved by reason	Disputes resolved by death/ exhaustion

As I have indicated already, my take is that Kafka runs aground in his legal fiction, offering no suggestions, programs, or prescriptions for reforming modern law; he seems to deny that law has evolved. Perhaps this is why Walter Benjamin said about Kafka, "He did not consider the age in which he lived as an advance over the beginnings of time."[22]

This makes his work more depressing, yet more interesting, than that of any other writer of legal fiction. He work is the polar opposite of courtroom dramas where lawyers use ingenious arguments to win cases and expose corruption. Not a single work is written from the perspective of a legal insider (such as a lawyer or judge), and for Kafka's protagonists the law remains forever inaccessible. This negativity is wedded to a persistent sense of absurdity and black humor.

He certainly hit on something dark about modern law, but he missed something light about it. As we have seen already, his own work as a lawyer and his ideas for social improvement through the existing legal system were grounded in fundamental concepts of modern law—so he certainly did not "practice what he wrote." This does not exactly make him a hypocrite because his fiction was a different activity than his professional life as a lawyer. But it does raise the question of why his fiction did not recognize that modern law, in one guise or another, would offer the way out of its own nihilism, or rather, that modern law is the only thing that can fix modern law.

PART II

Interpretation

5

Modern Law Has Come Unmoored from Its Normative Grounding

None of Kafka's protagonists make it to a hearing in front of a judge. Their hope of admission to the law is perpetually denied. In the parable "Before the Law," a man waits for admission to the law until his death, at which point he imagines that the law has radiance, but the reader has no way of knowing if the radiance is real or merely a projection of his wish for some kind of divine or transcendent grounding for the law. In "An Imperial Message" (a fragment from "The Great Wall of China"), a man imagines that the emperor has sent to him a message of great importance, but the distance is so far and the crowds are so thick that the message cannot be delivered, so the man dreams it to himself. The distance between the individual and authority—in this case, the emperor—is unbridgeable. The protagonist is cut off both spatially and normatively from any source of fundamental values, any decisive grounding for authority, as in the larger story ("The Great Wall of China"), where the workers building the wall have no idea which emperor is currently in power, so they humbly submit to whoever they think is in power. The need for authority is so great that a victim will wait interminably for the law or work themselves to death for an unknown emperor.

As I said earlier, the modern predicament is to expect and assume that one is due a hearing from the authorities and that the judge, the court, and the authorities are invested in one's situation. But as the priest tells Josef K. in *The Trial*, "The Court wants nothing from you; it receives you when you come and dismisses you when you go."[1] The law is not there to help you; it is indifferent to you.

Hui v. Castaneda is a US Supreme Court decision about penile cancer, amputation, and death.[2] The federal district court that first heard the case said that it should be studied by every law student in America to learn the meaning of the word "cruel" in the constitutional ban on "cruel and unusual punishment."[3] The Ninth Circuit Court of Appeals said that the victim had undergone a "Kafkaesque nightmare" at the hands of the government.[4] But the Supreme Court, in a curt opinion, washed the blood from the government's hands with a cheap technicality. The case is a classic illustration of Kafka's point that the law has become its own authority, such that judges become so wrapped up in the law that they forget the actual equities of the case and are indifferent to the humble subjects brought before them.

Castaneda was brought to this country illegally at the age of ten by his mother, who then died. Eventually he fell into trouble and was sent to prison, and then—this is important—he was switched to a separate facility for illegal immigrants; in all respects it was a prison as we know that term: he was locked up. By this point, Castaneda's penis was spraying urine, bleeding, and leaking pus. Since he was no longer in "prison," technically speaking, he was under the care of the doctors who were technically in the "public health system" instead of the "prison system," even though such doctors wore multiple hats and worked alongside the prison doctors, so no one could tell which doctor belongs to which system, and there was some overlap. The doctors were grossly negligent. Instead of diagnosing and treating Castaneda, the doctors gave him extra pairs of underwear and shuffled him through an endless labyrinth of negligent government doctors who misdiagnosed the cancer. This went on for years.

Upon release back into society, he went immediately to the nearest hospital and was found to have highly advanced penile cancer that should have been obvious to any doctor. His penis was amputated on Valentine's Day, but the cancer had already spread and he died shortly thereafter. His relatives sued the government under two theories: negligence under the Federal Tort Claims Act (a law that provides that a prisoner can sue for damages caused by intentional or negligent misbehavior by a federal worker such as a prison doctor, subject to draconian caps set by state law) and a separate doctrine called a "*Bivens* remedy" (named after a case called *Bivens*), which says that prisoners in custody can get a broader recovery of damages (not subject to state law caps under the Tort Claims Act) if they have suffered not merely a tort but a constitutional violation such as cruel and unusual punishment due to medical negligence. So his claim was not only that he had suffered negligence under the Tort Claims Act subject to the limits for claims in California, but also that he had suffered cruel and unusual punishment that allows recovery beyond such caps. Luckily for Castaneda's family, his case was picked up by advocacy groups such as the American Civil Liberties Union, so he had lawyers to take his case to court. He was one of the lucky ones; or so it seemed.

The trial court and the appellate court found in his favor. They reasoned that he was in government custody just like a prisoner, he was seen by doctors who were also working in the prison system, and therefore he should have the *Bivens* remedy to obtain full relief without a cap, given that his constitutional rights were violated while in custody. Things looked good. The press cited Castaneda's case as a reminder that society needs to treat everyone, even prisoners, with a modicum of civilization.

The euphoria ended when the US Supreme Court issued a ruling that the matrix of laws in this case precluded Castaneda's constitutional *Bivens* claims, and therefore Castaneda was limited to a state law negligence claim capping his damages at a pittance. In other words, he was denied full recovery.

This case is Kafkaesque not only because the victim was shuffled between doctors and facilities for years with an obvious case of penile cancer that no one would dare to diagnose, but because when the case finally came before the high court, no one mentioned the harm done to the victim.

I am now going to quote at great length from the oral argument before the Supreme Court so that the reader can see how the judges assiduously avoided addressing any of the equities in the case and focused exclusively on technicalities. I am quoting at length and verbatim so the reader can see that there was ample opportunity to talk about the tragedy that occurred, but no judge would seize on it:

MR. DOYLE (lawyer for Mr. Castenada): There are two relationships between the Westfall Act [an amendment to the FTCA, i.e., the Federal Tort Claims Act] and the Public Health Service Act. First, the Westfall Act simply applies on its face to all government employees. And this Court has held that, and so—

JUSTICE BREYER: Yes, right. They give the government employees the same kind of immunity that—a little more limited, and that's in paragraph 1. And then paragraph 2 says: Paragraph 1 doesn't apply to *Bivens* actions. It doesn't say anything about the earlier statute. It applies to a different group of people. It has all kinds of requirements, nothing involved with section 233. Okay, so what is it to do with this case? Now, what I'm thinking now from your hesitation is, it has nothing to do with the case; it's the *Carlson* thing that is the important thing. Now, you tell me why I'm wrong.

MR. DOYLE: Justice Breyer, if I could answer. This Court, in *Smith*, held that the immunity conferred by section 1 applies to all Federal employees. You have to read 1 and 2 together. I mean, you can't divorce them, because section 1 grants immunity, but subsection 2 affects it and—and helps define it by saying that—

JUSTICE BREYER: You are talking about the Westfall Act. Absolutely right. I just said: What does the act have to do with this older act?

MR. DOYLE: Well, it isn't—the older act refers to the Federal court claim that is providing exclusive remedy in this case. And the FTCA is the only remedial scheme in the case. So in other words, section 233 doesn't set forth within it different remedies that prospective plaintiffs can get against the Public Health Services. It decided to define it by referring to the FTCA. And when you go to the—

JUSTICE BREYER: Westfall—Westfall Act is not—is not the FTCA, is it?

MR. DOYLE: It is.

JUSTICE BREYER: Oh, it is the—in other words, you think—I thought the FTCA Act was an act that gives you action against the government.

MR. DOYLE: The Westfall Act is just simply an amendment to the FTCA.

JUSTICE BREYER: So it says: This act is the exclusive remedy—the FTCA is an exclusive remedy for all employees, but this provision which gives us an exception does not give you the exception, does not make it exclusive for *Bivens* actions. Okay. You go ahead. You explain it to me. I don't want to keep repeating my skepticism on this.

MR. DOYLE: Okay. Well, the first clause of section 233(a) states that the remedy against the United States provided by 1346(b) is available. And so you go to 1346(b) and Congress defined the 1346(b), I believe it's on page 5A of our appendix. It says that the remedy is subject to the entire provisions of the FTCA. So you have to look to the entire provisions of the FTCA to determine what the remedy is, because—

JUSTICE GINSBURG: What—what says "entire subject"—233(a), where does that say anything other than—I mean, it reads like it's immunity from any civil action. That's—those are the words I think that you have to overcome. It says: Plaintiff has a substitute remedy against the United States under the Federal Tort Claims Act, and the employee is immune from any civil action. And then you say, but any civil action doesn't include *Bivens* actions. And you must be saying that the later act shrinks the former act.

MR. DOYLE: The later act amended the former act; that's correct, Your Honor.

JUSTICE GINSBURG: It amended 233(a) without mentioning it?

MR. DOYLE: It did, in effect, because it's incorporated by reference through the Act. So 1346(b), the first sentence says: Subject to the provisions of chapter 171, which is the entire FTCA. And within that chapter, there's a provision entitled "exclusiveness of remedy." And that defines—and that really addresses the precise issue before the Court, whether the FTCA is the exclusive remedy here for a *Bivens* action. And it specifically says in that section that *Bivens* actions are excluded. And so if you want to find out what remedy is available to a prospective plaintiff, you have to look at how Congress defined the remedy, and it specifically defined it by limiting it under its Exclusiveness Clause to common law torts, not *Bivens* claims. But I think one of the key principles here that we have to acknowledge is that you deferred—the Court defers to Congress in policy considerations like this because presumably Congress is in a better position than the Court to—to weigh policy decisions like providing immunity to certain government employees. But the deference there is only appropriate where Congress has actually faced the issue and balanced the policy considerations. And it could not have done so in 1970, because *Bivens* hadn't been decided, *Estelle v. Gamble* hadn't been decided until 1976, which just—which established the deliberate indifference standard, and then *Carlson* wasn't decided until 1980. And when Congress, for the first time, actually looked at the issue—

JUSTICE SCALIA: Well, you say any—any other civil action that—that did not exist prior to the enactment of 233(a) would not be covered by its exclusion because Congress couldn't have known that this civil action existed, so that it only covered those causes of action that existed at the time the statute was passed?

MR. DOYLE: Only—only as the constitutional causes of action, Justice Scalia. I think—

JUSTICE SCALIA: Why? Why? I mean, if your theory is it doesn't preclude anything they didn't know about, if they didn't know about something, whether it's constitutional or not, what—what reason is there to say it's precluded?

MR. DOYLE: Well, I think that the issue here is, is that when Congress was going to—was going to abrogate a constitutional right or recognize a constitutional remedy, it has to do so in a clear way. And for example, *Webster v. Doe*, on effect, the *Latchford* case, has very similar language. It's all civil actions, and that's all in the context of whether Indians can bring an action against the State under the Eleventh Amendment. In that case, the Court held that all civil actions did not include the right to bring an action against the Eleventh Amendment, or State under the Eleventh

Amendment, because you are dealing with a constitutional issue. And in this case—I think it goes to Justice Kennedy's point—we are not saying that any cause of action, perhaps, was created after 1970 wouldn't be barred, but when you are talking about a constitutional cause of action there is a difference. And you—Congress has to at least consider the issue, balance the policy considerations, and make an informed decision in order for this Court to abrogate a constitutional right.

JUSTICE KENNEDY: And *Carlson* is your best authority for that? Even though I don't think *Carlson* is directly on point, *Carlson* is still your best authority?

MR. DOYLE: Well, *Carlson* sets forth the clear statement rule here, the explicit declaration test, and then—

JUSTICE KENNEDY: In a different context, but that—but *Carlson's* still your best authority for that proposition?

MR. DOYLE: I think *Webster v. Doe* is another example of a case where this Court would not abrogate a constitutional right based on fairly clear language that said the director of the CIA had discretion to terminate anybody. And in that case, he terminated a CIA employee because he was homosexual and he brought a variety of different constitutional causes of action. And then, you know, the Court held that to abrogate a constitutional cause of action, there has to be—there has to be a clear statement. So we don't believe there has been that clear statement, but—

JUSTICE STEVENS: I think your clear statement argument would apply even if *Carlson* had been decided before the statute was met?

MR. DOYLE: Well, that's true, Your Honor.

JUSTICE STEVENS: Okay.

MR. DOYLE: So, it's not—

CHIEF JUSTICE ROBERTS: I would have thought it wouldn't apply as strongly because they would have been saying any action at a time when they knew that particular action existed.

MR. DOYLE: It wouldn't—it wouldn't apply as—as strongly, but I—I don't think that the sequence of enactment is dispositive, I think is the point.

CHIEF JUSTICE ROBERTS: Oh, so you are saying—your response to Justice Stevens follows because you say they—unless they say a *Bivens* action is excluded, it's not?

MR. DOYLE: Or constitutional, but it has to be clear that Congress addressed the issue and considered abrogating a constitutional claim. I mean, that's what the cases are clear about. And so—

JUSTICE GINSBURG: So the Gonzalez Act is after *Bivens*?

MR. DOYLE: It is.

JUSTICE GINSBURG: But you say the same thing even though *Bivens* was before Congress and even though the Gonzalez Act doesn't have an exception for *Bivens* claims, you read one into the Gonzalez Act?

MR. DOYLE: Your Honor, I—I would say the Gonzalez Act also wouldn't bar *Bivens* claims, because it wasn't just the sequence of enactment—but I mean, if it was—but if it had shown in some way that Congress considered the constitutional issue, and the legislative history of the Gonzalez Act shows that it did not at that time, there was some indication in the—in the language of the statute or anywhere that a constitutional—

JUSTICE SCALIA: Legislative history will do the job, so you are abandoning the—the proposition that there has to be a clear statement by Congress?

MR. DOYLE: No, Your Honor. And if I—if I meant to imply, I misspoke.

JUSTICE SCALIA: That's what you said. I thought you said if—if it was clear from the legislative history that Congress considered *Bivens* actions and nonetheless enacted language similar to 233(a), that wouldn't be enough.

MR. DOYLE: It—it—I think that in the statute, in the—in the text of the statute itself, there has to be some evidence from Congress that it considered it. I think that you can look at other factors to try to figure out what—what Congress was thinking, of course. However, in this case, I think the point is clear that whether you look at the legislative history, whether you look at the alternative remedial scheme—[5]

Ok, it continues like this interminably, so let's take a step back. All of these judges know that a man was sent to a prison and then shuffled to a government detention center; that he had obvious penile cancer and should have been sent to an oncologist; and that his penis was amputated as a result of metastatic cancer because of *government* negligence while in custody of the *government*. The government killed him, and he was held without medical attention in a manner that was cruel and unusual—dying slowly from penile cancer while the authorizes stood idle. A simple question arises: does the fact that he was moved—by the government itself—from a prison to a detention center somehow prevent suing the government?

There ought to be some clear answer to this, right?

Wrong.

The "law" is a maze of statutes so thick that not even the Supreme Court can figure it out, but when it does gather its wits, it holds that the family cannot sue for what any person on the street would see as cruel and unusual punishment. To reach this result, the Supreme Court has tied itself into knots—it exercises a *kind* of reason—it has a particular logic, it conforms to conventions of language and argument, but something essential is missing. What we see in these passages is rationality—of a particular kind. It is purely instrumental and brackets any moral, social, or empathetic responses; it treats the law itself as the source of morality, never questioning the law itself. And so, bloodlessly, without compassion or empathy, they destroyed Castaneda even after his death. And he was the lucky one in a thousand who had a team of lawyers on his behalf and got his day in court.

Did the Supreme Court apply "the law"? Well, the lower courts were looking at the same cases and laws, and they certainly found that "the law" was different. They found that the government was at fault and should pay for the full damage it caused, whether or not the victim was in one government building or another. The lower courts looked at the justice of the case, the extreme negligence of the doctors, the sheer victimhood and humiliation of the victim, and the senselessness of it all, and they found a simple route to recovery for the victim.

The *Castaneda* case is unusual for its gruesome facts, but it is not unusual as an example of how modern law sucks the blood, the meaning, the empathy, and the justice out of every case. Judges and lawyers become technocrats who anchor their decisions in other decisions, which are anchored in other decisions, to infinity, so that they become so far removed from any normative grounding that the moral foundation falls out.

This is precisely the theme of Kafka's story "The New Advocate," and we should begin with that story because Kafka himself obviously thought it highly important. He chose it to be the first story in the anthology *The Country Doctor*, putting it ahead of "Before the Law" and "An Imperial Message," two stories that are often hailed by scholars as his greatest short parables.[6] When the publisher sent Kafka a revised sequence of stories for the volume, Kafka wrote back that there was a mistake because "the book must begin with 'The New Advocate.'"[7]

And yet scholars have for the most part ignored this story. Max Brod does not mention this story in his biography of Kafka; Frederick Karl writes about it for only a paragraph in his massive biography *Representative Man*; Nicholas Murray does not mention it in his well-regarded book on Kafka; Ernst Pawel does not discuss it in *The Nightmare of Reason*; Walter Sokel does not mention it in his highly praised book on Kafka's treatment of myth and power; and even Heinz Politzer, who wrote an entire book on the uniqueness of Kafka's parables (*Parable and Paradox*), devotes only a single sentence to it. The secondary literature has also been very quiet on this story.

I think there is tacit agreement that "The New Advocate" is not one of Kafka's more interesting parables. Once Kafka introduces the meme of Alexander the Great's horse becoming a lawyer, it seems to simply unfold downhill, without the characteristic Kafkaesque complexity, and since the bar authorities accept Bucephalus as a lawyer, there is no dramatic tension and no dialectic of interpersonal relationships. The language of the story is not particularly memorable, and the theme of dehumanization (man as animal, animal as man) is more deeply developed in many other Kafka stories. Why, then, did Kafka esteem the story so highly? Did he simply have bad self-judgment, or is there some hidden importance to the story that critics have missed?

I take the latter view. I think that the story is in fact important because it is really about law and modernity. Note the phrase, "*modern society* being what it is, Bucephalus is in a difficult position."[8] In other words, there is something about modernity that converts a daring horse into a domesticated animal sitting in a law library. At one point in the story, Kafka writes, "Of course, if you know his story, you are aware of something."[9] But what is his story?

According to Plutarch, the horse Bucephalus was brought to Alexander's father, Philip, but no one could tame it.[10] Alexander was merely a boy at the time, but he boasted that he could tame the horse, and to everyone's surprise, he did so and kept the horse, naming it Bucephalus ("ox-head"), due to its large head. The horse led Alexander beyond Macedonia to Central Asia, helping to make Alexander one of the greatest conquerors of all time. It was said that the horse eventually died of old age and received a massive funeral led by Alexander, who named a city after him.

The idea for this parable probably came from a mosaic of an Alexandrian battle on the wall at one of Kafka's schools. Years later in his notebook, Kafka writes, "Death is in front of us, rather as on the schoolroom wall there is a reproduction of Alexander's Battle. The thing is to darken, or even indeed to blot out, the picture in this one life of ours through our actions."[11]

This seems to suggest an admiration for Alexander, who mastered death through action. Nietzsche too was an admirer of Alexander, calling him "Dionysus incarnate," meaning that he could creatively build new life-affirming values.[12] Taking arms against fate is contrasted with persons who simply succumb to fatigue and stand immobilized, as Kafka later muses on a different course that Alexander could have taken:

> It could be imagined that Alexander the Great, in spite of his youthful triumphs in warfare, in spite of the superb army he built up, in spite

> of the energies he felt in himself that were directed to transforming the world, might have halted at the Hellespont [the waterway separating Greece from Persia, which Alexander eventually crossed on his way to conquering Persia] and not crossed it, and this not from fear, not from irresolution, not from weakness of will, but from the force of gravity.[13]

But Alexander did not halt—he went on. And that is what separates him from people like Kafka, who saw himself as a paralyzed bureaucrat and in a letter to his fiancée said that he often did not know whether he would have the mental fortitude to open the door to his apartment after climbing the stairs.

Beneath the humor is a critique of modernity, namely that we have lost the romance, danger, daring, and destructive power of the explorer/conqueror who has the capacity to think beyond the present system and create another system. The implication, of course, is that a person can become a member of the bar only by narrowing her vision.[14]

In other words, Kafka intended to show how the heroic greatness of former times has been transformed into mild-mannered conformity, how the conqueror has become a tame bureaucrat who adapts to the law instead of creating it. The story has a parallel in Max Weber's claim that today, "even the modern high-ranking officer fights battles from the office," adding, "The modern mass army, too, is a bureaucratic army, and the officer is a special type of official, *distinct from the knight, the chieftain, or the Homeric hero.*"[15] Here again, modernity reduces the gods to petty tasks. Just as Alfred Weber described a bureaucrat as a "climber" who gives up his soul for "the opportunity to climb his way up the apparatus,"[16] Kafka depicts a domesticated lawyer who "mounts the marble steps" of the law courts.[17]

In some versions of the Bucephalus story, it is reported that Alexander was able to tame the horse because he sensed that the horse wanted to submit, but only to a noble person. Thus in one version, we learn that "he became very manageable and obedient, yielding a ready *submission* to his master in everything. He would kneel upon his forelegs at Alexander's command, in order that he might mount him more easily."[18]

Kafka seems to be saying that figures like Alexander the Great had a certain "will to power" in the Nietzschean sense of taking responsibility for creating values and establishing a unique moral and political vision, whereas figures like Bucephalus are submissive, content to be organizational men who work within a framework created by others, and they think in an instrumental fashion. The message of this fable is reminiscent of Max

Weber's claim that the modern era suffers from "disenchantment," namely the loss of the magical/religious/substantive in favor of rational calculation and formal procedure.

A similar disenchantment can be found in Kafka's modernist renderings of Greek myths, such as his story "Poseidon." In the classic version of the Greek myth, Poseidon lives in an underwater palace, commands a golden chariot pulled by white horses with golden manes, and has the power to create and quell storms, to dry up rivers, to vex and punish; he effectively rules one-third of the universe, with Zeus ruling above and Hades ruling below. The myths surrounding Poseidon are full of magic and mysticism. Kafka's "Poseidon" gives us a beaten and powerless bureaucrat who sits at a desk going over figures, trying to keep track of assistants, and putting in requests for a change of job.

Unlike Nietzsche's (or Marx's), Kafka's critique of modernity does not point toward any sort of solution. Kafka's notebooks contain an admission that his work is negating without having the critical movement point to some imminent higher stage of political or social development: "The slight amount of the positive, and also of the extreme negative, which capsizes into the positive, are something of which I have had no hereditary share."[19] Here Kafka distinguishes himself from those critics of modernity who retain the modern insistence that there is some unique method of overcoming the dark side of modernity, whether through a Marxist revolution, or Lenin's vow to break up the bureaucracy, or the appearance of an Overman, or a charismatic leader, or even through some system of reform within the democratic tradition.

Kafka lacks this positive movement, as we can see in the passage known nowadays as "Couriers":

> They were offered the choice between becoming kings or the couriers of kings. The way children would, they all wanted to be couriers. Therefore there are only couriers who hurry about the world, shouting to each other—since there are no kings—messages that have become meaningless. They would like to put an end to this miserable life of theirs but they dare not because of their oaths of service.[20]

Here we have specialists without spirit, working in a narrow calling, who find themselves lost in a pantomime, powerless to create their own values, that is, to become kings. They persist, in words aptly used by Roberto Unger to describe certain law professors, "like a priesthood that had lost their faith and kept their jobs."[21]

In "The New Advocate," Kafka seems to be saying that if one wants to get the approval of the bar, one has to repress the ability to think for oneself, to create rules, to ask large questions, and instead become a page-turner who submits to the law. This is what the Supreme Court did in the *Castaneda* case. Modern lawyers and judges are like Bucephalus—domesticated.

The connection with Nietzsche here is particularly strong, and while Kafka did not often cite Nietzsche, I must agree with Kafka scholar Stanley Corngold that the spirit of Nietzsche hangs over Kafka's work even though we only have two concrete pieces of evidence. The first is Brod's description of the night that he met Kafka, where Brod gave a lecture denouncing Nietzsche, to which Kafka strongly objected. Second, we know that Kafka wooed a girl once by reading to her from Nietzsche's *Thus Spake Zarathustra*.[22]

Two Nietzschean themes run through all of Kafka's work: first, that God is dead (here, "God" is read in the broad sense of an established truth or foundation upon which the law can be grounded), and second, that humans are paralyzed by their inability to create new, fallible, tentative gods and values. Kafka was constantly writing about animals, and we must remember that Nietzsche refers to modern man as a "herd animal" that follows a "herd animal morality."[23] Under the spirit of modern submission, "the *lamb*, even more the *sheep*, gains in respect."[24]

The notion that modern law is self-grounding is a theme in the work of Max Weber and likely reached Kafka through his contact with Alfred Weber, who was Kafka's law school examiner and a friend of Max Brod. In 1910, when Kafka was a young lawyer, Alfred Weber published an article in the literary magazine *Der neue Rundschau,* which Kafka was known to read on a regular basis.[25] The title of the article was *Der Beamte,* variously translated as "The Civil Servant" or "The Official" or "The Functionary"—a word that Kafka once used to describe himself to his fiancée, Felice Bauer. Written at a time when Alfred Weber was very close intellectually to his brother Max,[26] the article borrows liberally from Max's earlier work *The Protestant Ethic and the Spirit of Capitalism,* with its trenchant portrait of modern man as a petty bureaucrat stuck in an iron cage of instrumental rationality. In this essay, Alfred cites Max's book and echoes a number of its essential themes, the central one being that the modern age is characterized by a loss of religious and traditional buttresses for institutions and practices. This is the result of Protestantism cutting off its own religious foundations. Originally, Protestantism was driven by the notion that each individual should pursue a "calling," whereby people prove their worthiness for the afterlife by spending their time on earth engaged in thrift, sobriety, and industrious activity, with an emphasis on logic, science, and calculability. They were businessmen, pragmatists, scientists, and empiricists who demanded rationality and order in all corners of life—political, economic, legal, medical, educational. This was to serve the greater glory of God and to earn a place in his good graces, but somewhere along the line, the movement destroyed itself. Eventually, the process of rationalization becomes an end in itself. Lawyers and judges become divorced from the fundamental principles that are supposed to hold the legal apparatus in check.

The future, says Weber, will be an ever-growing bureaucratic apparatus of narrow-minded "specialists without vision," a "polar night" of hyper-rationalization and a "shell of bondage," where we are caught in an "iron cage" of rationalization and bureaucratization in support of values that we no longer support.[27] Absent some imminent religious or cultural revival, rationalization is a driving force of its own power, no longer needing any justification other than itself. In fact, the exact moment of disaster for modern culture is when we abandon all hope of justifying the institutions around us and we adopt a fatalistic and pragmatic attitude: "Where the fulfillment of the calling cannot directly be related to the highest spiritual and cultural values, or when, on the other hand, it need not be felt simply as economic compulsion, the individual generally abandons the attempt to justify it at all."[28] At that point the individual no longer understands why she is working, what she is working toward, or how she would measure the value and meaning of her work. This is a description of a highly rationalized world of alienated people, but it resonates with anyone who has ever stood in line at a government agency and asked why certain paperwork was necessary, only to be told, "Those are the rules." At this point, rationality becomes rationality for its own sake, without purpose, toward no end.

The very rationality demanded by Protestantism undid itself, so to speak, finding that its own religious foundations were unbelievable. When this happened, we were left with social institutions divorced from any underlying normative commitments, such that they become freestanding in the sense of no longer being supported by (or measured against) external forces such as religion or tradition, but rather in circular fashion by the belief in the efficacy and legality of the procedures themselves. That is, the law becomes its own grounding. The question "Why?" does not go below the law to some fundamental value (freedom, security, natural rights, reason) but stays at the surface of the law in the form of "Law X is justified by Law Y which is Justified by Law Z, which is referenced by Law X," in a closed circle.

This circle befuddles all of Kafka's characters. They bounce between various supposed authorities but never get to the source of legitimacy. The higher purposes of the process drop out and the procedures are self-legitimating, or as Weber says, "Today the most common form of legitimacy is the belief in legality, the compliance with enactments which are *formally* correct."[29] This reduces justification to necessity: that is, the moral force of the law is the mere fact of its existence. Morality is reduced to power. And power is deified, godlike, since it is the only form of authority left to worship. This is why in the novel *The Trial*, Josef K. is told by a *priest* that in the parable "Before the Law" the doorkeeper is beyond human judgment because to doubt the doorkeeper is to doubt the law itself, which is impermissible: "It is not necessary to accept everything as *true*, one must only accept it as *necessary*."[30] In other words, legitimacy is no longer something that the law has to earn. And this, of course, takes us back to Kafka's messengers in the parable "Couriers," who slavishly obey their commitment to the dead kings even though the normative basis of their obligation no longer exists.

What does this mean for modern law? Quite simply it means that in a modern legal system the measure of a particular law or institution is not whether it harmonizes with a religious, traditional, or normative precept, but rather whether it was enacted in conformity with preestablished, formal procedures; similarly, court decisions increasingly turn not on the merits or substance of a case, but rather on arcane technical minutiae concerning procedures, standings, burdens of proof, and so forth. Justice—in the sense of conformity with some principle higher than the legal system itself—drops out of the picture, leaving only one standard by which a law can be judged—whether it was enacted legally. Modernity strips the moral grounding for the law, leaving the edifice of law and its legal institutions intact but hollow, as if the legal system splits off from its foundation and assumes its own teleology. What remains is a directionless superstructure of courtrooms, procedures, officialdom, and law books that is increasingly untethered to any substantive notion of justice and that posits itself as its own summum bonum.

Modern law, then, is unique in world-historical terms because of the degree to which it forms its own rationalized system that becomes autonomous from the pressures of religion, tradition, or charismatic leadership. The future, says Weber, will be an ever-growing bureaucratic apparatus of narrow-minded "specialists without vision"[31] who work on circumscribed tasks in a kind of empty role-playing "stripped of religious and ethical meaning."[32]

Weber was pessimistic about whether there was a way to stem this progression of hyperrationality, though he ominously (in retrospect) held out hope that a charismatic leader could push back against the bureaucratic apparatus in the name of the greater social good. Kafka was equally pessimistic: "There is hope. But not for us," he told his friend Max Brod.

Law is a strange social practice because while it is supposed to be anchored to some normative values, it is nevertheless quite easy for a lawyer to practice day to day without having a normative thought enter into his head. A lawyer may be an expert in, say, trusts and estates, and he may be a wonderful lawyer who can work the system on behalf of clients, all while disbelieving or even ignoring the fundamental tenets of probate law, namely the normative claim that persons have a natural right to unlimited property, that inheritance is justified, that the right to dispose of property can endure beyond physical life, and so forth. Or he may just simply not think about it. It is possible to be a specialist and to live one's life, and to take care of oneself and one's family, to function at the sociological average, all while bracketing the question of whether there are fundamental values driving the law. As Stanley Fish argues, the law *exists*, and that is enough; to ask a lawyer "why?" is often as pointless as asking a carpenter why he is using a hammer.[33]

Kafka reminds us that the bureaucrat is every bit as dangerous as the autocrat. Those who are merely following orders, delivering messages, or guarding the law are part of a system that can be ruthless. In this he was prescient; when the Nazi hunters finally located the evil genius of the Holocaust (Adolf Eichmann) and brought the supposed monster to Israel for the world to see, he proclaimed, "I merely sat at my desk and did my work."[34] The notion that rationality could lead to such irrationality was surely why Herbert Marcuse said that modernity "alters the relation between the rational and the irrational."[35]

So there is a trade-off inherent in modern law. We have cast aside the premodern irrationalities of unwritten and haphazard legal systems inspired by religious texts and administered by chieftains and elders, and in their place we have installed a rational, predictable, machinelike apparatus. Yet, the legal system has become so rationalized that all reasoning becomes immanent within it, such that the system becomes unfettered from its normative anchors and begins to appear pointless, arbitrary, and alien, while at the same time it also becomes deified because, after all, it is the sole remaining stand-in for the missing religious and traditional sources of value. Paradoxically, modern legal systems become so unknowable and impossible to navigate that their inner workings appear to modern persons to be as mysterious as the secret world of priests and shamans. Even to those inside the system such as lawyers and judges, there are whole areas of law that appear incomprehensible (for example, tax law, employee benefits law, and administrative law come to mind), and the system begins to look formally rational but substantively irrational: an "irrationality of rationality."[36]

And yet no matter how irrational the law is, there is always an aura of respectability surrounding it. This circular reasoning is captured in a speech given by radical lawyer William Kuntsler, who defended the Freedom Riders, the Chicago Seven, and the American Indian Movement:

> The terrible myth of organized society is that everything done through the established system is "legal." And that word has a powerful psychological impact. It makes people believe that there is an order to life and an order to a system, and that a person who goes through this order and is convicted has gotten all that is due to him, and therefore a society can turn its conscience off and look to other things and other times. And that is the terrible thing about these past trials, that they have the aura of legitimacy, this aura of legality. I suspect that better men than the world has known, and more of them, have gone to their deaths through a legal system than through all the illegalities in the history of man.[37]

This view is echoed by "people's historian" Howard Zinn:

> The modern era, replacing the arbitrary rule of men with the impersonal rule of law, has not brought any fundamental change in the facts of unequal wealth and power. What was done before—exploiting the poor, sending the young to war, and putting troublesome people in dungeons—is still done, except that this no longer seems to be the arbitrary action of the feudal lord or the king; it now has the appearance of neutral, impersonal law. The law appears impersonal. It is written on paper, and who can trace it back to what men? And because it has the look of neutrality, its injustices are made legitimate. It was not easy to hold onto the "divine right" of kings—everyone could see that kings and queens were human beings. A code of law is more easily deified than a flesh-and-blood ruler.[38]

Thus modern law is unmoored and untraceable to any normative foundation, but remains deified and respected for its bare existence.

To say that the law lacks a normative foundation is another way of saying that it has no center, and this is precisely how Hélène Cixous reads the parable "Before the Law." Why, she asks, does the doorkeeper deny entry to the man who seeks the law—what secret is the doorkeeper protecting? What is he really guarding? She thinks, and I agree, that the point of "Before the Law" is that there is no substance to be protected, or rather, that what we call "the law" is nothing other than the futile engagement with doorkeepers. We expect to get past the gates of the law and find a treasure chest of "law," but in reality the "law" is nothing more than this standoff with a lowly doorkeeper, this dialectic of force and counterforce between puppets who don't realize that one is seeking nothing and the other is guarding nothing: "The secret of the law is that it has no material inside it. The law especially defends its own secret, which is that it does not exist. It exists but only through its name. The entire force of the law consists in producing this scene so that it be respected."[39] This is the "law" as people find it: not the fundamental justice and rights enshrined in the Constitution, but a series of endless delays and doorkeepers who are hiding behind empty symbols. There is no "law for all of us" in the sense of clear rules; there is only an individual gate for each individual at which she must wait, and that is why, in the parable, the doorkeeper tells the man that the door was made only for him. To paraphrase Tolstoy, each of us is unhappy with the law in our own way, and yet, like the man from the country, we continue to wait, we continue to demand legitimacy and our day in court, even though the people whom we are petitioning are afraid to look at the people further inside the system, so they too are outside the law. In the end, we are undone by our belief in the law; like the man from the country, we stake our lives on it, to our peril.

This happens again in *The Castle*, where K. never reaches the authorities. Indeed, no one in the village ever has a meeting with the Count or ever gets to the interior of the Castle itself. This raises the interesting possibility that the Castle is empty. Could it be that the whole village is functioning day to day with the mistaken belief that there is a Castle when in fact there is none? In the novel, K. functions as an outsider/trickster who exposes the groundlessness of the system by demanding that the Castle authorities give an account of its structure and its legitimacy, that it recognize K. one way or another as an insider or an outsider to the village. K. never gets his answer, meaning that a person who demands rationality, who requires a clear answer, a meeting with authority—such a person will be disappointed. The legal system is empty at its core. There is no there, there. There is no transcendental signified to give it meaning. The belief in the Castle and the Count is what holds the villagers together, but when they press the issue they get nowhere; for example, the messenger Barnabas's father sits on the road to the Castle all day because his daughter refused the sexual advances of a Castle official and made the entire family outcasts in the village, yet he never gets a ride into the Castle to make amends. K. meets bumbling secretaries and agents of the Castle, even some who hint that they can help him, but no one does anything, and every road to the Castle leads in circles. Kafka seems to be saying that *this*—this shuffling—*is* all that there is. There is no engagement with the law or the authorities.

Once again this comes up in "The Problem of Our Laws," where the townspeople cannot decide whether there is any law at all or whether "the law" is simply an officious designation that the nobility gives to whatever it decides to do. In any event, one is subject to the nobility regardless of whether the nobility cloaks their power in the form of law. In this sense, the belief in the law is perhaps a mass delusion, but a necessary one nonetheless. As Frederick Karl reads the essay, "Whether meaningful or not, the law is all we have. Should we repudiate what gives us direction, even if the direction is not what we want? The illusion is important, not because one believes in the illusion, *but because one must believe in the belief*. The Kafka paradox is part of what makes Kafka Kafkaesque."[40] The modern predicament is to need, to require, to demand justification for the law, only to discover that the law no longer provides it. This is in keeping with Kant's demand that the Enlightenment requires that all social practices and institutions prove their justification in the light of reason, that is, that they can be traced to some moral foundation. But modern law provides only necessity, not justification. Its existence *is* its justification.

6

Modern Law Is Inherently Dystopian

Kafka's legal fiction adopts a perspective sometimes referred to as *third person limited*, meaning that the reader can understand the thoughts of the protagonist but not the thoughts of others. This heightens the sense of estrangement because we are within the mind of the central figure as his search for law comes up empty. He finds no justice, no day in court, no chance to encounter his accusers—in other words, no legal system worthy of the name. We follow his search for justice, and we feel his disappointments as they happen, in real time, as it were, with a creeping sense that things are getting increasingly worse without knowing precisely why. This is the perspective of an outsider—not because of the protagonist's gender, sexuality, ethnicity, race, or national origin—but rather because of his structural position in the hierarchy (or what seems to be a hierarchy) of authority. The struggle to get inside the law is most visible in "Before The Law," but always present in the other legal fiction. The protagonist assumes that there is an inside to the system, but the reader is always left in doubt.

To say that there is no "inside" to the legal system is to say that Kafka's characters always skirt the outside of what they think is the legal system, or rather, at the edge of what passes for officialdom. They come into contact with professed agents of the legal system—lawyers, doorkeepers, priests, warders, agents, court painters, and various officials—but never with the legal system itself. Kafka's point, of course, is that the legal system is nothing other than this encounter with officialdom. In *The Trial*, for example, Josef K.'s arresting officers, his lawyer, the court priest, and the court painter all profess to be agents of the court, yet despite encountering all these people, Josef K. never gets his day in court before an authorized judge, nor is there any proof that these people are truly connected to the court; when he returns to the attic courtroom in which he was interrogated, he finds that the examining magistrate's book is full of pornographic sketches. Similarly, Josef K.'s lawyer has another client, Block, who is reduced to living at the lawyer's house, and who is informed by the lawyer, cruelly, that despite the passage of years, his case has not even begun. Similarly, in "Before the Law," the man from the country sits next to a doorkeeper, yet this doorkeeper admits that he is the outermost in a series of doorkeepers, and he cannot bear to look at a more interior doorkeeper. In *The Castle*, K. spends much of the novel trying to get an audience with Klamm, the local official, even to the point of having an affair with his former mistress, yet it turns out that Klamm simply sleeps at his desk and does little if anything up at the Castle that purportedly runs the village. K. even hides outside Klamm's office in the village in an effort to surprise him en route to his carriage, yet it turns out that Klamm is hiding from K. as well. At one point in "The Refusal," the narrator reflects on the official (or seeming authority figure) to whom questions are posed: "Behind him is nothingness, one imagines hearing voices whispering in the background, but this is probably a delusion; after all, he represents the end of all things, at least for us."[1] Here again we see a point of connection with Nietzsche, who said that churches are merely empty tombs of a dead God, surrounded by alleged guardians and warders who believe in the illusion.

The customary way of looking at the law is as a vertical hierarchy—that is, one starts a case at the trial court, moves up to an appellate court, and then to a supreme court, making slow but steady progress toward resolution of the matter. At each stage, one gets closer to the inner core of power, until one reaches the dead center of the system. But for Kafka, characters do not move vertically, they move horizontally. He presents us with a paradox: a system where no one is on the inside, a system consisting solely of outsiders, some of whom wrongly view themselves as putative insiders. To see this point, consider "Before the Law." What is the status of the doorkeeper? Is he an insider or an outsider to the law? What about Josef K.'s lawyer in *The Trial*? They are guardians of the law, perhaps, but Josef K. dies without ever seeing the law and without ever knowing the status of his case. This is a truly nightmare scenario, a system where people disrespect others' rights, lie, enable, impose arbitrary restrictions, and even have the power to punish, delay, and execute—all in service of a system that has no inside.

Kafka's ability to depict legal outsiders was the result of two factors.

First, he was a multiple outsider in his personal life, since he was a German-educated, secular Jew in a Czech province of the Austro-Hungarian Empire. Kafka never qualified as truly German, Czech, or Jewish, and he remained forever an outsider to all three cultures. Second, he was an attorney for the state agency responsible for administering the workers' compensation scheme in Prague, a position where he represented injured Czech workers seeking protection under a complicated legal system conducted in German legalese, relegating the workers to a position of economic and linguistic subordination. Given Kafka's personal and professional life, it comes as no surprise that he produced an amazing body of stories that depict chronically alienated outsiders.[2]

None of Kafka's outsiders are members of a minority ethnic or gender group, but instead are outsiders by virtue of their positionality (their subordination) in relation to the dominant legal apparatus. Such people can be described as "situational outsiders" because they are outsiders by virtue of their situation, apart from whether they are also outsiders for other reasons. And in a macabre twist on the literary cliché of the crusading outsider who struggles until her rights are vindicated, Kafka depicts outsiders who never win their battle for justice, instead remaining forever confused, paranoid, ignorant, submissive, alienated, and self-defeating.

For Deleuze and Guattari, Kafka's outsider status is the key to his literature. By writing in a way that mirrored the dry and formal German of the bureaucracy in which he worked, Kafka exaggerated this language to the point of absurdity, creating a subversive "minor" literature in opposition to the "major" literary world of German arts and letters.[3] Kafka is effectively saying that if you (Germans) want to treat people as bureaucratic numbers and abstractions, than that is how I will write, and you will see a world denuded of color or emotion. Rather than a flowery world of literary device, I will give you name, rank, and serial number with no higher meaning.

Kafka's work also reflects the shifting political landscape of his day, since his stories always involve tenuous political systems that are constantly threatened with disintegration, leaving the citizens in exile and diaspora. During Kafka's formative years, his hometown of Prague was in the Kingdom of Bohemia in the Austro-Hungarian Empire, but the Czechs refused to acknowledge the legitimacy of the empire, and they bristled at the Germans who held the important posts in Prague. The central government in Vienna abolished the Kingdom of Bohemia in 1913, and in the years following World War I, the Republic of Czechoslovakia was created. Jews like Kafka were caught in the middle of a fight between Czech nationalists (who disliked the Jews) and the Germans (who also disliked, but tolerated, the educated Jews). Although Kafka was not overtly religious, he was unquestionably a person of Jewish identity, and he was clearly caught in the matrix of anti-Semitism among the Czechs and Germans. On several occasions, Kafka watched as the capital in Vienna sent troops to Prague to quell anti-Semitic riots spurred by Czech nationalists, once complaining to his Czech translator and love interest Milena Jesenská that staying in Prague was tantamount to acting like a cockroach that refuses to be driven from the bathroom. In his private communications, then, he saw his political situation as tantamount to being depersonalized.

Kafka's fiction is distinguished by its focus on situations instead of characters, and his characters are thinly sketched to avoid references to race, religion, class, and sometimes gender as well (although most of his characters are male). Perhaps this explains why the noted poet and critic W. H. Auden said, "Sometimes in real life one meets a character and thinks, 'This man comes straight out of Shakespeare or Dickens,' but nobody ever met a Kafka character. On the other hand, one can have experiences which one recognizes as Kafkaesque, while one would never call an experience of one's own Dickensian or Shakespearian."[4]

What does it mean to be a legal outsider? First and most fundamentally, the outsider lacks knowledge of the law. She is typically ignorant of both the substance of the law and the procedural process to which she will be subjected. This theme runs through nearly all of Kafka's stories. In *The Trial*, Josef K. is ignorant of the charges leveled against him, and he is informed that nobody understands the court structure; in "The Problem of Our Laws," the narrator can only speculate whether there is a legal system at all; and in "Before the Law," the protagonist waits at the entrance of the law until he dies.

Second, the outsider cannot distinguish law from brute force, living like a colonized person subject to imperial rule. This is demonstrated in "In the Penal Colony" and "Knock at the Manor Gate," which tell the story of makeshift judges who punish victims without informing them of the charges, and where the victim sees the law as brute force imposed despotically, not as a system of rules with legitimacy. This may seem like an extreme way to look at the law, but it is common among outsiders. Consider how Eldridge Cleaver, the former Black Panther, described the attitude of black prisoners during the turbulent 1960s: "One thing that the judges, policemen, and administrators of prisons seem never to have understood, and for which they certainly do not make any allowances, is that Negro convicts, basically, rather than see themselves as criminals and perpetrators of misdeeds, look upon themselves as prisoners of war, the victims of a vicious dog-eat-dog social system that is so heinous as to cancel out their own malefactions."[5] The outsider feels like a prisoner in his own country, adopting the nihilistic belief that the law is always drafted in favor of elites and interpreted in their favor.

A third remarkable feature of outsider status is self-contempt and numb submission to authority. This is counterintuitive. After all, we expect an outsider to harbor righteous indignation against the legal apparatus that has ensnared him. Yet Kafka's characters accept their fate as natural and inevitable: they have become adroit at "lumping it."[6] This phenomenon reaches degree zero in "The Problem of Our Laws," where the common people have no knowledge and no access to the law, yet they tolerate this depressing state of affairs because it is the one constant thing in their lives, so they dare not upset it with revolutionary action.[7] At one point the narrator says that the people do not hate their leaders for keeping the laws secret, but instead hate themselves for not being worthy of receiving the law. In "The Great Wall of China," the narrator depicts a political system in which the people don't even know who is running the country or whether the rulers have been duly appointed, yet he ends by suggesting that critical thoughts are dangerous since they are likely to undercut one's security. The same attitude surfaces in "The Refusal," where the citizens are relieved when their requests are routinely denied by the petty official who runs the town without being able to justify his position.

The nihilistic attitude of submission reaches an apex in those stories where the central character is an outsider who believes that there is no one on the inside, that the legal system is nothing more than concentric circles of outsiders surrounding an empty core, where life is a shuffling among doorkeepers who purport to represent the inside but who are not insiders themselves. The theme of a seeming insider who is really an outsider recurs in many of Kafka's stories, from the doorkeeper in "Before the Law" who guards the outermost gate of the law but is afraid to look at the inner doorkeepers, to the stalling lawyer Huld in *The Trial* who rarely leaves his bed, to the messengers in "Couriers" who carry messages from dead kings. Perhaps Kafka was painfully aware that he was a doorkeeper of sorts in his professional life—a bureaucrat standing between the injured workers and the possibility of remedy for their industrial accidents.[8]

Finally, there is a linguistic component to outsider status. The outsider not only lacks a forum for articulating his grievances, but also lacks the proper language to present his claim. This is evident in "The Refusal," where the townspeople never have a direct conversation with the official who runs the town, and in "The Stoker," where the plaintiff stammers when given the opportunity to speak (in "The Refusal" we find a similar petitioner who is overcome while trying to request relief from the colonel, even though he can be assured that his request will be denied). And of course, Kafka was painfully aware of the relationship between language and power, since he represented Czech-speaking workers who found themselves caught in a system where German was the official language.

While there is a longstanding tendency among mainstream legal theorists to privilege the insider perspective, there is a more recent tendency in academic circles (including legal studies) to valorize the outsider perspective as morally and epistemically superior while dismissing the insider perspective as a distorted rationalization. The outsider is often depicted romantically as a person of integrity and uniqueness who refuses to engage in the empty rituals of mass society and who understands social practices better than the participants precisely because of her disengagement. For example, the best-selling scholarly book on outsiders is probably Colin Wilson's *The Outsider*, which examines "outsiders" such as Nietzsche, Van Gogh, Camus, and Sartre, all of whom were talented, literate, and accomplished in their field.[9]

Kafka's fiction, however, presents a less flattering, but perhaps more accurate, view of the outsider. For Kafka, the outsider is confused and alienated. She understands what it is like to be crushed under the wheels of an unfathomable legal system, but she typically has very little constructive criticism to offer for the very reason that she does not understand the internal workings of the system that is crushing her. Kafka makes a bold move by refusing to ennoble the outsider perspective. Outsider status is not a guarantee of critical insight. In stories such as "The Refusal" and "The Problem of Our Laws," Kafka depicts narrators that are so far removed from the political/legal system that they are not sure whether there is any law at all, so they have nothing substantive to say about the internal workings of the law.

One wonders if it might be possible for there to be a system that consists solely of outsiders, without anybody on the inside, as it were? Such a frightening prospect might occur if each person was responsible for only a part of the whole and could not survey the entirety. This would be Hanna Pitkin's characterization of contemporary society: "No one takes responsibility for the whole; no one is in charge. Even those individuals still aware of personal choices construe them only in terms of their particular situation and interests. The large-scale, collective consequences of individual decisions and mass apathy thus confront everyone as an external force."[10]

This Kafkaesque possibility was played out recently in the science fiction movie *The Cube*, where seven strangers find themselves stranded in a giant iron cube, with a square portal in each wall looking out (up, down, sideways) into an endless chain of similar cubes. With no idea why they were brought there, or who was responsible, the strangers try to find a way out of the giant structure. As events unfold, we learn that one of the strangers worked on a part of the external structure, yet to the shock of the others, he is unable to give any advice on which direction they should be going since he was responsible for only a tiny portion of the whole. It turns out that each of them was involved in the creation of the cube, but only in a small capacity, with no sense of the whole. The end result is a giant monstrosity for which no single person is responsible, as each person only performed a small task. Thus nobody can say *why* it exists, that is, whether it is a government project, a military installation, a private corporate setup, or some other facility.

The Cube, like Kafka's tales from the outsider perspective, reminds us that a nightmare scenario develops when the insiders are permanently cut off from the outsiders. One of the fundamental tenets of modern law is that we are all insiders if we want to be. That is, the law is knowable, and we can all participate in the democratic process. As Aristotle said in *The Politics*, justice in a democracy requires that the citizens both rule and be ruled in turn, that they exchange roles as lawgivers and subjects of the law. Kafka seems to be saying that modern law fails in this aspiration.

Kafka stands utterly alone among writers in his depiction of the law from the perspective of alienated outsiders. Even Camus's alienated figure of Meursault in *The Stranger* gets his day in court after committing a senseless murder. Dickens brings us inside the Chancery Court in *Bleak House*, to expose the incompetency and obstinate rigidity that keep the probate case alive. But Kafka never takes us inside a courtroom, always refusing to provide a behind-the-scenes look at a trial, and never portrays a judge as a main character.

Kafka also stands in stunning contrast to fiction by other lawyers, especially popular lawyer-novelists such as Scott Turow and John Grisham, who tend to include the perspective of at least one character who understands the law and can maneuver his or her way through the legal system—usually a protagonist who is a crusading attorney or law student. Indeed, this is precisely why these authors are so popular, namely because they make the law knowable to readers who are outside the law and foster the illusion that anyone can get past the gatekeeper and see the inside of the legal machinery. They provide a glimpse of what goes on behind the scenes in the real workings of the law. Consider how Turow begins two books about law:

> This is a lawyer's story, the kind attorneys like to hear and tell. About a case. About a client. His name was Robert Feaver. . . . Last night two Special Agents of the Internal Revenue Service's Criminal Division had visited him at home. They had handed him a grand jury subpoena for all of his partnership's financial records and tried to ask Robert questions about his income tax returns. They knew. They knew what Robert and his law partner, Morton Dinnerstein, had been up to.[11]

> From the elevated walnut bench a dozen feet above the lawyers' bench, I bang the gavel and call the last case of the morning for oral argument. "People versus John Harnason," I say, "fifteen minutes each side." . . . The work of the appellate court in its simplest terms is to make sure that the person appealing got a fair trial. Our docket reflects justice in the American style, divided evenly between the rich . . . and the poor. . . . The issue today is well-defined: Did the State offer enough evidence to justify the jury's murder verdict against Harnason?[12]

Turow is a great writer and an insightful social critic, but in the fictional legal world that he has created, the characters have full names, the plot is framed as a "lawyer's story," and the issues are clearly stated—all of which masterfully brings the reader into a world that they did not know. Similarly, in John Grisham's *The Partner*, the defendant is an attorney charged with commission of a white-collar crime, in a trial held in a public courtroom. Grisham is also a great writer who creates ingenious plots. Turow and Grisham have a mass audience because they are demystifyers—they offer the possibility of pulling back the curtain and showing us the inner workings of the system; that is their talent, and it is to their credit. But how different all of this seems from Kafka's *The Trial*, which begins with the arrest of Josef K. on mysterious charges and ends with his execution by an unknown authority: "Someone must have slandered Josef K., for one morning, without having done anything truly wrong, he was arrested. . . . What sort of men were they? What were they talking about? What office did they represent?"[13] By the end of the novel, Josef K. is no closer to understanding the law, and his lawyer has proven completely useless. Kafka blocks the idea of access to the legal inside, often suggesting that there is no inside at all, only a series of doorkeepers guarding an empty house. Furthermore, Kafka's world is populated with people who are denied any voice in the political and legal system, but who internalize their subjugation to the point where they expect and even enjoy the denial of their demands for justice. The end result is a negative utopia, a nightmarish world where each person fears that she might be violating some unknowable law, creating a paradoxical condition where people cannot know the law but constantly fear that they have violated it. For Kafka, this is how the legal system appears to those who are caught up in it. Such characters have only an inchoate and vague sense of their own exploitation, and they seem doomed by an inability to challenge the system in which they are caught up, a state of mind that Kafka illustrates in the final act of *The Trial*, where the central character leads his executioners to the place where he will be slaughtered, too resigned to even run away or call a policeman.

Kafka must have felt that the outsider perspective was the key to understanding modern law, but, again, it is a system of outsiders without anyone on the inside. So what holds it together—how can a social practice be based on something that is empty?

Actually this happens all the time. As long as people believe that there is a center, then it will hold, much in the same way that currency holds its value despite consisting (physically, that is) of bits of colored paper held together by the belief that such paper has value. This runs contrary to the dominant view of modern law as having a hard center—judges, courtrooms, rules of law, due process, adequate counsel, an opportunity to defend oneself, and so forth.

Put this picture together and you get the following: a bureaucratic system that is unanchored in moral principles, that exists for its own sake, that is unnavigable even by those inside the system, that cannot be counted upon to prevent injustice or violence, and that is riddled by ambiguity. This is the legal system that Kafka depicted at a time when very few people were willing to take this view and where the safe stance was to extol the promise of modern law.

If Kafka had a progenitor in this view, it was, strangely enough, Alexis de Tocqueville, who asserted that America had assiduously destroyed the old European notion of aristocratic rule but had replaced it with an aristocracy of lawyers and judges: "If I were asked where I place the American aristocracy, I should reply without hesitation that it is not among the rich, who are united by no common tie, but that it occupies the judicial bar and bench."[14] He said that lawyers have a taste for formality and a contempt of the multitudes who would assert their power through popular action instead of in the formal, established, conceptual confines of current law. And in an eerie foreshadowing of Kafka, Tocqueville pointed out that the judicial apparatus maintains its power by an illusion of sorts, by holding a sort of privileged position in the minds of the public: "They are masters of a science which is necessary but not very generally known. . . . They are all powerful as long as the people respect the law, but they would be impotent against popular neglect or contempt of the law."[15]

This is very similar to David Hume's question of how "the few" can command obedience of "the many" who are much more powerful. Part of the answer lies in the ability of legal insiders to convince outsiders that there is an "inside" where the law functions as it is supposed to function, and the concomitant desire of the masses to hold this belief, even if the story is a lie. Kafka knew that modern people could not stomach the idea that the law is nothing other than the dysfunction and misery that we encounter when our number is called. Or as Hume puts it, that the law was held up by nothing other than what he called "opinion"—a truth that he said was too dangerous to teach children. Here is Hume:

> Nothing appears more surprising to those, who consider human affairs with a philosophical eye, than the easiness with which the many are governed by the few; and the implicit submission, with which men resign their own sentiments and passions to those of their rulers. When we enquire by what means this wonder is effected, we shall find, that, as force is always on the side of the governed, the governors have nothing to support them but opinion. It is therefore, on opinion only that government is founded; and this maxim extends to the most despotic and most military governments, as well as to the most free and most popular. The soldan of Egypt, or the emperor of Rome, might drive his harmless subjects, like brute beasts, against their sentiments and inclination: But he must, at least, have led his *mamalukes,* or *praetorian bands,* like men, by their opinion.[16]

The situation is exactly that described by Kafka in "The Problem of Our Laws," where the nobility rule the people by telling them that there is a sacred code of law that must remain unrevealed. Here is Kafka, sounding a lot like Hume:

> Actually one can express the problem only in a sort of paradox: Any party which would repudiate, not only all belief in the laws, but in the nobility as well, would have the whole people behind it; yet no such party can come into existence, for nobody would dare to repudiate the nobility. We live on this razor edge. A writer once summed up the matter in this way: The sole visible and indubitable law that is im-

posed upon us is the nobility, and must we ourselves deprive ourselves of that one law?[17]

In other words, we are a hairbreadth from anarchy, which can be triggered by any person who has the courage or knowledge to point out that the emperor has no clothes. But this does not happen. Dissenters are silenced, and no one wants the responsibility of designing a new system. This is why, for example, it is easier to watch a royal wedding in enthralled rapture than to stand on the side like social critic Christopher Hitchens and point out that a hereditary monarchy is as nonsensical as a hereditary doctor or mathematician. We prefer the illusion to the reality, and however much we harbor secret doubts about the illusion, the illusion is more stable and more real than any other "reality" that we see.

This reaches a kind artistic apex in the novel *The Castle*, which, I am convinced, is Kafka's most important and also most difficult work. The Castle turns out to be nothing majestic, just an ordinary set of buildings, and the Count is absent. Just as Hume thought it would be too dangerous to let the common people know that governmental legitimacy rests on mere opinion and blind submission, K. inquires about the Castle in front of schoolchildren, asking whether the schoolteacher has ever met the Count, or whether the people in the Castle are any different from the villagers, and the schoolteacher admonishes him not to say such things in the presence of innocent children!

According to Deleuze and Guattari, Kafka's central message about law is that it is merely an "exterior armature": "K will realize that even if the law remains unrecognizable, this is not because it is hidden by its transcendence, but simply because it is always denuded of any interiority: it is always in the office next door, or behind the door, on to infinity."[18] Here we touch base with the deconstructive notion of infinite semiology, endless deferral, and the absence of a transcendental referent.

There are literary parables of unreachable rules that have an affinity with Kafka's legal fiction. For example, in the novel *Catch-22*, the "catch" is that any person who asks to be removed from serving in the war is thereby deemed sane enough to fight in it, but this rule is nowhere to be found except as a kind of specter that haunts the soldiers. Since everyone acts as if it exists, the reality of its existence drops out, as it were. As the narrator says: "Catch-22 did not exist, he was positive of that, but it made no difference. What did matter was that everyone thought it existed, and that was much worse, for there was no object or text to ridicule or refute, to accuse, criticize, attack, amend, hate, revile, spit at, rip to shreds, trample upon or burn up."[19] Matt Taibbi described a similar situation after the breakup of the Soviet Union, a feeling that he finds in current America: "One thing I noticed about that dysfunctional wreck of a lunatic country was that it had two sets of laws, one written and one unwritten. The written laws were meaningless, unless you violated one of the unwritten laws, at which point they [the written ones] became all important."[20] This means that insiders can use the law as an instrument of exclusion, whenever they want.

Kafka's focus on outsiders is important because this country at least has a very long history of outsiders who were able to bring about legal change—from the American Revolution to the struggles for recognition by African Americans and women. A system that is not responsive to outsider perspectives will stagnate; the dialectic between the system and its "other" will grind to a halt. The system needs the other, the outside, as a check on the inside.

The question is whether Kafka holds out this possibility for dialogue between outsiders and insiders. Certainly his internal plot lines do not hold out this hope, but perhaps his entire corpus is itself a plea for the outsider perspective. Kafka may have known that the outside perspective holds value only when it is engaged with the inside, not when it is cut off completely, and in this sense his work is a harbinger of the dangerous trajectory of modern law toward a strict dichotomy of insiders and outsiders. A pure outsider has nothing meaningful to offer by way of critiquing the internal perspective, as Kafka shows, other than a vague jealousy of the insiders and an inchoate confusion, a longing for inclusion, and a sense of inferiority and sarcasm. Many of Kafka's characters who engage with the law are totally outside: Josef K. in *The Trial*, the old man in "Before the Law," the narrator in "The Problem of Our Laws." These characters are a parallel to the clueless animals and insects who inhabit Kafka's nonlegal fiction—the dog who cannot figure out how food is created, the ape who struggles to become a man, and the salesman who turns into an insect. Kafka's characters find no way to negotiate the insider and outsider perspectives, and that is truly nihilistic.

7

Modern Law Inverts Punishment So That It Predates the Crime

The legal systems depicted by Kafka have done away with the presumption of innocence. In the story "In the Penal Colony," the officer who administers the penalty and considers himself judge, jury, and executioner of the colony, tells the foreign explorer, "My guiding principle is this: Guilt is never to be doubted."[1] Similarly, in *The Trial*, Josef K. is informed that the court is attracted to guilt even if the person has not done anything demonstrably wrong. And in "Knock on the Manor Gate," the protagonist is imprisoned for an alleged impropriety (not a crime but an impropriety) committed by his sister, so his only "guilt" is by association.

In *Through the Looking Glass*, the second part of *Alice's Adventures in Wonderland*, the Mad Hatter is jailed prior to committing a crime. The Queen explains:

> "He's in prison now, being punished, and the trial doesn't even begin till next Wednesday: and of course the crime comes last of all."
>
> "Suppose he never commits the crime?" said Alice.
>
> "That would be all the better, wouldn't it?" the Queen said.
>
> "Were you ever punished?" said the Queen.
>
> "Only for faults," said Alice. "I HAD done the things I was punished for. That makes all the difference."
>
> "Yes, but if you HADN'T done them," the Queen said, "that would have been better still; better, better, and better."[2]

A more current fictional motif for this policy can be found in the science fiction story "Minority Report," by Philip K. Dick, where the police have a precrime unit that ostensibly predicts who will commit a crime in the future, thereby enabling the police to act preemptively and send the future criminal to a detainment camp. The predictions are based on the mental prognostications of three "precogs" (unique humans who have been trained to use the part of the brain that predicts the future) connected to computers, and when two of the three computers agree that a person is going to commit a future crime, it becomes the "majority report," which assigns criminal status. The founder's explanation to his assistant is remarkably similar to the logic of Lewis Carroll:

> "You've probably grasped the basic legalistic drawback to precrime methodology. We're taking in individuals who have broken no law."
>
> "But they surely will," [the assistant] affirmed with conviction.
>
> "Happily they don't—because we get them first, before they can commit an act of violence. So the commission of the crime itself is absolute metaphysics. We claim they're culpable. They, on the other hand, eternally claim they're innocent. And, in a sense, they *are* innocent. . . . In our society we have no major crimes, but we do have a detention camp full of would-be criminals."[3]

This leaves open whether crime has been eradicated due to the system's correct identification of would-be criminals or whether the mere presence of the system and the threat of arbitrary punishment is what drives the citizens to be law-abiding.

The big question is whether modern law has truly brought an end to arbitrary punishment and detainment. Those who have faith in modern law often point out the advancement created by the Magna Carta, which forbids detainment without a finding of guilt, a sentiment that found its best expression in the US Constitution, which provides due process protection and a right to jury trial prior to punishment. The "presumption of innocence" was supposed to do away with punishment prior to the offense, and the danger of wrongful arrest was considered so poisonous that Blackstone even said that it would be better if ten guilty persons were let free than for one innocent person to be found guilty.[4] In reality, however, it doesn't always work that way.

For Kafka, the presumption of innocence is a chimera. The real presumption is *guilt*. This is a highly controversial viewpoint, but it has some interesting backing among public defenders who spend all day defending the accused in the legal system. On a website run anonymously by a Connecticut public defender known only as "Gideon" (after the famous 1963

Supreme Court decision in *Gideon v. Wainwright*, requiring states to provide counsel to accused persons who cannot afford a lawyer), he vents his true feelings on the nearly impossible burdens facing an accused person:

> It's all a lie. A big, bold-faced, wool over your eyes lie. The presumption of innocence is dead, at least in practice. The real presumption, if you must, is that of guilt. From the absurdly low standard of probable cause needed to arrest a citizen, to the pitifully slanted pre-trial proceedings, to the trial itself, the presumption weighs heavily against all those who have been charged with a crime. The presumption of innocence exists in name only; a lofty ideal that we can thump our chests about and shout from rooftops. Look at this fine example of how just we are as a society. The real truth, hidden in the backrooms of courthouses and in the ugly, dirty trenches of everyday warfare is quite different. Every morning, the defendant and the defense lawyer face a nearly insurmountable task: overcome the fact that almost everyone but you thinks your client is guilty.[5]

This throws clients into an impossible situation where their assertion of innocence is taken as a sign of guilt. Jacques Derrida found this out when he went to Prague to do some research on Kafka and was detained on suspicion of bringing illegal drugs into the country, only to be released; when he told his attorney that he was obviously innocent because the police never produced any evidence of the alleged drugs, he was told that that is a standard excuse made by guilty people. This is almost an exact replica of the arrest scene in *The Trial*, where Josef K. tells his warders that he is innocent of any wrongdoing, and the warders respond that he cannot be sure of his innocence if he has no idea of the law under which he is (or will be) charged. Apropos of "Minority Report"—and note the irony of the word "minority"—the Chicago police are now using a computer algorithm designed at the Illinois Institute of Technology to identify persons likely to commit a crime in the future—and then arrange for such people to be interviewed by the police in order to prevent the crime that is coming in the future. According to the *New York Times*: "In this city's urgent push to rein in gun and gang violence, the Police Department is keeping a list. Derived from a computer algorithm that assigns scores based on arrests, shootings, affiliations with gang members and other variables, the list aims to predict who is most likely to be shot soon or to shoot someone. . . . They are warning those highest on the list that they are under intense scrutiny."[6] The city refuses to disclose the variables that make up the algorithm, such that no one can figure out whether they are on the list or what actions would tend to put them on it. This violates the basic tenet of jurisprudence that punishment follows an adjudication of fault; in this case, merely having one's name churned out by a secret algorithm is a basis for a visit by the police.

The most prevalent form of punishment without fault, in America at least, is pretrial detainment. According to US Department of Justice statistics, roughly 60 percent of the 700,000 Americans in jail are simply awaiting their day in court—detained but not found guilty or innocent.[7]

Many are detained and delayed for so many years that their lives are destroyed. Let's move to the Bronx in New York City, where the delays are so long that they amount to punishment even for defendants who are later found innocent. According to a federal complaint:

> The system more closely resembles punishment than due process. Each day, hundreds of people arrive at Bronx Criminal Court to wait for their day in court. Appearances are not scheduled for a particular hour or window of time, so everyone has to arrive at the beginning of the day. Arrest warrants may be issued for latecomers. People sit in packed courtrooms for hours —sometimes all day—waiting for their cases to be called. They take the entire day off of work; they miss school and doctor appointments; they rely on neighbors to watch their kids. When their case is finally called and they stand before a judge, the appearance usually lasts less than a few minutes and the case is perfunctorily adjourned for another date. Adjournment after adjournment, people wait for hours to see a judge only to be told to come back another day. The months often turn into years. For Sarah Bello, it took 1,166 days and 33 court dates, 30 of which were scheduled trial dates, before the charges against her were adjourned in contemplation of dismissal. For Joseph Bermudez, it took 1,258 days and 38 court dates before he could get his day in court, have a trial, and be acquitted. John Carridice waited 1,009 days and had 20 court dates before he finally got a trial and was acquitted. Though the cases were ultimately resolved in their favor, the damage inflicted by court delay—jobs and opportunities lost, lives disrupted, and relationships strained—had already been done.[8]

The reader must ask, How different is this from the seemingly phantasmagoric situation in "Before the Law," when a man dies while awaiting permission to enter the law?

We have already mentioned the existence of "black sites" in Chicago and other major cities, where the police bring suspects and punish them before giving them a hearing or determining if the suspect was at fault; further, the police in Chicago can stop anyone for any suspicion and write up a "contact card," putting the person in a giant database of troublemakers without actually arresting the person. In such cases, the punishment *precedes* the crime.

The same goes for widespread monitoring and data collection by the government under the auspices of the intelligence apparatus and the imprimatur of the court system—the constitutional harm predates the offense. This happened recently in Utah, when a firefighter was charged with theft of morphine from an ambulance, based solely on hypothetical speculation by the federal Drug Enforcement Agency combing through state medical records, and then determining that the man should be accused because his drug records indicate that he had once been given an opiate-based painkiller for a workplace injury and was therefore likely to be the thief. The federal government accessed his state records without a judge-ordered warrant and then accused him of the crime; he was put on the defensive and had to prove his innocence from a dozen felony counts.[9]

A more typical case, however, is when a law is fashioned after the fact to criminalize behavior, as is the case with the American base in Guantanamo, which one prominent law professor has called "a living museum of what it means to break the law by rewriting it."[10] Since the United States is party to the Geneva Convention protocols for the treatment of "prisoners of war," it would have an obligation to treat such prisoners humanely; and of course if they were brought onto American soil, they would have constitutional rights. To circumvent our own treaties, the government has brought them to a legal no-man's-land in the Caribbean where they will be tried, if at all, in an "Expeditionary Legal Complex," which is a makeshift court. The men are housed there at the cost of $3.4 million a year, originally labeled as "detainees" to get around the protections that would be owed to them as "prisoners of war"; then they were christened as "unprivileged enemy belligerents" because detention of people in this newly invented category—even in shackles and covered in their own feces—is not deemed an act of punishment. Nearly all of the men captured and sent to Guantanamo were released for lack of evidence, but a few are held on evidence that the government refuses to release, but that one defense lawyer calls "absolute bullshit," saying that "none of it would hold up in court."[11] In this manner, of the 780 original captures, some of whom have been held fifteen years without trial, President Bush released 538, President Obama released 196 as of January 2017, and the rest remain in legal limbo. As one of the defense lawyers says, "You don't pick up people and bring them to an island prison and decide you're going to figure out what to do with them later."[12] Yet this is exactly what happened in Kafka's parable "In the Penal Colony"—a place was created outside the law.

The Kafkaesque formula of "punish first and figure out later" has long been a specter haunting modern law. A central point of *The Trial* is that even in a modern legal system a person can be wrongfully accused and executed even though he "lived in a country with a legal constitution, there was universal peace, all the laws were in force," and the victim can go to his death asking, "Where was the Judge whom he had never seen? Where was the high Court, to which he had never penetrated?"[13] Although counterintuitive, this notion that a person can be persecuted for no reason despite living in a country with a modern legal system was echoed in the admission of Nuremberg prosecutor Robert Jackson, who said:

> With the law books filled with a great assortment of crimes, a prosecutor stands a fair chance of finding at least a technical violation of some act on the part of almost anyone. In such a case, it is not a question of discovering the commission of a crime and then looking for the man who has committed it; it is a question of picking the man and then searching the law books, or putting investigators to work, to pin some offense on him.[14]

Note the paradox: the specificity of modern criminal law—the "scientific" quest to catalogue and list a grand assortment of offenses—has enabled the abuse of discretion that it was designed to prevent. We created a massive assemblage of specific crimes with discrete elements that must be proven so that people would not be unjustly snared by vague accusations, but in the process we have created so many offenses that expand exponentially with the inherent vagaries of language, such that the vagueness that we sought to eliminate has crept back into the system, creating more ways that a person can be ensnared.

Kafka's point here is highly counterintuitive. We are accustomed to viewing the worst possible legal situation as lawlessness or anarchy—that is, the *absence* of legal rules—but Kafka is saying that same destabilization can take place when there is an overgrowth of rules without any inherent direction, meaning that the individual can live in a state with a full legal system and still be persecuted and crushed for no reason (as in *The Trial*) or as the result of bureaucratic bumbling, as in *The Castle*, when K. listens to a speech by the village mayor about the bloated Castle bureaucracy and responds, "It gives me some insight into the ridiculous tangle that may under certain circumstances determine a person's life."[15] The imagined seat of power (the king, the emperor, the judge, the Castle) is always an empty placeholder, since the power lies in the ability of lesser functionaries to endlessly defer, delay, and mystify. Our leaders are wrong to see lawlessness as the problem and modern law as the solution, because despite all the details of modern law, there is a pernicious lawlessness at its core. This view is dissonant to lawyers, judges, and legal scholars, and yet we know somewhere deep in our heart that Kafka is right, that for all the rhetoric about justice and equality and fairness and notice, the law does not offer the protections and processes that it promises.

The key point to Kafka's legal fiction is the inversion of the proper sequence of probable cause, arrest, defense, trial, and sentencing. Lechte correctly points out that modern law eliminates the causality which it purports to provide: "The nihilism of a society without God, the hyper-rationalization of bureaucratic domination, which strangles the innocent in its web, and the end of all idealism—including perhaps, the end of the notion of causality along with all first principles—is sketched out. Here in Kafka's *oeuvre* is an allegory of society without any particular end, but which is assuredly destined to come to an end in a *material* sense."[16] I have emphasized the word "material" here, because Kafka's point is that a case does not end in the *normative* sense with the determination of guilt or innocence, but rather with the material breakdown of the defendant prior to any such determination.

On my reading, the truly horrifying aspect of Kafka's legal fiction is not the horrific endings—the execution in *The Trial*, the impalement in "In the Penal Colony," the imprisonment in "The Knock on the Manor Gate"—but rather that there was no meaningful offense in the first place. This is especially true in "The Knock on the Manor Gate" and "In the Penal Colony," where the "crime" is simply the refusal to acknowledge the rank of a person above oneself, in the first case by shaking a fist or pretending to knock on the door of a manor, and in the second case by failing to arise every hour and salute a captain's door. The deeper implication is that society has no place for people who harbor disobedient thoughts or betray disobedience of any kind even when the crime is victimless, as in recent cases of whistleblowers who actually point out the injustice of the current political structure: they are branded as criminals for making public state secrets even when the secrets reveal reprehensible behavior by the government. The contemporary "crime" is having disobedient thoughts, reading disobedient books, visiting disobedient websites, telling the truth, and disobediently asserting one's right to assemble in public without getting pummeled by the police. It is hard to claim that one is "free" in a country that has more prisoners than any other in the world, where people are under surveillance and data monitoring, and where prisons are run for profit under agreements that they must be supplied with a certain percentage of occupancy.[17]

All of this is enabled by a kind of exception clause built into the protections offered by our modern legal systems, which allow them to give back the very rights that they provide. For example, note the last clause of Article VII of the French Declaration of the Rights of Man and Citizens: "No person shall be accused, arrested, or imprisoned except in the cases and according to the forms prescribed by law. Any one soliciting, transmitting, executing, or causing to be executed, any arbitrary order, shall be punished. *But any citizen summoned or arrested in virtue of the law shall submit without delay, as resistance constitutes an offense.*"[18] The exception buries the rule (i.e., it does not countenance that submission and endless delay are punishment in themselves), and in the course of explaining the rights of a citizen it creates a crime for refusing to submit to the law without delay. It is precisely these exceptions that end up eviscerating the point of the law, rendering modern law a serpent eating its own tail or tying itself in knots.

My analysis of "In the Penal Colony" as a critique of modern law is the exact reverse of its common interpretation as a *tribute* to modern law; it is commonly understood as a criticism of premodern forms of punishment that still exist only in remote outposts. This is far too easy a way to read the story because it relies too much on the metaphor of the explorer being spatially distant from a modern location. The key to the story is not the location but rather the disconnect between the severity of the offense and the extent of the punishment, coupled with the victim's lack of knowledge of his "offense" until it is engraved on his body, at which point he "radiates" with enlightenment. True, Kafka is saying that this method of punishment is premodern, but Kafka thinks we have not abandoned it, only placed it in a new guise; after all, *The Trial* takes place on the mainland—not on a remote outpost—and it ends with a summary execution. Kafka's point is that modern law is not a great improvement over premodern law. So in the story, the explorer is wrong to think that he can escape the colony and return to a more civilized method of punishment; indeed, he will return to only a different form of punishment, not one that is necessarily better. This is why Kafka told his publisher, "To explain this story, I can only add that not only is it painful; rather, the time in which all of us live, myself in particular, is painful."[19]

Kafka's position here is fairly close to Foucault's claim that punishment has gone through three stages: the first, where the victim is physically tortured to demonstrate the overwhelming power of the sovereign; the second, where the offense is seen as a violation of the social contract that requires removal of the offender from circulation in civil society; and the third, where the punishment is treated as a form of moral and physical reeducation, and where we now police ourselves, since punishment is internalized and self-applied in advance by the victim through a series of discourses, bodily demands, conformities, rituals, and micropunishments. For Foucault, the changes in punishment do not necessarily represent an advance, and in some ways the graphic abuses of the early forms of punishment were less harmful because they kept the interior world of the offender sacrosanct. As William Burroughs suggested, in a functioning police state there is no need for police, and indeed, in Kafka's legal fiction we rarely see any police in the strict sense.

"In the Penal Colony" also functions as a parody of the hyperrationalization of modern law, for example, the attempt to make justice efficient and machinelike. Here we are reminded of Justice William Douglas's statement, "The law is not a series of calculating machines where definitions and answers come tumbling out when the right levers are pushed."[20] In America, at least, the Fourth Amendment has always been the bulwark against the state detaining a citizen without *prior* reasonable cause; the state and its representatives are not supposed to shop around for a pretext to arrest and charge the individual. But in a recent case, the Supreme Court upheld the conviction of a man for drug possession, even though he was stopped for no reason other than that he had walked out of a house that officers were watching as a potential "drug house," and they then ran a warrant search on him, conducted a physical search, and found drugs; he was not stopped on suspicion of anything. The Fourth Amendment would normally require reasonable cause before a search and seizure, but this is not how the law works. As a dissenting judge on the Supreme Court explained, the Court has eviscerated the moral principle behind the amendment:

> This Court has allowed an officer to stop you for whatever reason he wants—so long as he can point to a pretextual justification after the fact. That justification must provide specific reasons why the officer suspected you were breaking the law, but it may factor in your ethnicity, where you live, what you were wearing, and how you behaved. The officer does not even need to know which law you might have broken so long as he can later point to any possible infraction—even one that is minor, unrelated, or ambiguous. The indignity of the stop

is not limited to an officer telling you that you look like a criminal. The officer may next ask for your "consent" to inspect your bag or purse without telling you that you can decline. Regardless of your answer, he may order you to stand "helpless, perhaps facing a wall with [your] hands raised." If the officer thinks you might be dangerous, he may then "frisk" you for weapons. This involves more than just a pat down. As onlookers pass by, the officer may "feel with sensitive fingers every portion of [your] body. A thorough search [may] be made of [your] arms and armpits, waistline and back, the groin and area about the testicles, and entire surface of the legs down to the feet." The officer's control over you does not end with the stop. If the officer chooses, he may handcuff you and take you to jail for doing nothing more than speeding, jaywalking, or "driving [your] pickup truck with [your] 3-year-old son and 5-year-old daughter without [your] seatbelt fastened." At the jail, he can fingerprint you, swab DNA from the inside of your mouth, and force you to "shower with a delousing agent" while you "lift [your] tongue, hold out [your] arms, turn around, and lift [your] genitals." Even if you are innocent, you will now join the 65 million Americans with an arrest record and experience the "civil death" of discrimination by employers, landlords, and whoever else conducts a background check.[21]

This is not some rogue accusation. It is a summary of the current state of the law from a member of the US Supreme Court, the highest authority for interpreting the law of the land. Notice: this justice is *not* complaining that such actions are tolerated as the free whim of police officers; rather, this is what courts have made of the law.

At this point, I would like to speak personally about how modern law has influenced my own life with its "punish first" mentality. After all, I was sent to jail in the fall of 2013 without committing a crime. Apparently, I was a great threat to the community.[22]

The story begins in 1997 when I was teaching at Florida State University and met a woman at the library who was getting her MBA on an exchange program from Kazakhstan. She soon returned home, and we met briefly a few times in the next years, but the long-distance relationship broke up for good in 1999. Fourteen months later she called me to say that her company (an international corporation) was sponsoring her to take the CPA exam, and she wanted to stay with me while preparing for and taking it. I found it odd when she insisted on staying with me in Florida when the CPA exam was administered in rural Maine. During her stay, we had sex and she assured me that pregnancy was not possible. Three months later I got a phone call that she had gotten pregnant "by accident." By this time, I had just started dating my current wife, to whom I am still married and with whom I have two wonderful girls. I told her that I could not marry her, since we were not even a couple and I had a new girlfriend (soon to be a wife), but I agreed that I would take a paternity test and support the child.

The law in most states begins with a presumption that the noncustodial parent (typically the father) pays 20 percent of his net income in child support and receives ample visitation with the child. This presumption can be altered where 20 percent would create a windfall to the child and his mother, or if there were unusual circumstances such as the father not having access to the child. Here, my child was born and raised in Kazakhstan by his mother, came to America only for a few weeks every other year, and never learned to speak English, nor would she allow him to stay in my home. I admitted paternity, got my son an American passport, sent him packages, and called him often (with his mother translating). She said that she needed some paperwork to assure the authorities in Kazakhstan of my parentage, so we agreed that I would supply 15 percent of my income to her, and in return I would have custody for the summer and in the winter school break. I dutifully paid her regularly, not 15 percent of my salary but enough so that my money alone placed her in the top rung of Kazakh society and exceeded her own salary as an executive of an international company.

She then found some obscure way to get a green card (the truth of which has never been revealed), moved from Kazakhstan to five miles from my home in Chicago, and immediately sued me for 20 percent of my salary in arrears and into the future. She was asking for hundreds of thousands of dollars.

The time came for the hearing on child support in Lake County, Illinois, and my attorney argued that there was fault on both sides—I had not given her the full 15 percent of my salary for the past two years (which would have amounted to well over $50,000 for one child in a third-world country), and conversely she had not given me any visitation, so it was a mutual default. It also turned out that she had come to America pretending to be broke and had me cosign for her car and apartment, and she sought help from my parents—all while having $250,000 in the bank. If there was any comparison, then certainly I had performed our agreement better than she.

The judge took out a calculator, punched in some numbers based on my tax returns, and asked me to stand up. She told the sheriff to handcuff me and escort me to the Lake County jail in Waukegan, Illinois, where I would be held indefinitely until I came up with $56,000 in cash bail, which is what the judge had just determined on her calculator as the minimum amount that I owed.

My attorney objected that this was an unconstitutional punishment for a debt that had been calculated on the spot—with no notice. Nor could the judge impose punishment on one party without considering the nonperformance by the other party. The judge responded that I was being jailed for contempt, not for a crime. She then ran—not walked—out of the courtroom.

The next day my parents arrived at the jail with $56,000 in $100 bills. This was perhaps the largest bail set in Lake County in many years, and I learned from the jail staff and prisoners that even bank robbers and attempted murderers were being given less bail. Shortly thereafter, the judge was found embroiled in controversy because, during her judicial election process, her car was found with election signs from her opponent that had been pulled off lawns around town.

And thus a lawyer of twenty-five years with a spotless record went to jail, in a suit. What did I find in jail? Other than the usual collection of accused men, I found a host of other men there for the same reason as myself. One man—an architect—had been transferred from the more dangerous Cook County jail after sheriffs burst into his office and arrested him during a meeting, taking him to jail in a suit, all over a dispute of less than $10,000, without a hearing. He had been in the prison system for ten days already with no end in sight, the only "evidence" against him being the word of his ex-wife. Later I met another man who was an executive at a leading pharmaceutical company, and he sought my advice on how to move outside of America to escape, after giving his ex-wife many millions of dollars and leaving him with nothing, as the court was attempting to "impute" income to him and threaten him with jail for not earning this imputed income. No crime, no hearing, no weighing of faults between the parties—just a judge, a calculator, and a nearby prison. I never got my day in court. I immediately settled and broke off all contact with my son and his mother at the advice of the court-appointed psychologist. I was relieved of hundreds of thousands of dollars for a son whom I never had the right to see and who grew up speaking a different language and being taught to hate me, even though I had consistently offered to raise him as part of my loving family.

Now, what are we to make of this personal story?

It is tempting to read it as showing merely that there is a difference between "law on the books" versus "law in action." But that would be to assume that the actions taken (the "law in action") were lawful. In fact, they were arbitrary and spiteful, not reasoned. And so if you ask me what was the "law" in my own situation, I would give you two answers: (1) in one sense, the law consists of the Illinois statutes on child support and the laws of civil procedure under Illinois law and the judicial circuit for Lake County, Illinois, which grants the judge discretion to determine past amounts due and to consider a host of factors in assessing what the father owes, if anything; and/or (2) the law is that a man can be jailed without notice, without being accused of a crime, without a hearing, even though he has given massive amounts of money for a child raised overseas to hate him, by a woman who did not honor her obligation to provide any meaningful visitation. The "law" is both of these; ideologically, it is the rules laid down in advance, but simultaneously, it is the indifference toward and abandonment of those rules.

What does this have to do with Kafka? Well, the difference between Kafka and those who extol the virtues of modern law is that Kafka is willing to see that the second description is not merely some perversion of the first description, but is integral to the meaning of modern law. The law falls short of its aspirations, every time. That is what modern law is.

Finally, a word must be said about a little-discussed aspect of "In the Penal Colony," namely the social practice of tattooing; after all, the criminal learns of his crime only when it is tattooed onto him. Here we must go back to the history of tattooing to recognize that it began as a kind of branding of outlaws, in both the Greek and the Judeo-Christian traditions, going back to the mark of Cain placed by God. Slaves were tattooed in ancient times, and in some cultures criminals were tattooed by the state with their offenses written on their face or bodies. This practice gradually faded, though it reemerged with the tattooing of Jews and other undesirables in the Nazi concentration camps.

But tattooing among criminals is now primarily self-administered, often prior to any punishment or sentencing. Thus singer and activist Tupac Shakur famously had the tattoo "Thug Life" on his midsection, while other gangs have elaborate tattoos that provide details into their backgrounds, affiliations, and crimes. This represents a kind of internalization of state power to classify the individual; the person stigmatizes himself as proof of his autonomy. It was Charles Manson who carved an X (later converted into a swastika) into his forehead and told the newspapers that it was a symbol of what society had done to him: "I am what you are making me. For you as a group of people have shown me no mercy. The mark on my head simulates the dead head black stamp of rejection, anti-church, falling cross, devil sign, death, terror, fear. I wanted to be a good guy but you didn't let me."[23] As crazy as Manson was, and still is, there is truth in his statement, for he was indeed the product of institutions from a young age. The truly scary aspect of the Manson "family" was not the viciousness of its crimes, but rather that a group of all-American kids could be so easily turned into murderers who x-ed themselves out of society. Tattoos are now ubiquitous, and by tattooing themselves a new generation has taken it upon themselves to find strength in administering their own banishment from society rather than letting society do it; it is a kind of "You can't fire me, I quit," approach to life.

"In the Penal Colony" works by a similar trajectory of state-sponsored to voluntary tattooing. The officer begins by demonstrating the administration of an involuntary tattoo on a prisoner, but then changes it to a self-administered tattoo. The punishment no longer comes from outside, but from inside. And rather than having broken a particular law, the officer is tattooed with "Be Just," which is more of a moral expression than a penal violation. This is where Kafka's work ties into Foucault's work on the internalization of punishment. Kafka seems to be saying that to tattoo oneself is a last grasp at having some control over the otherwise incomprehensible forces that turn a person into an outcast. Or rather, that we have tattooed our own brains, so to speak. Victims may try to tattoo themselves to convince themselves that their fate was chosen instead of being imposed.

Critics have erred for decades by assuming—along the lines of modern law—that Kafka's characters *must* be deserving of punishment for having done something wrong. This leads these critics to come up with a laundry list of possible things that the protagonists have done wrong: losing their spiritual connection to God, refusing to conform, becoming too bourgeois, or simply suffering guilt by virtue of being a human being.

This search for a reason is a blind alley because it starts from the false premise that these people have done something wrong in the first place. The search is pointless because it merely replicates the pointless search of Kafka's characters. They have no idea why they are being punished and neither do we; and there is no answer to why the punishment gets worse the more they try to fix the situation. The only thing we can say is that the characters and the readers both feel the dislocation between what we have been taught exists under the law and what really happens. In *The Trial* and in "The Knock on the Manor Gate," the protagonist comforts himself with the notion that he cannot possibly be subject to arbitrary arrest and punishment because he had done nothing that would be recognized as wrong under any lawful system. This turns out to be cold comfort because modern law does not care whether you are innocent or guilty. Kafka is saying that when your number comes up, there is nothing you can do. The system needs enemies in order to function, and it will manufacture these enemies for its own sake.

8

Modern Law Fails to Accept the Ambiguity of Texts

Kafka was trained in the Austrian Civil Code of 1811, which supplied rules for the interpretation of legal texts. Section 6 of the code said that courts should not impose any interpretation other than the plain meaning of the words; if any confusion still existed, a court must look to the intention of the legislature, then to similar cases, and then to the natural principles of right.[1] Notice that the interpretive directive is framed as a prohibition: *thou shalt not interpret the text in any other way*. The idea here is to set sufficient limits to language so that words come to an ending point where they find a referent; words hit bedrock. This view has a parallel with the logical positivist notion that each word in a sentence somehow refers to a unique and particular object or concept. This is the viewpoint underlying the modern approach to law—namely that the law is publicly proclaimed and available for inspection by all citizens, so they cannot plead ignorance of the law. This assumes a certain mapping of language onto the world.

Yet for Kakfa this process—however well-intended—leads to its opposite. The constant attempt to clarify keeps rationalizing the law until it becomes a massive wall that is insurmountable and indecipherable under the weight of the interpretations ad infinitum. Peter Goodrich is a little too careful in calling this a "paradox" of modern law, namely that we are all commanded to know the law, but legal language is structured so that it is the exclusive province of a highly trained elite.[2] To my mind, "paradox" is too mild a word; are we not talking about a "bitter contradiction"? The former dean of Stanford Law School seems more on target in asserting that this disjunction is a threat to legitimacy, as he threw up his hands in exasperation when the Treasury Department issued 110 pages of regulations to clarify the distinction between debt and equity under Section 385 of the Income Tax Code: "The legal system of a democratic society cannot operate—and that means that a democratic society cannot operate—if the law is allowed to become so elaborate that it is beyond the reach of the informed, literate citizen who would like to be law-abiding."[3] The point here is that modern law cannot fulfill its pretension of clarity, notice, and due process, because this very idea is based on an outmoded concept of language and semiotics.

The "plain meaning" requirement of the Austrian Code under which Kafka was trained is the same injunction that applies in common law countries, where lawyers have been trained to look for the "plain meaning" of a text for so long that the injunctive seems axiomatic. But recently Judge Richard Posner of the Seventh Circuit Court of Appeals, a towering figure in judicial and academic circles, said that he did not understand the term: "When interpreting a statute, you're supposed to look for 'plain meaning,' and I don't know how 'plain meaning' would differ from 'meaning.'"[4] In a recent concurring opinion, he agreed with the result reached by the majority of judges, but he was perplexed by the jargon that they used: "What does the term 'actual guilt' and 'actual innocence' mean that guilt and innocence without the adjectival 'actual' do not mean?"[5] If a leading judge and scholar cannot figure out the meaning of the terms used by lawyers and judges, then we have a situation where lawyers are trained to use language robotically without seeing how it obscures rather than illuminates.

Kafka's legal fiction does not accept the notion that words can map onto referents, and in this sense he anticipated the notion, likely attributable in theoretical form to Charles Peirce, that the meaning of a word is a representation that refers to other representations, coming to rest only from sheer exhaustion or practical necessity. This entails a kind of infinite semiosis that is the bugaboo of literalists and others who would impose strict prohibitions on the interpretation of texts, but it nicely explains why so many of Kafka's legal writings don't have any ending in the traditional sense—they are an unending sequence of signification without rest.

In Kafka's legal fiction, there are three possibilities that the main characters face when dealing with texts. One possibility is that there is no text at all, or rather, that the text of the law is merely a projection of the victim's belief or desire that there is some master text; he cannot believe that authority can rest on mere power, so he comes to believe that there must be a foundational text bestowing authority.

The second possibility is that the text exists but is unintelligible. This happens in the story "In the Penal Colony," where the officer of the colony repeatedly shows the explorer the texts of the old commander, which are illegible scratches. In *The Trial*, the examining magistrate uses a book filled with doodles and pornography, and in *The Castle*, there is always an unintelligible humming on the telephone connecting the Castle to the village.

The third possibility is that the text exists, but it cannot be finally interpreted, so the interpretation is cut short, leading to some extreme act of violence or destruction. This is most clearly illustrated in *The Trial*, in the discussion between Josef K. and the prison chaplain, where they discuss various readings of the parable "Before the Law" without reaching any conclusion other than the chaplain's morose recognition that Josef K. must accept that the law cannot be wrong and that it has legitimacy simply because it exists.

In *The Castle*, K. receives two mysterious letters from the purported Castle official who oversees the village—Klamm—both of which are unclear. The first letter recognizes his appointment as a land surveyor and instructs him to take direction from the village mayor. Accordingly, he makes an appointment with the mayor, who tells him that the letter is not an official communication even though it is from an official, and in fact the letter may be a total mistake; it may be a relic from a previous time when the villagers floated a proposal for inviting a land surveyor to solve a boundary dispute, but this letter was likely meant for another person, was sent to K. in error, and therefore is a document without effect. The mayor then explains to K. that there are so many departments in the Castle that mistakes are inevitable and that despite the language seemingly in K.'s favor, such proclamations do not grant K. any privileges. When K. inquires whether there are any "control" departments, he is told cryptically that there is nothing other than control departments. The letter has a liminal status: it *might* mean something. Or rather, it means something to K., but has no recognizable meaning because he cannot establish or find any community in which there is intersubjective agreement on its meaning.

When the letter cannot be deciphered, K. is offered a makeshift position as janitor for the local school. In short order, he receives a second letter congratulating him on his land surveying work so far and urging him to complete his work soon. This letter is unnerving to K. because of its falsity: in fact, he has not yet done any work and has no idea of his assignment, which indeed suggests the mayor may have been correct that the prior letter was a mistake. At the same time, these letters are some kind of acknowledgement of his presence and his mission, and just when the reader is about to feel sorry for K., we recall that he came to the village and the Castle without any letter of appointment and with no instruments for land surveying, so he may in effect be trying to defraud his way into the village. The text of the narrative is unclear, the text of the main character's life is unclear, and the text of the book is unclear. There is just semiosis in all directions.

Here we reach Kafka's main point, namely that meaning is intersubjectively determined according to rules of an interpretive community, such that there is no "plain meaning" to be found in the letter and no safe place to rest when interpreting legal documents and laws. The semiosis is interminable, and it stops only when those in power make it stop. The struggle for power is a struggle for language, or rather for setting the limits of language or the place where interpretations end.[6] Kafka's characters are constantly asking for a full discussion of the semiotics of a document, but they are confronted by authorities who cut off the discussion to their advantage.

The intersubjectivity of meaning is evidenced most clearly in the story "The Judgment," which lacks an omniscient narrator who knows the "truth" and shares it with the reader; there are only different viewpoints and a power struggle for recognition and authority. In the story, a young man works and lives with his aging father, who is widowed and depressed. The young man writes a letter to a friend in Russia who has experienced hard times, hesitatingly deciding to inform the friend of his engagement and imminent marriage. The young man comes into his father's room to tell his father about the letter and notices that the father is decrepit and seemingly showing traits of senility. When he informs the father of the letter, his father insists that there is no friend in Russia, and that the friendship is imaginary. The young man is befuddled and tries to comfort and relax the father, only to find the father shift tactics and tell the son that the friend does in fact exist, that he (the father) has been secretly writing the friend and informing him of the wedding, and that the father and the son's Russian friend were in league together and laughing at the son. The father then insults and mocks the son's fiancée, accuses the son of neglect, and then announces that he sentences the son to death by drowning. Immediately the son runs out of the house and jumps off a bridge and drowns. The reader is left not knowing if the son was correct (namely that the father was insane) or the father was correct (namely that the son was disgraceful). When the father refuses to acknowledge the son's reality, cutting off his dialogue, the son is undone; he lacks the independence and power to assert his own view of the situation, and the authority wins out. Authority is destabilizing because it causes one to cast doubt on one's internal reading of texts.

Much of Kafka's writing on law consists of an individual who has a preconceived notion of interpretive reciprocity yet finds herself incapable of finding a mirror, an "other" who acknowledges her position. In the context of law, Kafka's characters believe that there is a legal system that all of the actors hold in common—that it is accessible, that it is public, that it is verifiable, and so on. Yet it turns out that there is none. This is the theme of "Before the Law"—the individual assumes that the law exists and that the doorkeeper can point the way. But it turns out that even the doorkeeper is afraid of the inner doorkeepers, so there is no way to gauge the system as a whole. Similarly, in both *The Trial* and *The Castle*, the lead character assumes that he can find a direct audience with the authorities and is continually frustrated by his inability to meet them. His view of the legal system can never be mirrored; he is alone in vigorously pushing his case to the point where he is blocked by those who flatly refuse to see it the same way as he does. There is something of this failure in all of Kafka's work. His characters seek recognition from the law, and they never get it. This has a direct parallel with Kafka's own life, given that he began his *Letter to His Father* with the paradoxical beginning: "You asked me recently why I maintain that I am afraid of you. As usual, I was unable to think of any answer to your question, partly for the very reason that I am afraid of you."[7] This reminds us of the power relations at work prior to any proceeding, and the sense in which any contest is framed by the status of the parties. One cannot but speculate that this was the mix of emotions felt by Kafka when he proudly gave a volume of his writing to his father, who told him to place it on the bedside table, where it sat unread; the child's need for recognition, for a parent reflecting back the pride that he felt, hit a brick wall.

Kafka's legal fiction can be read in an even more expansive way to assert that not only texts but all relationships have this dialectic of dependence and struggle: we need the other to reflect back on us in order to form a view of ourselves, but at the same time we are victim to the view that they reflect on us. This insight—that people seek recognition and meaning from authority figures but are dependent for their self-concept on this recognition—runs through all of Kafka's fiction about the law. Indeed, most of the stories are about people who seek recognition from the law, and are either refused such recognition or else have to deal with a reflection that is humiliating or degrading.[8]

Social reality as well as psychological reality is constructed intersubjectively, which means that it is subject to contestation, disruption, subversion, and indeterminacy. This accounts for the radical loss of reality in Kafka's work, since "reality" is an intersubjective creation. When reading Kafka we are inclined to ask, "Well, what is *really* going on here? Is there something going on that the narrator or the protagonist doesn't see?" And the answer is that we don't know. We can't know. Kafka refuses to say what is *really* going on, because the only reality is the contest for who will be allowed to determine reality. For example, the narrator of the story "The Problem of Our Laws" is not sure whether there are any laws at all, or whether they are a secret kept secure by the nobles—and the reader has no way of knowing either. As we saw in "The Judgment," a young man tells his father that he has just written a friend in Russia, and the father tells him that there is no such friend—and the reader will never know the truth. In *The Castle*, we learn that Kafka's companion Frieda is pretty, then we hear another person call her old and withered—and the reader never knows which is accurate; we are led to believe that the protagonist was called to the Castle as a land surveyor, but all indications suggest that he came to the village of his own free will and may be wrongfully asserting his claim to a position in service to the Castle, but in any event we will never know—it is forever undecipherable. In *The Trial*, Josef K. never discovers whether there is a real court or a judge to whom he can appeal—and the reader does not know either.

This inability to know reality or, alternatively, the notion that there is no reality "out there" to find that does not involve our own participation, is at the heart of Kafka's work. It is what drives the protagonists of his fiction into a rage, an almost childlike obsession that he be granted some affirmation, some grounding in reason and legitimacy, some hard facts, some solution, some clear interpretations, some resolution. The characters are utterly alone, and at best they find a temporary friend or a woman to give some solace, but not a clear answer.

This struggle, which was certainly noted as early as Hegel's master-slave dialectic, was echoed in Sartre's notion that "hell is other people," meaning that we are reliant on others to establish the "truth" about ourselves, but we cannot fully control their subjective assessments of us; this creates a kind of struggle for recognition as well as domination, that is, the domination of how meaning is established. Author Jerzy Kozinski captured this struggle very concisely:

> Hell is the inability to escape from others who prove and prove again that you are as they see you. Hell is also the inability to be alone, to see yourself as your self sees you. Both convert the subjectivity of the other into a menacing object and originate the sadomasochistic struggle to impose our will upon the Other more dominantly than the Other can impose his will upon us. At stake is the retention of the dominant position. This enables one to pronounce judgment, for only the subject can judge; the object can only be chosen.[9]

Notice how this maps onto the conversation between K. and the landlady in *The Castle*:

> "What actually is it you are?"
>
> "A land surveyor."
>
> "What *is* that?'"
>
> K. explained, the explanation made her yawn.
>
> "You're not telling the truth. Why won't you tell the truth?"
>
> "You don't tell me the truth either."
>
> "I? So now you're beginning your impudent remarks again? And if I didn't tell the truth—do I have to answer for it to you? And in what way don't I tell the truth then?"
>
> "You are not only a landlady, as you pretend."
>
> "Just listen to that! All the things you discover! What else am I then?"[10]

This is useful to keep in mind when reading Kafka's fiction, because all of his stories have a fulcrum based upon the need for the protagonist to affirm his self-concept with some authority figure, who refuses to engage. That is why Josef K. spends the entire novel *The Trial* trying to find someone in authority to agree that he is innocent; it is also why K. spends the entire novel *The Castle* trying to find someone in authority to affirm that he is truly a land surveyor called to the village to perform services.

And yet perhaps Kafka's characters are not entirely blameless. They seek recognition as individuals from people who are part of a social system (law, politics, economics) that necessarily deals in large numbers and reduces everyone to a social role (defendant, land surveyor, petitioner). The demand to be treated as an individual is deeply grounded in our sense of autonomy and freedom, but it comes into conflict with the bureaucratic organization of a large state apparatus. Walter Benjamin said that Kafka was driven by "fear of the ant-colony state: how people become estranged from themselves by the forms of their communal life,"[11] but I think Milan Kundera was closer to the target when he said that Kafka's characters are caught in situations where their official file becomes more real than their actual life. No matter that a person is innocent, or wants to prove or convince others of this: if the file says that he is guilty, then he faces a presumption of guilt.[12] The formality of law reduces people to roles—it *de*-personalizes them—squeezing the particular facts of their life into the strictures of legal doctrine. The ideology of law is framed in terms of individual rights and freedoms, but the actual practice of law and modern legal systems is to treat people as exemplars, as cattle, as things, and not as persons.

These problems occur at a macro level ("Who am I?" "What is the meaning of my life, or my job?") but also at the micro level ("What does a particular word mean?"). In terms of meaning, Kafka is close to T. S. Eliot's notion that "Words strain, / Crack and sometimes break, under the burden, / Under the tension, slip, slide, perish, / Decay with imprecision, will not stay in place, / Will not stay still."[13]

This is not a mere academic point, since most recent legal controversies are about language and definitions. Consider this question: what does the word "relevant" mean in terms of the government's ability to obtain "relevant" materials about Americans from Internet service providers without a police warrant? According to the Foreign Intelligence Surveillance Court, which the *New York Times* describes chillingly as "almost a parallel Supreme Court, serving as the ultimate arbiter on surveillance issues," the word "relevant" can be broadened to include an entire database of records on millions of people. The word "relevant," therefore, includes massive data dumps of irrelevant material. Traditionally the word "relevant" requires some link between the information sought and a particular investigation that is under way; for example, if a person is suspected of terrorism, it would be "relevant" to view his telephone records, but if the person is not suspected of wrongdoing, then it would be a constitutional violation to review his phone records. Even though the new meaning of "relevant" creates a dragnet so wide that it ensnares innocent people with an unjustified search and seizure of information, the Supreme Court has struck down a challenge to such overreach brought by civil rights groups—on the grounds that they did not have "standing" to sue because they could not prove they were being spied upon, since that information was not available to them.

What does the word "trial" mean, as used in the US Constitution, which guarantees the right to a speedy "trial"? The US Supreme Court recently adumbrated the term "trial" to exclude the sentencing phase, thereby meaning that a person could sit unsentenced indefinitely and still have been given a speedy "trial." Imagine sitting in jail for years without a sentence, or possibly receiving a sentence that is shorter than the time you have already spent in jail, and being told by the court that you are receiving a *speedy* trial.

In these cases, and in Kafka's legal fiction, we see an inversion of Lewis Carroll's playful insistence by the character Humpty Dumpty that a word has whatever meaning one wishes to assign it. Kafka is saying that this is the wrong way around. A word has the meaning that those in the interpretive community assign to it, not what the individual assigns to it. To those in power, the word makes sense, even if outsiders see their interpretation as a perversion of language. For example, in *The Trial*, Josef K. is informed by telephone that he is to appear in a courtroom on a weekend, but he is not told what time to show up. Reasoning that the courts typically open at nine o'clock in the morning, he shows up at that time, only to be told that he is an hour late. It does not matter that he is not late according to the normal hours of other courts in the city, or according to local custom, or by any other measure. He is told that he is late; therefore he is late.

The power of definition is tied up with the power to end the semiotic chain, that is, to pronounce a definitive end to the conversation. The scene from Kafka's legal fiction that excites the most ambiguity is the conversation between Josef K. and the priest in the cathedral. After being told the parable "Before the Law," which is ostensibly a story that takes place before the beginning of the text of the law itself, K. reaches the initial conclusion that the doorkeeper deceived the man from the country by not telling him straightaway that entry to the law would be impossible. The priest counters this interpretation by insisting that the doorkeeper told the truth, namely that the man could not enter at this time, and there was nothing to indicate that the ban was permanent. Far from being a despicable figure, the doorman may have exceeded his strict duty as a doorkeeper by engaging the man in idle conversation and other activities not required of his post.

The priest then offers an interpretation that reverses K.'s initial stance, by claiming that perhaps the doorkeeper is the one who is deceived because his knowledge is limited to the exterior of the law and he cannot enter the law nor abandon his post, making him truly inferior in terms of knowledge and options, since at least the man from the country has the power to walk away. Based on this reading, K. then concludes that both the doorkeeper and the man were deceived. But the priest suggests that we cannot reproach the doorkeeper since he serves the law, and we cannot doubt the law. K. rightly objects to this admonition because if the doorkeeper is placed beyond the pale of doubt, we must submissively take everything that the doorkeeper says as true, even if it is not. As we have seen, the priest responds that K. needn't take what the doorkeeper says as *true*, but he must take it as *necessary*. In other words, the semiosis must stop somewhere, and here it stops with pure necessity: the doorkeeper is the authority and that ends the discussion. Yet for K. this is a depressing opinion, because it means that we must accept what the doorkeeper says even if it is not true, thereby elevating lying into a universally accepted practice. The discussion ends without resolution, but with the sense that the priest (who belongs to the court) is himself implicated in the parable as the latest in a long line of doorkeepers preventing K. from reaching the law. The dialogue ends with one party asserting its power—its necessity—and not on normative grounds. The better interpretation does not win in the real world, and the better legal argument does not win.

A truly unnerving scene of this kind unfolds in *The Castle*, when K. is assigned a messenger and two new assistants who claim to be his old assistants, yet K. has never seen them before and they have no tools or experience in land surveying. In a desperate attempt at clarity, he decides to call the Castle to request a meeting, but is told that he needs a permit from the Castle's warden, whom they call on the telephone only to be told that K. may not come up to the Castle for a meeting, "neither tomorrow nor any other time." In exasperation, K. grabs the phone and pretends to be one of his assistants: "When can my master come to the Castle?" The answer is, "Never."[14] In his left hand, he is holding a letter that seems to grant his appointment as a land surveyor, plus a letter congratulating him on his work, and on the other hand he is absolutely prohibited from visiting the very authority from which these letters are supposed to have been issued.

K. is actually a human version of unlimited semiosis, a kind of empty signifier shuffling around the inhabitants of the village in a horizontal movement, but never landing on the object that he seeks—the Castle. And yet just as "the law" may be nothing other than our own projection of desire for a stable edifice, "the Castle" may be nothing other than the desire of the villagers for something solid at the center of their lives. When K. remarks that he is unsure whether he will fit in with the Castle and may feel more comfortable among the villagers, he is told, "There's no distinction between the local people and the Castle."[15] Indeed, K. sets out to the Castle but finds that all the roads are circuitous and that the Castle is unreachable. What to make of this? It certainly seems that there is no Count and no "insiders" except a few people (such as Klamm or Sordini) who may have some connection to the Castle, but in the main, the Castle is just a figment of a stable signifier among the villagers, something that they need to believe.

This is why Kafka's novels cannot end on a point of meaning, where the protagonist learns the system and finds his place within it. Words refer to other words and concepts refer to other concepts in a massive process of intermediation, so that there is no stable meaning and therefore no possible ending. As we have seen, the American philosopher Peirce thought that unlimited semiosis was not a practical problem in the "real world," so to speak, because interpretations must come to an end for practical reasons. That is, I can think about my computer, and then the concept of computing, and the relation to the word "computation," and perhaps the Chinese term *dian nao*, which means "electronic brain," and that would lead me to think about artificial intelligence, and so forth, forever; but in the real world, I have legal work to do, I have demands, and this forces me to cut the chain of semiosis and to join a community of others who have cut the same chain in roughly the same places—in other words, I have to get back to work. This is what allows me to think about my computer without setting off an infinite chain of reference in the real world.

In a similar way, courts and authorities put a practical limit on semiosis, but this always involves cutting off some aspect of the case, and many times what gets cut off is the most important part, having to deal with human feelings, emotion, relationships, fairness, and identity. What Kafka seems to be doing in *The Trial* and *The Castle* is to play with the reader's desire—her need—for the semiosis to end at some point where the words and letters and communiqués hit some sort of moral and emotional bedrock, however temporary. This could happen if the accused person learns the charges against him, if the man from the country is granted access to the law, if the land surveyor can reach the Castle. But he is saying that this *cannot* happen in our technocratic and robotic legal system, where the words and concepts are merely twisted until they come to rest with the exhaustion or death of the victim. Kafka's message to litigants is that your case will end because at some point people will tire of your demand for meaning, and they will respond by delaying or killing you. In other words, modern systems and bureaucracies cannot give you the level of semiotic clarity that you desire (and that they promise); they can only send you spinning in circles. As Ritchie Robertson explains in his introduction to the new edition of *The Castle*, "It may be that the Castle contains no secret and has no power, except the power that the villagers bestow on it by projecting onto it their own hopes and desires."[16]

The Castle is Kafka's ultimate masterpiece about the ambiguity of texts and the anxiety of establishing any fixed meaning. The novel is frustrating and frankly brutal, yet exhilarating, because it contains so many multiple readings that there is no fixed point on anything. In fact, despite hundreds of pages of dense language, nothing is firmly established.

The ultimate question, "What is the Castle?" is never clearly answered. When K. finally spies the Castle, he sees "neither an old knight's fortress nor a magnificent new edifice, but a large complex, made up of a few two-story buildings and many lower, tightly-packed ones," akin to a "miserable little town, pieced together from village homes."[17] K. walks in circles trying to find a way to the Castle, but gets lost. He meets the schoolmaster and asks if he knows the Count, only to be told, "What makes you think I would?" and "Kindly recollect that we are in the company of innocent children."[18] K. then throws a snowball at a house, which turns out to belong to the master tanner Lasemann and contains a mysterious girl with a baby at her breast; she claims, perhaps sarcastically, to come from the Castle, but this too is never really made clear. K. is forcibly removed from the house and meets Gerstacker, a coachman, who gives K. a ride back to the inn where he is staying. At this point, K. meets his two similar looking assistants, Jerimias and Artur, who have ostensibly been sent by the Castle to assist him, yet have no tools or training in land surveying, and it later turns out that perhaps they were sent by a person with tenuous ties to the Castle solely in order to cheer up K. When K. asks them to call the Castle for instructions, they are denied.

A second question is whether K. was asked to come to the Castle. He has no equipment, no history, no proof of being called. Eventually, a uniformed messenger named Barnabas arrives with a note from a certain Klamm, a director who ostensibly has ties to the Castle but sits in a room at the inn and never speaks directly to anyone. Later it turns out that Barnabas's uniform is not official and that this is the first message that he has been asked to deliver in years, and it is probably an old note that was simply grabbed from a pile and instructed to be given from Klamm to K. So it is not clear if the note is meant for K.

K. eventually has an affair with a certain Frieda who works in the bar of the Gentleman's Inn (ostensibly for Castle officials), and she professes to be the mistress to Klamm, the author of the letter that K. received. Later in the story it is revealed that Klamm never spoke to Frieda nor had any physical or social interaction other than occasionally saying the word "Frieda"; K. would later learn that the landlady of the Bridge Inn was also a mistress to Klamm under similar circumstances. At K.'s request, Frieda allows K. to observe Klamm through a peephole, but he seems to be sleeping at his desk. After a night of sexual activity, Frieda leaves her position at the taproom in order to join up with K., announcing her decision to Klamm from the other side of a door, to which he has no reaction.

The next day, K. visits the council chairman, who explains that there is no need for a surveyor and that the entire affair is likely a mix-up caused by a confusion among different departments at the Castle. One department may have requested a surveyor at some point long ago, and it was overruled by another department, yet the two departments did not coordinate. After explaining the massive bureaucracy and how the Castle has control systems for avoiding such miscommunications, K. suggests that the Castle be contacted to straighten out the confusion, but the chairman states that the phones have been turned off. K. leaves the meeting with no resolution, but a little while later the village schoolteacher arrives with an offer from the chairman to hire K. as the school janitor while his case is settled. After initially rejecting the offer, K. moves himself and his assistants into the schoolhouse.

Meanwhile, K. goes back to confront Klamm about K.'s relationship with Frieda. He waits for Klamm outside to intercept him before getting into his coach, but Klamm never shows up. Instead, K. is brought inside, where he is told that Klamm would not leave while K. was standing in wait for him and that K. must give a deposition of the matter to Momus, one of Klamm's village secretaries. K. refuses and heads back to the school building where he is now the janitor. On the way, a message arrives via Barnabas in the form of a new letter from Klamm stating that K.'s work so far is good and that it is hoped that he will carry his work to a successful conclusion. Of course, K. has not started any work, has no tools, and has not been formally given any task or met with any officials. He also learns that Barnabas has never delivered his response letter to Klamm. At this point K. begins to sense that he is caught in a massive bureaucratic confusion that can be straightened out only if he has access to the Castle.

That night, K. returns to the schoolhouse but impulsively steals wood from the school's supply; later he is awakened by the children while still sleeping in the classroom in his underwear. During the night he had punched the assistant Artur for stealing his spot near the fire. He is summarily fired by the schoolteacher and then temporarily rehired. He meets a student named Hans, who is the son of the shoemaker Brunswick and was in the house that K. visited on his first day, when the woman with the baby at her breast claimed to be a girl from the Castle. K. shows interest in the boy and floats various schemes for meeting this woman, who (he thinks) might lead K. to the Castle. Frieda now suspects that K. is pursuing relationships only for access to the Castle.

At this point K. has no idea what to believe and no concept of who or what is at the Castle. K. decides to go to Barnabas's house to wait for Barnabas in case he has another letter from Klamm. At the house, K. meets the decrepit and beaten parents of Barnabas and his older sisters, Olga and Amalia. The sisters tell him the story of how the family came to be shunned by everyone. The father was a shoemaker who also worked as a fireman, and one day a Castle official named Sortini came down to oversee the fire department demonstration, at which time he fell in love with Amalia. Soon a messenger arrived at Amalia's window summoning her to come to Sortini's room and describing graphically the sexual acts that Sortini wanted Amalia to perform. She then tore up the letter and did not show up. Soon the family was ostracized, the father was relieved of his fireman's duties, his diplomas were confiscated, and his business faltered and was taken over by Brunswick. The father journeyed every day to the Castle but was continually denied entrance; he even took up the habit of sitting on a fence leading out of the Castle so that he could catch the eye of an official, but this was equally useless. Gradually the family's fortune faded and they were near collapse, living in poverty and as outsiders. To remedy the situation, Olga came up with the plan of having Barnabas dress up like a messenger and go to the clerks' office in the Castle, in hopes of being given a message to deliver in the village, thereby building a relationship with the Castle that might inure to the benefit of the family and bring it out of disrepute. Olga spent her nights sleeping with various Castle messengers to find the one who has a link to the dreaded Sortini so that the matter can be resolved, but she never meets him. Although the family has been destroyed by Amalia's rejection of Sortini, Olga says she is not sure whether or not Amalia loved Sortini (whom she has never met), saying that even Amalia cannot decide if she loved him.

This conversation with the Barnabas sisters takes up most of the night, and in the early morning, K.'s assistant Jeremias arrives to inform K. that Frieda is distraught at his involvement with the Barnabas family, that Frieda has left K. for Jeremias, and that Artur filed a grievance against K. Frieda resumes her old position. K. is informed by Barnabas that a certain Erlanger, a secretary of Klamm, has summoned K. for a meeting at 5 AM. Apparently the secretaries meet with the village petitioners at night to avoid seeing them in daylight.

K. arrives early for the meeting with Erlanger, and while searching for Erlanger's room, K. knocks on a door and meets a different secretary, named Brugel, who gives an interminable bureaucratic speech about Castle procedures. At one point in the speech, as K. is drifting off to sleep, Brugel says that even though a secretary cannot help a party reach a particular result of a matter with the Castle, there arises a hypothetical situation where a person accidentally enters the room of a secretary such as Brugel who might have minor jurisdiction over his case, and such a situation would make the secretary vulnerable to helping the aggrieved person, if only he would ask for such help. Brugel appears to be referencing his current meeting with K. and suggesting that he might be able to help K. if he would only ask Brugel. However, Brugel's speech has put K. to sleep, and he is awakened only by the knock of Erlanger, who is in the room next door. Just as in *The Trial,* when Josef K. misses a crucial meeting due to being distracted by the housekeeper, in *The Castle* he misses a crucial opportunity due to falling asleep.

Shortly thereafter, K. stands in the hallway and watches as clerks deliver files to each of the doors, behind which stand the secretaries who mediate between the Castle and the village. Eventually, there is one file left over; the clerk motions for K. to be silent and then tears up the file, as K. speculates that it could be K.'s file that is being torn up. The officials behind the doors soon make a racket because K. (a mere villager) is lingering in the hallway instead of going back down to the taproom. As the novel draws to a close of sorts, the coachman Gerstacker (the man who gave K. a sleigh ride at the beginning of the novel) offers K. a job, and a salary, even though K. lacks all knowledge about horses and coaches. K. speculates that Gerstacker cares about him only because of his relationship with Erlanger and the Castle officials (however tenuous and one-sided), to which Gerstacker says, "Certainly, why else would I be interested in you?"[19] K. follows Gerstacker home to a dimly lit room where Gerstacker's mother is sitting. The novel ends with this incomplete sentence: "She held out her trembling hand to K. and had him sit down beside her, she spoke with great difficulty, it was difficult to understand her, but what she said . . ."[20]

K.'s fate is to remain stuck in the village forever.

Now, what is the point of all this miscellanea? Kafka seems to be saying that a seeming pastoral arrangement of a Castle and a village, which seems to be the most easy to read "text," actually turns out to be an impenetrable and unending maze of signification. Even personal identity is up for grabs: at one point, Olga suggests that the person known as Klamm might not be the real Klamm and that her brother the messenger might not really be inside the Castle when he is getting messages; even the landlady tells K. that he is not really a land surveyor, and K. tells her that she is not really a landlady. In short, the novel is a constant doing-and-undoing, often for pages and pages without a single paragraph break.

What does all of this have to do with modern law? Quite simply, it describes the agony and indecision involved in any interpretive process, and it is this anxiety that is denied by modern law, which presumes a certain kind of mapping of words onto the world and then sets rules of interpretation to make this happen. But language and signification cannot be so constrained; they are the return of the repressed, the inherent uncertainty and messiness that underlie even the most basic legal decision.

Kafka's semiosis can be applied to Kafka's legal fiction itself, and the best example of this is Jacques Derrida's dissection of "Before the Law." Derrida asks what Kafka means by "before." Does he mean "temporally prior to the law," or "standing spatially before the law," or "conceptually prior to law, like a kind of introduction to the law"? And what "law" is at stake here—the parable does not say if it is a moral law, a religious law, a political law, or some other kind of rule. For Derrida, the ending is also enigmatic because the doorkeeper closes the door when the man from the country dies—the text closes, but it "closes on nothing." In other words, it does not close because the man (or the reader) finds the law or even gets a definitive prohibition from entry; rather, the door closes when the man dies, meaning that we sit before the story just as the man sits before the gates of the law, and the story is closed on us just as the door is closed on the man.[21] We are left wondering: what, if anything, lies at the center of the law and at the center of the story? Or is the story itself about us as readers, about how we desire a story to have some point? In fact, when the story reappears in *The Trial* as a parable told by the priest, he disclaims, "I am only showing you the various opinions. . . . The comments often enough merely express the commentator's despair."[22]

For Derrida the secret of the parable is that the doorkeeper is guarding nothing: "We do not know what it is, who it is, where it is. Is it a thing, a person, a discourse, a voice, a document, or simply nothing that incessantly defers access to itself, thus forbidding *itself* in order thereby to become something or someone?"[23] This does not mean that there is no law; it merely means that "the law" is highly unstable as a referent, and it consists of categories, definitions, and boundaries that are constantly moving—a movement that is contrary to the assumed stability of reference that modern law promises when it tells us that it is clear enough for each person to understand, to the point where ignorance of the law is no excuse since every person is capable of understanding it. Derrida makes this point brilliantly by stating that the protagonists in Kafka's legal fiction seek to enter the law as it if were at territory or place because they assume that the words of the law mark out a clear boundary; what is maddening to us is the process of mediation and interpretation: "He [the protagonist in "Before the Law"] wants to see or touch the law, he wants to approach and 'enter' it, because perhaps he does not know that the law is not to be seen or touched but deciphered."[24]

This is the point at which Kafka draws the interest of so-called postmodern thinkers, who read his legal fiction as depicting the law as an indeterminate text shaped by power relations.[25] For these thinkers, Kafka is essentially a demystifier of the liberal rule of law, showing that "the law" is not a ready-made set of rules but an empty signifier that is actively constructed in a symbolic struggle between social forces vying to establish a fixed, state-sanctioned interpretation of a fluid text.[26] The law is a kind of game where we create a rule through interpretation and then pretend that the rule predated our interpretive effort; to paraphrase Stanley Fish, we walk on the bridge while we are building it, then declare that it was there all along. To use a classic example, the criminal law may have a statute that says in black and white, "No motorized vehicles are permitted in a city park," but this does not answer the question of whether a person who enters the park on a motorized wheelchair is suddenly a criminal. The prohibition that at first seems so clear and stable starts to dissolve in the process of interpretation. Kafka takes this to the extreme where the indeterminacy of texts means that one never gets to the center—to the court, to the tribunal, through the gates of the law, to a clear rule. Instead, three horrible outcomes are possible: death ("Before the Law," *The Trial*), exhaustion (*The Castle*), or resignation ("The Great Wall of China," "The Refusal").

The postmodern notion that the law is empty is difficult to grasp at first. It sounds quite bizarre to say that the law is "empty." After all, there is a set of laws and case decisions at the library and in every courtroom, and there is a huge legal apparatus in place consisting of judges, lawyers, administrators, police, law schools, and so forth. We can go to the law library and see the texts of the Illinois law, so what sense is there in saying that it is "empty"?

There are two analogies for this that help to make it clear; the first is philosophical and the second is literary. In philosophy, consider Hegel's critique of Kant's categorical imperative—the notion that all ethical behavior by rational beings must be grounded in the principle of reason and that one should act as if one's conduct could be made into a universal rule; that is, whether one's conduct is possible of universalization. Thus Kant concluded that lying could not satisfy this requirement, since lying—if made universal—would destroy the institution of truth telling and thereby destroy the distinction between lies and truth. Hegel said that this norm was empty because it was so formalistic as to lack any connection to a particular society from which morality arises. In this sense, it has no content until placed into context and applied to a particular lie.

Kafka actually suggests that the courtrooms are empty in *The Trial*, where he describes a surreal scene where a court official is so angry with the endless motions of the lawyers that he physically bars them from entering the courtroom by throwing them down stairs, but the lawyers create a plan to tire out the official and soon he leaves: "The lawyers down below would not believe it at first and send one of their number up to peep behind the door and assure himself that the place was actually vacant. Only then were they able to enter. . . . The only sensible thing was to adapt oneself to existing conditions."[27]

On the literary side, consider the poem by Schiller called "The Veiled Statue at Sais," where a man yearns to find the truth and hears that there is a statue of the truth behind a veil in a museum. There is a rule against opening the veil. He sneaks into the museum at night and pulls back the veil. The next morning they find him pale and grey, shaken to the core, and finally admitting that one should never pull back the curtain on truth. Presumably he saw nothing, or simply his own reflection, meaning that truth is constructed and not discovered. Similarly, as Derrida reminds us, Hegel tells the story of Pompey entering the holiest of holy Jewish sites only to find nothing. That is, there is nothing at the core, only people who are protecting the secret that there is nothing. One could analogize this to other religions, which are based on impossible and preposterous myths and legends that can never be verified, yet have given rise to a superstructure of priests, popes, bishops, schools, seminaries, temples, and the like—all in service of an empty core. Again, we come back to Roberto Unger's statement that certain law professors are "like a priesthood that had lost their faith and kept their jobs."[28]

Kafka's legal fiction is modern in that his victims are not undone by a tragic flaw (as in Shakespeare, for example, where Othello is undone because he loved too much), nor are they undone by the gods or the vagaries of fate (as in Greek tragedy). Rather, they are victims of artificially constructed systems of language perpetuated by authority figures. The victim is any person who demands that the system (whether it be the state, the courts, the family, the employer) provide some account of its legitimacy, to justify itself rationally. Since the system can never offer a justification, it can offer only disappointment, delay, punishment, shunning, and curses. In most of the stories, the protagonist sticks out precisely because he is hell-bent on forcing the system to justify its existence and procedures, while those around him go quietly into the night, as it were, and submit to whatever reasons are doled out to them.

This raises the question of whether Kafka's victims are normal or pathological. Eric Fromm sees the victims as heroes who expose the "pathology of normality," namely that Kafka's victims at least have the temerity to force the system to give an account of itself, as opposed to simply adapting like a child.[29] As Pierre Bourdieu observes, the problem with people who are well adapted is precisely that they move seamlessly within established institutions: "The State does not necessarily need to give orders or exert physical coercion to produce an ordered social world, so long as it is able to produce incorporated cognitive structures attuned to the objective structures and thereby to secure doxic submission to the established order."[30] On this view, the key to being normal—or pathological depending on how you see it—is precisely the ability to adapt to the prevailing social reality. Like all things in Kafka, we are left without an answer, other than to say that his protagonists are both sane and pathological. Take the example of the Barnabas family in *The Castle*. One of their daughters refused the sexual advances of an official connected to the Castle, with the result that the whole family is ostracized in the village, and the father spends his days sitting on the road hoping for some kind of meeting with an official who can remove the black cloud hanging over the family, while the other daughter makes herself sexually available to strangers in the hopes of hooking up with a Castle official who will restore the family to its good graces. And the landlady of the inn where K. takes his room and board spends her days wistfully recalling her days as Klamm's favored woman, even though she has been replaced by a string of others, including K.'s onetime girlfriend Frieda. These people function, they eat and sleep and work, and they consider everything in their lives to be pretty normal in comparison to K., whom they find objectionable. But who is the crazy one here—the outsider to the village or the villagers who function from day to day? Is K. sane or insane for simply wanting some kind of definitive answer from the Castle about his role in the village? Does the key to sanity rest on a posture of indifference and shrugging disregard about authority, or does it rest on putting authority to the test of justifying itself? These are questions that Kafka raises but does not answer. And so perhaps Adorno was right when he said of Kafka, "Every sentence says 'interpret me,' and none will permit it."[31] The chain of signification will end only when those in power draw it to an end, and that will be a place where they want it to end. The system is not built to give you an answer to your satisfaction.

9

Modern Law Is Comic and Carnivalesque

Humor can be found everywhere in Kafka's work, once the reader is trained to look for it. And it is an important and often overlooked component of his critique of modernity and modern law. It is widely known that when Kafka read the first chapter of *The Trial* to his friends, both Kafka and his audience were laughing. They were listening to a story about a man arbitrarily arrested, condemned, and then executed without getting a chance to appear before a judge—and they were laughing. This would hardly seem to be funny material, but the first chapter of *The Trial* is indeed funny. There is something comical about the contrast of the protagonist's self-assurance that his rights will be vindicated versus the reality that he is caught in an apparatus that does not recognize his claims. He is arrested by two warders who enter without a warrant, eat his breakfast, attempt to take some clothes, and refuse to say why he has been arrested; but Josef K. stands earnestly and self-righteously, assuring himself that all of this is impossible in a country that has a constitution and in which all laws are in effect and that a great injustice has been perpetrated that will soon be set right. He is like a sailboat that refuses to get out of the way of an ocean liner because it has the right of way under nautical rules. This is humor in which a person is about to get crushed.

This is dark humor. Consider Kafka's remark to his love interest and Czech translator, Milena Jesenská, about his decision to stay in Prague despite anti-Semitic riots: "The heroism of staying on is nonetheless merely the heroism of cockroaches which cannot be exterminated, even from the bathroom."[1] He refers to the street where he lives as "Suicide Lane," a launching ramp for suicides because it bottomed out onto a half-built bridge over the river.[2] And who can miss the humor in his journal entry of October 18, 1917: "Dread of night. Dread of not-night."[3]

In a letter to his fiancée at the time, he said, "I can also laugh, Felice, have no doubt about this; I am even known as a great laugher."[4] To illustrate this, he related an incident at work in which Kafka and other clerks were granted an audience with the president, who according to Kafka was held in the same esteem as an emperor. He carried himself with a pompous air and spoke in platitudes of self-righteous aggrandizement, which sent Kafka into spasms of laughter that he had trouble controlling. The clerks were supposed to offer solemn and heartfelt thanks to the president, but something in the situation made Kafka giggle, choke, and then laugh: "The president listened in his usual posture adopted for solemn occasions, somewhat reminiscent of our Emperor when giving audience—which, if one happens to be in a certain mood, is a terribly funny pose. . . . Needless to say, like anyone exposed to clear and general scrutiny whose position does not quite correspond to his achievements, this man invites ridicule."[5] These are not examples of jokes as we commonly understand the term, but rather situations where one person is faced with the humorous underside of power.[6] In other words, his humor is subversive.

The humor in Kafka's writing has always been underestimated, probably due to Max Brod's insistence that Kafka's work was a kind of religious quest about which it would be impertinent to joke. And indeed there is a passage in *Letter to His Father* where Kafka pedantically admonishes his father for laughing in the synagogue during the Passover ritual. There were certainly a lot of passages in his diaries and letters that were self-absorbed and overdramatic, hardly the stuff of comedy.

Another roadblock to recognizing the humor in Kafka's writing is that he simply does not fit within the standard taxonomy of types of humor. For example, Simon Critchley's thoughtful introductory text on the philosophy of humor lists three classic explanations of humor—as an expression of superiority (e.g., ethnic jokes); as a release of anxiety (e.g., jokes about sensitive subjects like sex, politics, and money); and incongruity (logical puzzles, word games)—but none of these categories fit Kafka's sense of humor.[7] In other leading books on humor, no mention is made of the humor that one finds in Kafka.[8]

One contemporary figure who grasped Kafka's humor was the writer David Foster Wallace. In "Laughing with Kafka," Wallace was keen to point out that Kafka's humor is not easily categorized; there are no jokes in the contemporary sense, but there is something funny going on. He described the difficulty in conveying this to his students who equate comedy with the timeworn categories of slapstick, situation comedy, scatological humor, and other clichés. Wallace tries a unique approach with his students:

> You can ask them to imagine his art as a kind of door. To envision us readers coming up and pounding on the door, pounding and pounding, not just wanting admission but needing it, we don't know what it is but we can feel it, this total desperation to enter, pounding and pushing and kicking, etc. That, finally, the door opens . . . and it opens outward: we've been inside what we wanted all along. *Das ist komish* [That is comic].[9]

There is a strong streak of the surreal, comic, and phantasmagorical in Kafka's writings on law (what some have called Kafka's "looniness"). For example, *The Trial* is shot through with wild passages such as the sadomasochism of whippings in the bank vault, a court official throwing lawyers down the stairs, and the bizarre sleeping arrangements of clients at the lawyer's apartment. These elements (which run through all of Kafka's writings on law, by the way) are a critique of the absurdity and paradoxes of power in modern legal systems. Kafka is saying that the system that prizes formality and solemn ritual based on supposed natural rights and reason in the end comes down to brute force, dependence, and the arbitrariness of favors and disfavors. What is at stake in modernity is the preposterous attempt to put something *beyond* comedy, to create a edifice of such significance and solemnity that one cannot laugh at it. Here we are reminded of Dostoevsky's claim that he would not want to live in a crystal palace (a glass monument popular at the time as a paean to modernity) for the simple reason that you could not stick your tongue out at it. In other words, it would be an edifice of such greatness and authority that comedy would be forbidden.[10]

There are elements of slapstick and physical humor in Kafka's work, characterized primarily by the reduction of humans to things or animals, which is a visible demonstration of their dehumanization and depersonalization. Consider Gregor Samsa, the salesman who wakes up transformed into an insect, or the ape who gives a speech on his efforts to act as a human, or an animal that constructs an elaborate protective burrow that is essentially a place where he will die.

But the physical humor runs parallel to a deeper strand of humor, which is the description of situations where the legal apparatus gets tied into knots and makes a fool of itself. Consider again in greater length the passage from *The Castle*, as K. meets with the chairman (mayor) of the village who has been appointed his superior by a mysterious letter sent by Klamm, the local official with alleged ties to the Castle. The mayor launches into an impossibly boring tirade about the complex bureaucratic procedures for issuance of letters:

> "But," said the chairman, interrupting himself as if he had gone too far in his eagerness to tell the story, or as if it were at least possible that he had gone too far, "does the story bore you?"
>
> "No," said K., "it amuses me."
>
> At that, the chairman said: "I am not telling you this for your amusement."
>
> "It amuses me," said K., "only because it gives me some insight into the ridiculous tangle that may under certain circumstances determine a person's life."[11]

K.'s treatment of the chairman creates an imminent rebuke from the village schoolteacher, who thinks that K. has not shown enough respect for authority. To this, K. responds: "I'm not aware of being impolite, though you are quite right that I have more important things to worry about than fancy manners, for what was at stake was my livelihood, which has been jeopardized by the ignominious machinations of officialdom, the details of which I needn't fill you in on, since you yourself are an active part of that official apparatus."[12] This is humorous because K. is refusing to play the game of the bureaucracy—he is forcing the bureaucrats in the village to earn their esteem instead of merely deriving it from their title. This is not an accepted move within the game. Similarly, in *The Trial*, after being summoned to his first hearing without being given a time for the hearing, the prosecutor admonishes him for being late and then wrongfully inquires about whether Josef K. is a house painter.[13] This shows the ridiculous double standards of authority figures: they require obedience and respect as a matter of course, even as they bumble and cause reckless harm to the very people over whom they exercise their supposed expertise.

This brings to mind a hilarious incident that occurred during the trial of the Chicago Seven: two defendants showed up to court wearing judicial robes. Their point was to demystify the role of the judge by pointing out that the robe was just a vestment that anyone could purchase; in other words, the judge was just a man, the same as the defendants, and we should not fetishize his accouterments of power. The judge did not find the humor clever and issued nearly 160 contempt citations to the defendants, prompting their defense lawyer to say, "This is no longer a court of order, your Honor.

This is a medieval torture chamber."[14] This fits in with the notion of humor provided by anthropologist Mary Douglas, who said that comedy involves "the leveling of hierarchy, the triumph of intimacy over formality, of unofficial values over official ones."[15] This is Kafka's humor because it takes the perspective of the victims instead of the members of the judicial apparatus.

The closest analogue to Kafka's sense of humor can be found in a work by fellow Czech writer Milan Kundera, whose early novel *The Joke* is both a story about a joke and a meditation on humor itself. The story is set in motion by a postcard that a man sends to his girlfriend, who, like him, is in the Communist Party. He had planned a romantic getaway for the week, but instead she went to a party retreat that stressed the need for "optimism" and a "healthy atmosphere" while echoing the party line about the inevitable triumph of orthodox Communism (as opposed to Trotskyism). To express his disappointment, he sends her a postcard saying, "Optimism is the opium of the people! A healthy atmosphere stinks of stupidity! Long live Trotsky!"[16] Naturally this postcard finds its way to the party authorities, and it ends up in the hands of a certain party official who is instrumental in sentencing him to hard labor in the mines. Upon his return to society years later, he plots revenge by seducing the officer's wife, in which he is successful. But he finds out—and here is the "joke"—that this is precisely what the man wanted; in fact, the woman becomes clingy and a burden on the protagonist, and so the joke is on him, so to speak. Upon thinking over the situation, he concludes that history itself had simply put him at a time and place where he was caught in a bizarre situation where he was not allowed any sense of humor: "What if history plays jokes? And then I realized how powerless I was to revoke my own joke when throughout my life as a whole I was involved in a joke more vast (all-embracing for me) and utterly irrevocable."[17]

In other words, the joke is at a metalevel, the level of the situation. This seems to be what Kafka is getting at in his legal fiction: namely that comedy derives from situations where a person's plans are destroyed and his path toward recovery is only a dead end. We are talking, then, about the humor rooted in a historical epoch (modernity) in which a certain kind of laughter is not permissible.

Kafka's use of humor as social criticism is best appreciated through the lenses provided by Michel Foucault and Mikhail Bakhtin, who have written forcefully about humor as an antidote to power. Foucault's seminal study *Madness and Civilization* asserts that from the late Middle Ages through the Renaissance, certain forms of madness and folly were socially tolerated, and the insane were not institutionalized, segregated, or branded as deviant. Indeed, as literature of the period makes clear, madness was often respected as an alternative vision exposing the arbitrary and socially constructed elements of authority that are mistakenly taken as natural or inevitable. Madness engages in a dialogue with reason; it is the other of the accepted pretensions and illusions of the social order. For example, we find in this era stories such as "The Emperor's New Clothes," originally written in the fourteenth century, which upbraids the pretensions and pretense of royalty and puts their sanity into question.

Yet in the eighteenth century, according to Foucault, a "classical age" emerges where madness becomes an object of disciplinary regulation: the mad were no longer able to circulate freely and to mock the social order, but were assigned a deviant status, subsumed under a host of legal, medical, and psychological classifications, and isolated both physically and socially. In the modern age that is heir to the classical age, madness no longer interrogates and engages in a dialogue with the accepted wisdom, but the mad become objects of analysis and control rather than subjects with a voice. This is a "transition from the medieval and humanist experience of madness to our own experience, which confines insanity within medical illness."[18] Put in simple terms, the madness and folly that once offered an avenue of critique, that was an interlocutor and a debater with reason, has been largely neutralized and forgotten. The mad were now those who could no longer function as part of the social contract and therefore had to be removed from society. As the mad were banished, so too was a certain strand of social criticism—the kind that mocked authority and reminded us all that even kings and queens were humans who ate, defecated, and had sex.

Yet, and this is the important point as far as Kafka is concerned, Foucault insists that a substratum of madness continues to exist in the work of certain writers and thinkers, such as Sade, Nietzsche, and Artaud. In these writers, the subversive notion of madness continues. In their work, the existing social order is interrogated by art. Often these "mad" thinkers are not recognized in their lifetime, but only later does it appear that they stood outside and presented a well-grounded criticism of the existing social order of their time, and in this limited sense, madness gets the last word despite all attempts to domesticate it. Madness—in the older sense of parody, folly, physicality, absurdity—performs a kind of return of the repressed by mocking authority.

This line of argument finds expression in the work of Russian literary critic Mikhail Bakhtin, particularly in his study of folk humor and the "carnivalesque" in the Middle Ages, which he sees as permeating the writings of the French author Rabelais. Bakhtin points to festivals and feasts in the

Middle Ages as a social practice where hierarchies, authorities, and dominant institutions and persons were openly mocked: "Carnival celebrated temporary liberation from the prevailing truth and from the established order; it marked the suspension of all hierarchical rank, privileges, norms, and prohibitions."[19] Bakhtin emphasizes two ways in which the carnivalesque inverts the established order: laughter and the grotesque. Laughter, for Bakhtin, is liberating. It mocks and pierces the solemnity demanded by religion and stately rituals: "Laughter purifies from dogmatism, from the intolerant and the petrified; it liberates from fanaticism and pedantry, from fear and intimidation, from didacticism, naiveté, and illusion."[20] Alternatively, the grotesque is exemplified mostly by the body and its physicality and basic functions such as defecation and sexuality, serving as a reminder that humans are always tied to a downward movement toward the earth and animality, as opposed to a purely upward path of spirituality. And it has the leveling effect of reminding us that even the authorities are subject to the same infirmities of the body as their subjects.

Bakhtin makes clear that humor is not a withering negative critique of the type that sets up an alternative social system. Its goal is to remind everyone that there is a common denominator of absurdity to all human endeavors and to all people, regardless of social rank or position, and that in fact human existence is tied to death, suffering, renewal, and eventual rebirth. Like Foucault, Bakhtin thinks that the carnivalesque came to an end with the rise of nation-states, at which time power was consolidated in the state apparatus and the authorities sought to rule out alternative viewpoints that cast shame or ridicule on the political or ecclesiastical. However, says Bakhtin, the tradition of the carnival and the grotesque continues to exist as a substratum in various literary genres. Although he does not mention Kafka, he specifically mentions Alfred Jarry, the surrealist, and Thomas Mann, who was in fact a fan of Kafka's.

A contemporary example of Kafkaesque humor can be found in an article by Ralph Nader, the consumer advocate and former presidential candidate. Nader had been receiving what he mockingly called "touching letters from Barack Obama."[21] Many of these letters solicited feedback and even included a comment card on which Nader and other recipients were encouraged to submit comments to the president to help him stay connected. According to the president, "my ability to lead the country depends on listening to you"; "I pledged that I would always keep the lines of communication open—and I meant it"; and "I need your voice." The president, it seems, wanted to hear from Nader.

Or did he?

In point of fact, Nader had been writing to the president for years and had yet to receive a single reply, nor even an acknowledgment of receipt. He had also written to First Lady Michelle Obama but had not received any response from her either. In exasperation, Nader sent a letter to both of them asking for an explanation of their nonresponse policy guidelines; paradoxically, this letter itself drew a nonresponse. Finally, after sending all these unanswered letters to the president and his wife, Nader opened his mail to find yet another card from the president, with the boldly underlined words, "I'd like to hear from you."

Here we are, nearly a century after Kafka's miscommunication with the Revenue Department in Prague, and we have two public figures, living in the same city, whose paths might cross at any number of events, expressing an interest in speaking with each other, yet being unable to communicate despite the myriad ways to communicate today—letter, fax, email, telephone, text message, and so on. Surely there is something Kafkaesque going on here amid the crossed letters, the distance between authorities and their subjects, the self-righteous proclamations about democracy and connection to the people, and the black humor of impossible communication with a person who professes an open desire to communicate. The contemporary world, *our* world, is still Kafkaesque.

This can be a cause for laughter, but also for alarm. There are contemporary events in American law that are Kafkaesque and highly disturbing: secret tribunals, indefinite detentions, courts that disown their own opinions, government agencies that act in direct opposition to their mandates, domestic spying, and pretrial execution of a US citizen by remote-controlled drone anywhere in the world. These are developments that have direct parallels in the darker reaches of Kafka's legal fiction.

But it is not just criminal law that cries out with humor. Opening the financial news one day, I came across a headline that caused me to burst out laughing: "New Hedge Fund Buys Barclay's Toxic Assets with $12.6 Billion Loan from Barclays."[22] Recently in the financial news, I found that "Apollo [hedge fund] Paid Itself Some Fees and Gave Itself Some Loans," which—according to the author—"isn't really so bad because *you pay the interest to yourself.*"[23] The Supreme Court tells us that corporations are "people" with the full panoply of rights, and yet this "person" is able to use his left hand to loan money to his right hand. In this same vein, I recently saw this posting on the message board for hedge fund lawyers:

> Is anyone aware of any guidance that would allow a "feeder vehicle" to rely on a different Regulation D exemption than the underlying

> vehicle itself? The facts at hand are: (i) an adviser makes investments on behalf of itself and its clients in underlying investments; (ii) the underlying investments are typically real estate investment vehicles or operating companies, but generally not private investment funds so we do not need to worry about 3c1/3c7 exemption at the underlying vehicle level and potential look through issues; and (iii) while the feeder vehicle is clearly formed for the purpose of investing in the underlying vehicle, it is not marketed as a simple "access" vehicle, but as a means of investing in private investments with the oversight of the adviser. Investors in the feeder vehicle will effectively be giving up the right to vote or participate in any action involving the underlying investment and there will be fees and carried interests applied at the feeder level. The general rule of thumb as I understand it is that an entity that is formed for the purpose of investing in another is effectively collapsed with the underlying entity for securities law exemption purposes. I would, however, be interested in hearing if anyone is aware of any guidance or any thinking as to whether any particular features could deem the feeder vehicle to be different enough to lead to a different result. I will note that I believe that for purposes of determining whether the feeder vehicle is an "accredited investor" with respect to its investment in the underlying vehicle, it will not be able to rely on Rule 501(a)(3) irrespective of the response to the above.

Upon reflection, what took me aback about this query was that I understood it. I could think this way. But is it not comical in a strange way? Is there not a black humor in the fact that the law—a way of regulating human behavior—can become lost in a level of abstraction so far removed from any human emotion or need?

Is it not a sign of "reason" gone amok—yet comical—when we learn that Enron Corporation had 900 offshore subsidiaries and some 3,000 partnerships and joint ventures, some of which were not distinguishable from Enron itself?[24] How about when we learn that "persons" who are corporations can become citizens of other countries such as Ireland while keeping their headquarters in America, in order to lower their tax burden—something that natural "persons" are not able to do? All of this is outrageous, preposterous, and yet comical in a Kafkaesque kind of way, for it resembles nothing so much as Kafka's story about how his two hands got into a fight, and he wasn't sure whether to be a neutral referee or to assist the left because he had inadvertently favored the right hand for most of his life. The ability to call a law or a process "Kafkaesque" is to say that it lacks the dignity that it purports to have, that it falls short of its stated pretentions. And that is the fate of modern law.

It can lead in two directions.

On the one hand it can lead to relatively harmless stunts, as when a man in Virginia recently paid the tax on his son's car in pennies—300,000 pennies contained in five large wheelbarrows, which kept the employees at the Department of Motor Vehicles working into the night.[25] He had called the local authorities to ask which county was the proper recipient of the tax on the car, since the man had several homes in different counties, and wasn't sure which county was officially the home of his son's car. He was placed on hold and routed to a call center that refused to give him the telephone number for the local office of the Department of Motor Vehicles, so he then filed a Freedom of Information lawsuit to find the phone numbers of the local Departments of Motor Vehicles, a process that he "won" in court when the state of Virginia agreed to post the phone numbers, but the whole thing cost himself and the taxpayers at lot of money. As he said, "If they were going to inconvenience me then I was going to inconvenience them."

But the humor and absurdity of the law can turn deadly. Take the example of software engineer Joseph Stack, who flew his airplane into the Austin, Texas, office of the Internal Revenue Service in a suicide mission, killing himself and one man, and injuring others. Stack had spent years fighting with the tax authorities, first over the question of why religious institutions get a tax exemption while ordinary people cannot; it appears that he tried to form a church in his home to obtain the exemption, but this was denied. Later, Stack lost everything when the Internal Revenue Code was rewritten as a favor to IBM Corporation by giving them a tax break in exchange for imposing new penalties on freelance engineers like Stack, destroying his client base. Even after the sponsor of the law found that it was useless, the Treasury Department published a study that confirmed the pointlessness, and sixty senators called for its repeal, it remained on the books.[26] In his suicide note, which is widely available, Stack said:

> How can any rational individual explain that white elephant conundrum in the middle of our tax system and, indeed, our entire legal system? Here we have a system that is, by far, too complicated for the brightest of the master scholars to understand. Yet, it mercilessly holds accountable its victims, claiming that they're responsible for fully complying with laws not even the experts understand. The law "requires" a signature on the bottom of a tax filing; yet no one can

say truthfully that they understand what they are signing; if that's not "duress" than what is. If this is not the measure of a totalitarian regime, nothing is. . . . Well, Mr. Big Brother IRS man, let's try something different; take my pound of flesh and sleep well.

Now, is this madness? On one level, yes, a normal person does not fly an airplane into a government building to protest the tax laws, even when the laws are universally acknowledged by that same government to be useless and nonsensical. On another level, no, he is simply raising some good questions that have never been answered, such as why religions get a preference over atheists. Even Noam Chomsky pointed out that Stack's suicide note had some good points about the inequalities in our medical and legal system, and that his mood captured the "rustbelt rage" felt by millions. This is the bewilderment felt by K. in *The Castle* when K. concludes that the authorities exist only to "guard the distant and invisible interests of distant and invisible masters, while he fought for something vitally near to him, for himself."[27] And after he is told by the mayor that there is no clear explanation of why K. is in the village or whether he has been summoned or can stay, K. sarcastically summarizes his situation: "So the only remaining conclusion is that everything is very uncertain and insoluble, including my own being thrown out."[28]

My point is that Kafka's legal fiction is filled with humor, but it is situational humor based on the destruction of the individual in the face of a massive and uncaring bureaucratic apparatus. This is humor on a knife's edge and cuts close to the bone. These are not jokes as we commonly use the term. They are—as in Kundera's novel *The Joke*—about life and death situations.

The legal apparatus can function only by excluding its own ridiculousness, by believing its own pomposity. There is no laughing allowed in court, no self-critical humor, and no place for unfiltered human emotion. This was illustrated nicely in a case from Delaware where a plaintiff tried to point out the silliness and bumbling formality of the court, only to be rebuffed and told that his situation was *not* Kafkaesque.

This was a case brought by Michael Kelly, a certified public accountant who invested—and then lost—a lot of money in a Chinese jewelry company called Fuqi that had gone public in America. Kelly suspected early on that something was amiss with the company—and he was correct. As it turned out, Fuqi was engaged in fraudulent transfers to private accounts in China; it was unable to hold an annual meeting of shareholders or to provide financial statements; its directors resigned rather than remedy the situation; and the company was eventually delisted by the stock exchange and punished by the Securities and Exchange Commission.[29] But before all of that came out, Kelly thought he could take the company to court by acting as his own lawyer and speaking in plain English.

First, he tried to contact the directors of the company, some of whom lived near him in California. No response. He contacted the company's lawyers. No response. Finally Kelly sued in California court to compel the company to release its books and records. On the court date, he was thrilled to see the people that he wanted to interrogate show up at the courthouse, until the judge told Kelly not to get excited since the defendants were only there to argue that they could not be sued in California since the company was incorporated in the state of Delaware. In other words, the defendants were there—physically that is—but were not really there. Kelly blithely said to the Court, "So the company's representative standing here is a hologram?" The California lawsuit was dismissed, and Kelly was told to go across the country to Delaware and file his lawsuit even though he was trying to get an answer from defendants that lived near his home in California.[30]

Kelly filed his case in Delaware Chancery Court. He also wrote letters to the judge saying that the company was a "con" and had "gone dark," and that no one was answering his calls and messages. His pleadings were colorful and amateurish, even sophomoric, but hilarious. He ridiculed the legalese of the company's lawyers:

> Rather than share information with the court, the [lawyers] muddy the waters and prostitute themselves for money. Derivative / Direct / First Filed / Collateral Estoppel / Res Judicata / Improper Service and a Partridge in a Pear Tree. This is all form and no substance. I may not have articulated the arguments like lawyers do, or illuminated the right path forward and I undoubtedly have made mistakes—but this should be about JUSTICE. Shut Fuqi International down.[31]

The Court took Kelly to the woodshed. It said his passion had become debased and transformed like Kafka's character Gregor Samsa (from "The Metamorphosis"), and that Kelly wrongly "considers himself the victim of a meaningless bureaucratic labyrinth reminiscent of another work of Kafka, *The Trial*." The case was dismissed on a technicality—that a shareholder's claim must be brought by a lawyer for the shareholder and not by the shareholder himself. The court told Kelly that it was also sitting as judge in a different case dealing with the same company—namely, a different shareholder was suing to demand that the company hold an annual meeting—and that case would probably give him the information and relief that he sought.

After Kelly's case was ignominiously dismissed, it slowly became clear that he had been right all along and had good reason to be angry in his court filings. Eventually the SEC ruled that the company had engaged in securities fraud relating to transfers of money to China, and the Delaware court noted in the other lawsuit that the technical dickering of the company's lawyers stood the purpose of corporate and securities law on its head. The Delaware Chancery Court eventually appointed a receiver for the company—the exact remedy that Kelly had sought. And the SEC revoked the licenses of the brokers who sold the stock.

It is certainly true that Kelly's claims were somewhat eccentric, but what is striking is that the Court took the side of the formality and process orientation of the lawyers for the company, never striking out at those lawyers with the same vituperative indignation it directed toward Mr. Kelly; after all, it was the company's lawyers who were delaying justice, not Mr. Kelly. The court could see that Kelly was in distress and driven to madness by the loss of money and the stonewalling of the company and its law firm. Why was the court willing to play the "game" of the law with the company lawyers but not willing to listen to Kelly's heartfelt and clear warnings?

And what does this say about the ability of an average citizen to access the court system? It says simply that an average person cannot represent herself because courts will elevate decorum about substance and cannot handle any raw emotion. The system is incapable of laughing at itself, incapable of assimilating or understanding any behavior other than pious and supplicant restraint, and anyone who enters the system and points out that the emperor has no clothes will become an instant object of scorn.

Kafka is saying that there is humor in the legal system, but it exists at a metalevel, because the entire system is ridiculous. On the ground level, day to day and in the courts, it is humorless and punitive.

Conclusion: Was Kafka Correct about Modern Law?

The central claim of this book is that Kafka is an important thinker with a unique vision of modern law as a social institution. This claim is somewhat broader than what is typically found in the existing legal scholarship. As I pointed out in the introduction, Kafka's legal fiction has often been used to illuminate a particular aspect of modern law (say, the law of punishment), but he was not considered to have anything to say globally or at a metalevel about modern law as an institution. If I am correct, Kafka is not merely a writer who can be approached from various interpretive perspectives or whose work illuminates a particular area of law, but instead he can be understood as a legal theorist in his own right.

It is worth asking why the secondary literature has not sought a metamessage in Kafka's legal fiction. There is no great mystery here, only a historical accident of sorts. Much of the current interest in Kafka's legal writing arose as a consequence of the intense and widely read debate between Robin West and Richard Posner in the 1980s on the question of whether Kafka's fiction refuted the assumption of rational behavior that was a key component of the law and economics approach then favored by Posner.[1] West used Kafka's depiction of self-defeating and conflicted characters as a challenge to the law and economics model of rational behavior, while Posner deflected the criticism with his own interesting take on Kafka that relegated him to more of a personal rather than a political (legal) thinker. In any event, the exchange sparked a renewed interest in Kafka, and that is to the credit of both. However, one consequence that neither intended, I believe, was that subsequent scholars would continue to approach Kafka narrowly from a particular angle with respect to discrete questions (such as whether behavior is rational, or whether punishment is truly a deterrent, and so forth). This narrowing of the discussion was somewhat paradoxical because Posner himself turned from this debate with West to broader questions of the relationship between law and literature, writing a formative book of the same name. But while he was starting to think on a metalevel, other thinkers were reading Kafka at a microlevel. The end result is that Kafka is safely ensconced in the "canon" of law and literature,[2] but he is not treated as a theorist with a global approach to law.

Among the more microapproaches to Kafka's legal fiction, some critics read his fiction as a historical account of the legal system in Austro-Hungary during the first few decades of the twentieth century,[3] others see *The Trial* as primarily a commentary on Austrian criminal law and procedure,[4] and still others see his work as a prescient foreshadowing of totalitarianism exemplified by the Nazis and the Stalinist purges.[5] Still others mine Kafka's writings for material that is relevant to issues of law and psychology, or such disparate topics as family relations, mental destabilization, and capital punishment.[6] All of this research is welcome, but its proliferation can obscure the larger question of Kafka's attitude toward modern law as a whole.

A further cause of ambiguity is the widespread use (or rather, misuse) of the term "Kafkaesque," which has even prompted the dictionary company Merriam-Webster to warn that the term is losing its meaning.[7] The judiciary is no exception here,[8] as they use the term "Kafkaesque" rather often.[9] By recent count, this term has been used over 500 times in court opinions in the last few decades,[10] and the tendency is even more pronounced among journalists, who use it to describe everything from global conflicts to the reams of paperwork that one must fill out to get a driver's license. On the positive side of the ledger, this shows the continued relevance of Kafka's work, especially among the educated classes from which judges and lawyers are drawn, but constant use threatens to reduce the word to a stock phrase that is increasingly divorced from Kafka's actual writings.

In researching this book, I have come across only one writer who has attempted, rather sketchily, to claim that Kafka had a general take on modern law. This is Frederick DeCoste, who claims that Kafka presents a picture of modern law as inherently dystopian. That is, law always creates an insular cadre of insiders and a larger class of alienated outsiders, and this phenomenon is an inherent and inescapable feature of all modern legal systems. As he puts it, "Kafkian jurisprudence is a jurisprudence of despair. . . . There is no possibility of a coherent future, and no opportunity to reshape our moral and communal lives and commitments."[11] I think this is generally correct, if overly simplistic, and I have tried to describe in detail the components of this "jurisprudence of despair."

But at some point, however, we must ask whether Kafka got modern law right, and here is where I have to lay my cards on the table and say that Kafka's critique of modern law strikes me as only half-convincing. The negative movement—that is, the illumination of the glaring failure of the law to meet its own ideals—is sketched with precision and power. But this negative movement stands alone in Kafka's legal writing. There is no counterbalancing recognition of the emancipatory features of modern law. In the end, there is no dialectic.

I have no intention of confusing the artist with the art, as it were, but we must say that something odd is going on when Kafka was a lawyer who sought to use modern law to improve the lives of workers, injured soldiers, and the powerless, yet his fiction nowhere recognizes the possibility of such remediation through modern law. One almost suspects that his fiction is a kind of working through of his frustrations of his professional life. That is fine, but it raises the question of why he discounted the emancipatory side of modern law in his fiction when it was standing before his eyes every day.

Again, the negative movement in Kafka's writing is hard to gainsay: the legal system has indeed failed to live up to its own standards. I have already cited many instances where the promises of freedom, privacy, and autonomy have been severely compromised by the current American legal system. But to get the broadest possible perspective on this failure, let's look at the Illinois preamble to the state constitution, which contains the aspirational language of modern law for the state of Illinois:

> We, the People of the State of Illinois—grateful to Almighty God for the civil, political and religious liberty which He has permitted us to enjoy and seeking His blessing upon our endeavors—in order to provide for the health, safety and welfare of the people; maintain a representative and orderly government; eliminate poverty and inequality; assure legal, social and economic justice; provide opportunity for the fullest development of the individual; insure domestic tranquility; provide for the common defense; and secure the blessings of freedom and liberty to ourselves and our posterity—do ordain and establish this Constitution for the State of Illinois.

Now let's compare it to the facts as we find them on the ground in Chicago, the biggest city in Illinois. Safety and welfare? The city—half-jokingly known as "Chiraq"—has a high number of killings and shootings. Orderly government? The majority of recent governors are currently in jail, and the city is rife with corruption. Elimination of poverty and inequality? The city is plagued by poverty, and the wealth distribution is abysmal. Legal, social, and economic justice? Most people cannot afford a lawyer, most wrongs go without remedy, and most people live one paycheck from homelessness. Domestic tranquility? Common defense? Posterity? These are almost comical in light of what life is like for most people. The law has set aspirations that it cannot meet, which is not unusual, but what is striking is the gulf separating the aspirations from any hope of realization.

One could go even deeper and ask whether modern law has truly become modern, that is, governed by reason instead of superstition, ritual, and magic. For example, a recent *Time* magazine feature about the Supreme Court inadvertently revealed the law's premodern aspects: "Cloaked in secrecy and long black robes, issuing oracular pronouncements with scant warning, the court carries a vaguely medieval air . . . the Supreme Court still occupies an island of elite authority, a sanctum sanctorum. . . . No one witnesses their deliberations—not even the clerks who serve them like votaries—but their decisions are often the final word in society's most intense disputes."[12] So at the heart of *modernity* are nine unelected members of the elite who dress in quasi-religious outfits and operate in secret. Kafka's writing on law plays on this question raised by Bruno Latour to the effect of whether we have ever been fully modern, let alone *post*modern, because modernity is premised on the impossible prospect of fully rationalizing all institutions and projects so they are pure and not mixed up with the irrational (resulting in what he calls the "hybrid").[13] Law is particularly equivocal on this point, because it professes to chart certain rights that are natural and time-honored (that is, grounded in human nature and time immemorial), yet it sees itself as a rational science devoid of superstition and arbitrariness. One cannot have it both ways, and when the chips are down, the law is not a very effective bulwark against tyranny, arbitrary rule, injustice, and violence; indeed, law is just as likely to be a weapon of these monstrous forces, and in this regard we need not be reminded that even Hitler came to power under the rubric of German law (via its allowance for rule by emergency decree) and that when eminent jurists and legal scholars are put to the test, they switch parties and alliances with great speed: Andrey Vyshinsky was a Menshevik lawyer who turned into the Bolshevik bulldog who led the horrific purges for the Soviets, while Carl Schmitt was a German law professor who joined the Nazi Party and was soon burning books and was so unrepentant that he refused denazification after the war. In our own country, the Supreme Court has a very mixed legacy of some horrendous decisions such as forced sterilization, internment, and segregation, and has pretty much stood with business interests and the elite against the interests of minorities and common people. All of this suggests that Kafka's negative critique is on point.

And yet as we have seen, Kafka pointed to the limits of his nihilism in his journal entry when he admitted, "I have vigorously absorbed the negative element of the age in which I live," but without the extreme negativity that could "capsize into the positive."[14] This is oblique, but what he means is that other thinkers like Nietzsche and Marx offered extremely bleak portraits of modernity, but only in order to set the stage for the emergence of a higher ("positive") arrangement. With Kafka, negativity prevails as homeostasis. Just as Kafka himself was never politically active,[15] neither do his characters or stories offer any solution to the problems of modern law, suggesting that these problems are insoluble.

To see this extreme negativity, it is worthwhile to compare Kafka's writing on law to the work of Marx and Engels, who admittedly did not write fiction, but were equally suspicious of modern law's ability to fulfill its pretensions. In *The Communist Manifesto*, Marx and Engels say that modern law is simply a reflection of capitalist relations of production (owner/renter, employer/employee, lender/borrower) and that modern law reifies these roles as issuing from reason itself: "In a word, compared with the splendid promises of the philosophers, the social and political institutions born in the 'triumph of reason' were bitterly disappointing caricatures. . . . We know today that the idealized kingdom of reason was nothing more than the idealized kingdom of the bourgeoisie."[16] Engels, whose family had businesses in northern England, in particular was appalled to see how the law could be an instrument of class rule, and his observations on the conditions of the working class in England reveal his shock at the draconian antilabor regulations that made illegal more than two people quitting a job at the same time, thereby criminalizing a walkout by the workers! But for Marxism, there is a way out, because law is—like everything else—a dialectic; it contains the seeds of its own destruction and subsequent elevation to a higher level. Thus Marx and Engels could look forward to the day when modern law collapses, or rather "withers away," finally bringing the freedom that was merely an ideological construct under capitalism: "Man, at last the master of his own form of social organization, becomes at the same time the lord over Nature, his own master—free."[17] This did not turn out as predicted, of course, but it illustrates a dialectical project that points a route through modern law as a way of overcoming itself. In *State and Revolution*, Lenin set his goal as "reducing officialdom to naught," but this kind of ambitious project (however poorly it turned out) is nowhere to be found in Kafka's legal fiction.

Perhaps this is why Kafka received a cold reception among the more trenchant Marxists, exemplified by Georg Lukács's notion that Kafka's writing was a cry of bourgeois self-pity: "The world of modern capitalism, seen as a form of hell on earth, and the helplessness of all human endeavor in the face of the power wielded by that world: such is the stuff of which Kafka's fiction is made."[18] The problem, again, is the overwhelming angst with a lack of dialectic: "The question is not: is *x* present in reality? But rather: does *x* represent the whole of reality? Again, the question is not: should *x* be excluded from literature? But rather: should we be content to leave it at *x*?"[19] Lukács criticized German intellectuals as living in "The Grand Hotel Abyss," which he described as "a beautiful hotel, equipped with every comfort, on the edge of an abyss, of nothingness, of absurdity. And the daily contemplation of the abyss between excellent meals or artistic entertainments, can only heighten the enjoyment of the subtle comforts offered."[20] The patrons contemplate the absurdity of the modern world without seeing it in broader historical context as a contingent phenomenon that can be overcome. I have to admit that there is little or nothing in Kafka's legal fiction to indicate any method of transcending, sublating, or even reforming the law. But surely Kafka's supporters will fire back that Lukács was forced to eat his words when the Marxist system arrested him and held him captive in a *castle* fortress, where he reportedly said, "Kafka was right after all."[21]

Kafka's supporters will also point out that Max Weber, the very person who influenced him the most, or at least developed similar ideas along the same lines, came to the lugubrious conclusion that a socialist revolution would involve the same degree of strangulating bureaucracy and usher in a new kind of subservience to nameless and faceless authorities. For Weber, and seemingly for Kafka too, there is nothing in the toolbox of modernity to enable us to make ethical choices, and we are left with merely a free-floating rage for order and a kind of blind hope that a charismatic leader will come along to restore our values and tame the bureaucracy. That did not work out as expected in Germany.

But Kafka did not need to adopt a full-blown Marxist or Weberian solution to modern law—all he needed to do was to acknowledge that while modern law is often an instrument of oppression, it remains a necessary component to liberation. For example, Christine Sypnowich has argued convincingly that a socialist system with a rule of law is possible, echoing the sentiment of historian E. P. Thompson that the rule of law is often an

NOTES

Introduction: An Outline of the Project

1. Jeffrey Alexander, *The Dark Side of Modernity* (Cambridge: Polity Press, 2013), 2.

2. Franz Kafka, *The Blue Octavo Notebooks*, ed. Max Brod, trans. Ernst Kaiser and Eithne Wilkins (Cambridge, Mass.: Exact Change, 1991), 52.

3. This distinction is attributable to Roscoe Pound, but its spirit permeated the legal realist movement in later years. For example, see Jean-Louis Halperin, "Law in Books and Law in Action: The Problem of Legal Change," *Maine Law Review* 64, no. 1 (2011): 45–76.

4. Jacques Derrida, "Before the Law," in *Acts of Literature*, ed. Derek Attridge, trans. Avital Ronell and Christine Roulston (New York: Routledge, 1992), 191–192.

5. Several decades ago, Christian Goodden mentioned seven distinct interpretations of Kafka in the secondary literature: magic-religious, existentialist, ontological, psychoanalytic, social critical/Marxist, literary, and literary-historical. See his essay, "Points of Departure," in *The Kafka Debate*, ed. Angel Flores (New York: Gordian Press, 1977), 4. To update this list, I would add the broad category of "postmodern" approaches (encompassing "postcolonial theory"), which focuses on Kafka's deconstruction of hierarchies and power relations, and his alleged use of the dominant German language in a subversive way to highlight colonization of the ethnic Czechs. Much of this approach has its roots in Jacques Derrida's essay, cited above, and Giles Deleuze and Felix Guattari, *Kafka: Toward a Minor Literature* (Minneapolis: University of Minnesota Press, 1986).

6. Terry Carter, "A Justice Who Makes Time to Read, and Thinks That All Lawyers Should, Too," *Chicago Daily Law Bulletin*, January 26, 1993, 2; emphasis mine.

7. James Hawes, *Why You Should Read Kafka before You Waste Your Life* (New York: St. Martin's Press, 2008), 226–227, 231.

8. Tina Rosenberg, "Have You Ever Been Arrested? Check Here," *New York Times*, May 24, 2016, http://www.nytimes.com/2016/05/24/opinion/have-you-ever-been-arrested-check here.html.

9. Justin Fenton, "Groups Applaud Police Reform," *Baltimore Sun*, June 23, 2010, http://articles.baltimoresun.com/2010-06-23/news/bs-md-ci-naacp-aclu-settlement-20100623_1_arrests-david-rocah-police-officers.

10. Tony Plohetski, "Despite Negative Blood and Breath Tests, Man Arrested for DUI," *Austin American-Statesman*, February 24, 2014, http://www.statesman.com/weblogs/investigations/2014/feb/24/despite-negative-breath-blood-tests-man-arrested-d/.

11. "New York City Settles with Occupy Protestors Pepper-Sprayed by Police," *New York Times*, July 7, 2015, A16.

12. Max Ehrenfreund, "The Biggest Question about Police Militarization That

Obama Hasn't Answered," *Washington Post*, May 21, 2015, https://www.washingtonpost.com/news/wonk/wp/2015/05/21/the-biggest-question-about-police-militarization-obama-hasnt-answered/.

13. Jeremy Gorner, "Police Stops Raise Suspicions," *Chicago Tribune*, November 5, 2013, http://articles.chicagotribune.com/2013-11-05/news/ct-met-contact-cards-20131105_1_chicago-police-cards-officers.

14. Monica Davey, "Chicago Police Try to Predict Who May Shoot or Be Shot," *New York Times*, May 24, 2016, A11.

15. Glen Greenwald, *No Place to Hide: Edward Snowden, The NSA, and the U.S. Surveillance State* (New York: Metropolitan Books, 2014).

16. David Jackson, "Obama Takes Heat over 'Transparent' FISA Court," *USA Today*, June 23, 2013, http://www.usatoday.com/story/theoval/2013/06/21/obama-politifact-fisa-court/2445809/.

17. "Homan Square Revealed: How Chicago Police 'Disappeared' 7,000 People," *Guardian*, October 19, 2015, https://www.theguardian.com/us-news/2015/oct/19/homan-square-chicago-police-disappeared-thousands.

18. National Defense Authorization Act for Fiscal Year 2012, Pub. L. 112-81, 125 Stat. 1298 (Dec. 31, 2011), at §1021; emphasis mine.

19. See *Hedges v. Obama*, 890 F. Supp. 2d 424, 432–433 (S.D.N.Y. 2012).

20. "Unspeedy Trial in Louisiana," *New York Times*, January 14, 2013, A22.

21. Michael Schwirtz and Michael Winerip, "Kalief Browder, Held at Rikers Island for 3 Years without Trial, Commits Suicide," *New York Times*, June 8, 2015, A20.

22. Tony Mauro, "Supreme Court Declines Review of NSA Wiretapping Program," *Legal Intelligencer*, February 21, 2008, 4.

23. Conor Friedersdorf, "Am I on the 'No-Fly' List?," *Atlantic*, May 18, 2012, http://www.theatlantic.com/national/archive/2012/05/am-i-on-the-no-fly-list-0151-and-other-faqs-to-the-fbi/257316/.

24. Nate Raymond, "Chicago Hacker Tied to Anonymous Given Ten Years in Prison," *Reuters*, November, 15, 2013, http://uk.reuters.com/article/uk-crime-hacking-hammond-idUKBRE9AE0X320131115.

25. Joshua Kopstein, "Hacker with a Cause," *New Yorker*, November 21, 2013, http://www.newyorker.com/tech/elements/hacker-with-a-cause; his statement to the court, which was ironically redacted by the judge, can be found here: https://freeanons.org/jeremy-hammond-sentenced-10-years.

26. Dan Eggen and Josh White, "Memo: Laws Didn't Apply to Interrogators," *Washington Post*, April 2, 2008, A1.

27. Dan Froomkin, "White House Torture Advisers," *Washington Post*, April 10, 2008, http://www.washingtonpost.com/wp-dyn/content/blog/2008/04/10/BL2008041002069.html; John Yoo, "Terrorists Have No Geneva Rights," *Wall Street Journal*, May 26, 2004, http://www.wsj.com/articles/SB108552765884721335.

28. Eliot Spitzer, "Predatory Lenders' Partners in Crime," *Washington Post*, February 14, 2008, A25.

29. Juliet Eilperin, "EPA Is Sued for Answers on Emissions," *Washington Post*, April 3, 2008, A4.

30. "Transcript: Attorney General Eric Holder on 'Too Big To Jail,'" *American Banker,* March 6, 2013, http://www.americanbanker.com/issues/178_45/transcript-attorney-general-eric-holder-on-too-big-to-jail-1057295-1.html.

31. Jo Becker and Scott Shane, "Secret 'Kill List' Proves a Test of Obama's Principles and Will," *New York Times*, May 29, 2012, A1; Amy Davidson, "The President's Kill List," *New Yorker*, May 30, 2012, http://www.newyorker.com/news/daily-comment/the-presidents-kill-list.

32. William Robinson III, "Letter to President Obama from the American Bar Association," December 30, 2011, http://www.americanbar.org/content/dam/aba/administrative/litigation/materials/sac_2012/525_agr_2011_12_30_aba_letter_to_obama_re_signing_statements.authcheckdam.pdf.

33. Danielle Douglas, "Holder Concerned Megabanks Too Big to Jail," *Washington Post*, March 6, 2013, https://www.washingtonpost.com//economy/holder-concerned-megabanks-too-big-to-jail/2013/03/06/6fa2b07a-869e-11e2-999e-5f8e0410cb9d_story.html; "Return of Debtor's Prisons," *New York Times*, July 14, 2012, A16.

34. Luz Herrera, "Training Lawyer Entrepreneurs," *Denver University Law Review* 89, no. 4 (2012): 894–939.

35. Michael Zuckerman, "Is There Such a Thing as an Affordable Lawyer?," *Atlantic*, May 30, 2014, http://www.theatlantic.com/business/archive/2014/05/is-there-such-a-thing-as-an-affordable-lawyer/371746/.

36. Noah Feldman, "When a 'Speedy Trial' Includes a 14-Month Delay," *Bloomberg View*, May 20, 2016, https://www.bloomberg.com/view/articles/2016-05-20/when-a-speedy-trial-includes-a-14-month-delay.

37. Lauren E. Glaze and Danielle Kaeble, *Correctional Populations in the United States, 2013* (NCJ 248479), December 2014, http://www.bjs.gov/content/pub/pdf/cpus13.pdf.

38. Adam Gopnik, "The Caging of America," *New Yorker*, January 30, 2012, http://www.newyorker.com/magazine/2012/01/30/the-caging-of-america.

39. Fareed Zakaria, "Incarceration Nation," *Time Magazine*, April 2, 2012, http://content.time.com/time/magazine/article/0,9171,2109777-2,00.html.

40. Debra Cassens Weiss, "Middle-Class Dilemma: Can't Afford Lawyers, Can't Qualify for Legal Aid," *ABA Journal*, July 22, 2010, http://www.abajournal.com/news/article/middle-class_dilemma_cant_afford_lawyers_cant_qualify_for_legal_aid.

41. Anais Nin, *Ladders to Fire* (Athens: Ohio University Press, 1995), xiii.

42. H. L. A. Hart, *The Concept of Law* (Oxford: Oxford University Press, 2012), 117.

43. Antonio Negri, *The Labor of Job* (Durham, N.C.: Duke University Press, 2009).

Chapter 1: Kafka's Life in the Law

1. Kafka's law school transcript, with a list of courses and examination topics, can be found in Klaus Wagenbach, *Franz Kafka: Pictures of a Life* (New York: Pantheon Books, 1984), 59.

2. Peter Mailloux, *A Hesitation before Birth: The Life of Franz Kafka* (Newark: University of Delaware Press, 1989), 100.

3. Franz Kafka, *Letters to Milena*, trans. Philip Boehm (New York: Schocken Books, 1990), 146 (letter of August 8–9, 1920).

4. Franz Kafka, *Letter to His Father*, trans. Ernst Kaiser and Eithne Wilkins (New York: Schocken Books, 1966), 95.

5. Ibid., 95.

6. Elias Canetti, *Kafka's Other Trial: The Letters to Felice* (New York: Schocken Books, 1974), 58.

7. Wagenbach, *Franz Kafka: Pictures of a Life*, 107.

8. Klaus Wagenbach, *Kafka's Prague: A Travel Reader* (Woodstock, NY: Overlook Press, 1996), 79.

9. The best anthology in English of Kafka's office writings, with analysis, can be found in Stanley Corngold, Jack Greenberg, and Benno Wagner, *Franz Kafka: The Office Writings* (Princeton, N.J.: Princeton University Press, 2009); hereafter, *Office Writings*.

10. Frederick Karl, *Franz Kafka: Representative Man* (New York: Fromm International, 1991), 237.

11. Wagenbach, *Franz Kafka: Pictures of a Life*, 212.

12. Franz Kafka, "In the Penal Colony," in *The Complete Stories*, ed. Nahum Glatzer (New York: Schocken Books, 1995), 143.

13. Kafka, "The Scope of Compulsory Insurance for the Building Trades," in *Office Writings*, 69.

14. Kafka, "Workmen's Accident Insurance and Employers," in *Office Writings*, 153.

15. Max Brod, *Franz Kafka: A Biography* (New York: Da Capo Press, 1960), 82.

16. Franz Kafka, *Letters to Felice*, ed. Erich Heller and Jurgen Born, trans. James Stern and Elisabeth Duckworth (New York: Schocken Books, 1973), 20 (letter of November 1, 1912).

17. It may seem out of character, but Kafka considered going to war on the German side, and he had no objection to supporting the war by buying war bonds. This may not be as odd as it seems in retrospect, as a lot of Jews who were later persecuted under the Nazis in World War II had served for Germany in World War I.

18. Kafka, "Speech on the Occasion of the Inauguration of the Institute's New Director," in *Office Writings*, 52.

19. Ibid. (emphasis mine).

20. Kafka, "A German Society for the Establishment and Support of a Military and Civilian Hospital in Prague for the Treatment of Nervous Diseases in German Bohemia," in *Letters to Felice*, 580–581.

21. Jan Kuklik, *Czech Law in Historical Context* (Prague: Karlinum Press, 2015), 72.

22. Ibid., 72–73, 80.

23. Theodore Vondracek, *Commentary on the Czechoslovak Civil Code* (The Netherlands: Martinus Nijhoff, 1988), xx.

24. Gilles Deleuze and Felix Guattari, *Kafka: Toward a Minor Literature* (Minneapolis: University of Minnesota Press, 1986).

25. Kafka, "The Problem of Our Laws," in *The Complete Stories*, ed. Nahum Glatzer (New York: Schocken Books, 1995), 437 (emphasis mine).

26. Richard Weisberg, "Comparative Law in Comparative Literature: The Figure of the 'Examining Magistrate' in Dostoevsky and Camus," *Rutgers Law Review* 29 (1976): 237–258.

27. Walter Sokel, "Kafka as a Jew," *New Literary History* 30, no. 4 (1999): 837–853.

28. In a letter to his fiancée Felice Bauer, he says that "I am not only a clerk, but also a manufacturer. For my brother-in-law owns an asbestos factory, and I (although only through money my father put into it) am a partner, and as such am on the board. The factory has already caused me enough pain and worry, but I don't want to talk about that now; in any case, I have neglected it for some time (i.e., I withhold my anyway useless collaboration) as much as I can, and more or less get by with it." Kafka, *Letters to Felice*, 22 (letter of November 1, 1912).

29. Sander Gilman, *Franz Kafka* (London: Reaktion Books, 2005), 102.

30. Franz Kafka, *Letters to Friends, Family & Editors*, trans. Richard and Clara Winston (New York: Schocken Books, 1977), 89.

31. Kafka, *Letter to His Father*, 9.

32. Franz Kafka, *Diaries*, ed. Max Brod, trans. Joseph Kresh (New York: Schocken Books, 1976), 205.

33. Ibid., 179.

34. Kafka, *Letter to His Father*, 55–57.

35. Franz Kafka, *Dearest Father: Stories and Other Writings*, ed. Max Brod (New York: Schocken Books, 1954), 408n58.

36. Ibid., 391–392.

37. Franz Kafka, *The Castle*, trans. Mark Harmon (New York: Schocken Books, 1998), 63.

Chapter 2: Isolating the Relevant Texts

1. Stanley Corngold, Jack Greenberg, and Benno Wagner, *Franz Kafka: The Office Writings* (Princeton, N.J.: Princeton University Press, 2009), xi.

2. Indeed, this output was so meager that once Kafka was "discovered" by English readers and became widely read after World War II, at least one noteworthy literary critic felt compelled to take a "dissenting view" of Kafka based in part on the lack of finished material. Edmund Wilson, "A Dissenting Opinion on Kafka," in *Franz Kafka: A Collection of Critical Essays*, ed. Ronald Grey (Englewood Cliffs, N.J.: Prentice-Hall, 1962), 91–98.

3. Kafka's instructions are set forth by Max Brod in his Postscript to *The Trial*, and while there has been some debate about the dating of the wills as to which version preceded the other, the main point of both is that Kafka sought the nonrepublication of his published works and the destruction of all non-public materials. Max Brod, "Postscript to the First Edition," in Franz Kafka, *The Trial*, trans. Willa and Edwin Muir (New York: Schocken Books, 1992), 264–271.

4. Judith Butler, "Who Owns Kafka?," *London Review of Books* 33, no. 5 (March 3, 2011): 3–8.

5. Richard Heinemann, "Kafka's Oath of Service: '*Der Bau*' and the Dialectic of Bureaucratic Mind," *PMLA* 111, no. 2 (March 1996): 256–270.

6. See, for example, Stanley Corngold, *Lambent Traces: Franz Kafka* (Princeton, N.J.: Princeton University Press, 2004).

7. Niels Bokhove and Marijke van Dorst, eds., *A Great Artist One Day: Franz Kafka as Pictorial Artist*, trans. Rachel Ward (Prague: Vitalis, 2007).

8. Claude Gandelman, "Kafka as an Expressionist Draftsman," *Neohelicon* 2, no. 3–4 (September 1974): 237–277. Gandelman makes much of the resemblance of the figures to the letter K, but it is clear that this shape is a common motif in industrial drawings and warnings, of the type reproduced in this chapter and photographed by myself in China.

9. Ibid., 263–267.

10. See Christian Klemm, in collaboration with Carolyn Lanchner, Tobia Bezzola, and Anne Umland, *Alberto Giacometti* (New York: Museum of Modern Art, 2001). Giacometti knew Albert Camus, who wrote about the importance of Kafka's work, as well as playwright Samuel Beckett, whose theater of the absurd plays used minimalist settings that reflected the isolation and alienation found in the work of both Giacometti and Kafka.

11. Joyce Carol Oates, "Kafka as Storyteller," in *Franz Kafka: The Complete Stories and Parables,* ed. Nahum N. Glatzer (New York: Quality Paperback, 1971), ix.

12. Ofer Aderet, "After Bitter Battle over Kafka's Papers, a Daunting Task: Tracking Them Down," *Haaretz*, July 7, 2015, http://www.haaretz.com/israel-news/.premium-1.664741. The case could go on even further: "The judges noted that some of the manuscripts, which the Hoffe family sold at public auction in previous decades, didn't even belong to Hoffe. Will the National Library now embark on an international crusade for the return of these manuscripts? Time will tell."

13. Max Brod, "Postscript," 267 (emphasis mine).

14. Ibid., 265, 267.

15. Joyce Carol Oates, "The Art of Suicide," in *Suicide: The Philosophical Issues*, ed. M. Pabst Batten and D. J. Mayo (New York: St. Martins, 1980), 162–169. Oates argues that a suicide attempt can be like an art performance, and the same logic can extend to a will. Kafka's fate of having his will ignored is not unusual. The Marquis de Sade left a detailed will with careful instructions for his burial in an unmarked area without any ceremony, as well as a wish that his memory fade from the face of the earth. But his son insisted on giving him a Christian funeral in the cemetery of the very asylum where Sade was held for his final years. The will was clearly an expression of his atheism and materialism (the concept that all matter becomes other matter), but his son disobeyed his instructions. In both Kafka and Sade, we see the artistic ambivalence of issuing a will that is intended to erase one's legacy. See John Phillips, *How to Read Sade* (London: Granta Books, 2005), 104–105.

16. Milan Kundera recognizes that Brod was put into a conflict, but suggests that it could have been handled by publishing the major stories without also publishing every little letter and private note: "And thus did Brod create the model of disobedience to dead friends; a judicial precedent for those who would circumvent

an author's last wish or divulge his most intimate secrets." *Testaments Betrayed*, trans. Linda Asher (New York: Harper Collins, 1993), 276.

17. Nili Cohen, "The Betrayed (?) Wills of Kafka and Brod," *Law & Literature* 27 (2015): 1–21, at 19.

18. Walter Sokel, *The Myth of Power and the Self: Essays on Franz Kafka* (Detroit: Wayne State University Press), 23.

Chapter 3: Narrative Summaries

1. Source texts may be found in Franz Kafka, *The Complete Stories*, ed. Nahum Glatzer (New York: Schocken Books, 1995); Franz Kafka, *The Trial*, trans. Breon Mitchell (New York: Schocken Books, 1998); and Franz Kafka, *The Castle*, trans. Mark Harmon (New York: Schocken Books, 1998).

Chapter 4: Kafka's Target—Modern Law

1. Stephen Toulmin, *Cosmopolis* (New York: Free Press, 1990), 16, 200.

2. Zygmunt Bauman, *Modernity and Ambivalence* (Ithaca, N.Y.: Cornell University Press, 1991), 20.

3. Karl Gareis, *Introduction to the Science of Law* (New York: A. M. Kelley, 1911), 13.

4. John Merryman, *The Civil Law Tradition* (Stanford, Calif.: Stanford University Press, 1985), 61.

5. Edward McWhinney, "Code Law Systems," in *International Encyclopedia of the Social Sciences*, ed. David L. Sills (New York: Macmillan, 1968), 9:214–217.

6. William Blackstone, *Commentaries on the Laws of England: Facsimile of the First Edition of 1765–1769*, vol. 1 (Chicago: University of Chicago Press, 1979), 5.

7. Lawrence Friedman, *Law and Society: An Introduction* (Englewood Cliffs, N.J.: Prentice-Hall, 1977), 42.

8. Francis Bacon, *Advancement of Learning* (New York: American Home Library, 1902), 413.

9. Jeremy Bentham, "The Limits of Jurisprudence Defined," in *The Great Legal Philosophers: Selected Readings in Jurisprudence*, ed. Clarence Morris (Philadelphia: University of Pennsylvania Press, 1959), 287–288.

10. Max Weber, *Economy and Society*, vol. 2, ed. Guenther Roth and Claus Wittich (Berkeley: University of California Press, 1978), 866.

11. Rudolph Von Ihering, *Law as a Means to an End*, vol. 5, trans. Isaac Husik (Boston: Boston Book Company, 1913), 290.

12. Ronald Dworkin, *Law's Empire* (Cambridge, Mass.: Harvard University Press, 1986).

13. Tom Bingham, *The Rule of Law* (London: Penguin Books, 2011), 8.

14. And here we must remember that while Tom Bingham has written perhaps the best recent book on the rule of law, he relies on quotes from a law minister from Singapore, where corporal punishments such as "caning" are meted out for "offenses against modesty," and he quotes a law minister from Zimbabwe, which has descended into mob justice, and where the rule of law has been so corrupted by selective prosecution that some commentators have wondered if there is even a justice system worthy of the name.

15. Barack Obama, "Remarks by the President on National Security," *The White House*, May 21, 2009, https://www.whitehouse.gov/the-press-office/remarks-president-national-security-5-21-09.

16. Marc Hauser and Michael Shermer, "Can Science Determine Moral Values: A Challenge and Dialogue about the Moral Arc," *Skeptic Magazine* 20, no. 4 (2016): 18, 20–21.

17. Boaventura de Sousa Santos, *Towards a New Legal Common Sense: Law, Globalization, and Emancipation* (London: Reed Elsevier, 2002), 7.

18. Friedrich Engels, *Socialism: Utopian and Scientific*, trans. Edward Aveling (New York: Cosimo Classics), 32.

19. Dirk Kasler, *Max Weber: An Introduction to His Life and Work* (Chicago: University of Chicago Press, 1988), 15.

20. Karl Marx and Friedrich Engels, *The Communist Manifesto*, ed. and trans. L. M. Findlay (Toronto: Broadview Press, 2004), 64.

21. At the same time that Kafka mirrored these contemporary thinkers, his stance on modernity anticipates the postmodern critique of totalizing modern institutions, which perhaps explains why his work has caught the attention of so many influential figures in the late twentieth century, including Jacques Derrida, Hélène Cixous, Jean-François Lyotard, and Slavoj Žižek, each of whom has addressed Kafka's treatment of law. Like many of these postmodern writers, Kafka stresses the fluidity of identities, the indeterminacy of language and interpretation, and the dialectic of domination and resistance. For this reason, Kafka's work forms an interesting link between the classical social theorists and more contemporary figures in critical theory.

22. Walter Benjamin, *Illuminations: Essays and Reflections* (New York: Harcourt Brace Jovanovich 1968), 130.

Chapter 5: Modern Law Has Come Unmoored from Its Normative Grounding

1. Franz Kafka, *The Trial*, trans. Willa and Edwin Muir (New York: Schocken Books, 1992), 222.

2. *Hui v. Castaneda*, 599 US 799 (2010).

3. Adam Liptak, "Justices Agree on Detainee Death Case," *New York Times*, May 4, 2010, A20.

4. *Castaneda v. US*, 546 F.3d 682 (9th Cir. 2008).

5. 2010 WL 710089 (US) (Oral Argument).

6. For example, these two stories are found at the beginning of Franz Kafka, *The Complete Stories*, ed. Nahum Glatzer (New York: Schocken Books, 1995).

7. Franz Kafka, *Letters to Friends, Family & Editors*, trans. Richard and Clara Winston (New York: Schocken Books, 1977), 207.

8. Franz Kafka, "The New Advocate," in *The Complete Stories*, ed. Nahum Glatzer (New York: Schocken Books, 1995), 415 (emphasis mine).

9. Ibid.

10. Plutarch, *Plutarch's Lives*, vol. 4 (Boston: Little, Brown, and Company, 1868), 165.

11. Franz Kafka, *The Blue Octavo Notebooks*, ed. Max Brod, trans. Ernst Kaiser and

Eithne Wilkins (Cambridge, Mass.: Exact Change, 1991), 39. In his private notebooks, Kafka wrote a fragment about a lawyer called Bucephalus who was called to represent his brother (a greengrocer) in a suit against a firm, though the nature of the suit is not specified.

12. Friedrich Nietzsche, *Ecce Homo*, trans. Duncan Large (Oxford: Oxford University Press, 2007): 11.

13. Kafka, *Blue Octavo*, 26.

14. "The New Advocate" should not be confused with the similarly titled "Advocates," a brief, nightmarish first-person tale where the narrator (again nameless) finds himself trapped in a large building where the corridors are filled with people dressed in huge striped aprons. The narrator believes that the building is a law court on account of the endless droning noise. He is looking for advocates because they are needed everywhere. Although the story is very brief and cuts off abruptly, it contains an interesting passage reminiscent of *The Trial*, in which the narrator says that one cannot question whether the law is being administered unfairly because life would be impossible if one suspended belief in the legitimacy of the law. This echoes the statement by the priest in *The Trial* to the effect that one need not consider the law as true but rather as necessary, and it also echoes the scene in "The Refusal" where the narrator says that without the refusals issued by the authorities, the villagers simply could not get along. Apart from these parallels, "Advocates" is a bit too sketchy to offer major insights into Kafka's view of the law.

15. Max Weber, "Parliament and Government in a Reconstructed Germany," in Max Weber, *Economy and Society*, ed. Guenther Roth and Claus Wittich (Berkeley, Calif.: University of California Press, 1978), 1393.

16. Austin Harrington, "Alfred Weber's Essay 'The Civil Servant' and Kafka's 'In the Penal Colony': The Evidence of an Influence," *History of the Human Sciences* 20 (2007): 41–63, 51.

17. Kafka, "The New Advocate," 415.

18. Jacob Abbott, *Alexander the Great* (New York: Harper, 1901), 29.

19. Kafka, *Blue Octavo*, 52.

20. Franz Kafka, "Couriers," in Franz Kafka, *The Basic Kafka*, ed. Erich Heller (New York: Pocket Books, 1984), 185.

21. Roberto Unger, *The Critical Legal Studies Movement* (Cambridge, Mass.: Harvard University Press, 1986), 119.

22. Stanley Corngold, *Lambent Traces* (Princeton, N.J.: Princeton University Press, 2004), 95.

23. Friedrich Nietzsche, *Beyond Good and Evil*, trans. Walter Kaufmann (New York: Vintage, 1989), 115.

24. Friedrich Nietzsche, *Basic Writings of Nietzsche*, trans. Walter Kaufmann, (New York: Modern Library), 783.

25. Alfred Weber, "Der Beamte," *Die neue Rundschau* 21 (1910): 1321–1339, translated and reprinted in Harrington, "Alfred Weber's Essay," 47–59. Weber was better known for his theory about where industries were located, namely *Theory of the Location of Industries* (Chicago: University of Chicago Press, 1929).

26. See, for example, Eberhard Demm, "Max and Alfred Weber and the *Verein fur Sozialpolitik*," in *Max Weber and His Contemporaries*, ed. Wolfgang Mommsen and Jurgen Osterhammel (London: Unwin Hyman, 1987), 88; Wolfgang Mommsen, *The Political and Social Theory of Max Weber* (Chicago: University of Chicago Press, 1989), 175.

27. See Douglas Litowitz, "Max Weber and Franz Kafka: A Shared Vision of Modern Law," *Law, Culture, and the Humanities* 7, no. 1 (2011): 48–65.

28. Max Weber, *The Protestant Ethic and the Spirit of Capitalism* (New York: Routledge, 1992), 124.

29. Max Weber, "Parliament and Government in a Reconstructed Germany," in *Economy and Society*, 36; emphasis added.

30. Kafka, *The Trial*, 220 (emphasis mine).

31. Ibid., 124.

32. Ibid.

33. Stanley Fish, *There's No Such Thing as Free Speech, and It's a Good Thing Too* (New York: Oxford University Press, 1994), 222.

34. Peter Papadatos, *The Eichmann Trial* (London: Stevens & Sons, 1964), 29.

35. Herbert Marcuse, *One Dimensional Man* (Boston: Beacon Press, 1964), 247.

36. George Ritzer, *The McDonaldization of Society* (Thousand Oaks, Calif.: Pine Forge Press, 2000), 11.

37. William Kunstler, "The Terrible Myth" (transcript of speech February 1970), in *William Kunstler: Disturbing the Universe*, PBS, *POV*, http://www.pbs.org/pov/disturbingtheuniverse/audio-speeches-and-interviews/2/.

38. Howard Zinn, *Declarations of Independence* (New York: Harper Perennial, 1991), 11.

39. Hélène Cixous, "Writing and the Law: Blanchot, Kafka, and Lispector," in Hélène Cixous, *Readings*, trans. Verena Andermatt Conley (Minneapolis: University of Minnesota Press, 1991), 18.

40. Frederick Karl, *Franz Kafka: Representative Man* (New York: Fromm International, 1991), 645 (emphasis mine).

Chapter 6: Modern Law Is Inherently Dystopian

1. Franz Kafka, "The Refusal," in Franz Kafka, *The Complete Stories*, ed. Nahum Glatzer (New York: Schocken Books, 1995), 264.

2. The term "outsider jurisprudence" is often credited to law professor Mari Matsuda. See Mari Matsuda, "Public Response to Racist Speech: Considering the Victim's Story," *Michigan Law Review* 87 (1989): 2320–2381. The term is often used synonymously with critical race theory and/or the various related approaches such as critical race theory, LatCrit theory, feminist legal theory, and queer legal theory for their common goal of seeking justice by focusing "attention to the experiences and perspectives of subordinated persons, communities, and peoples." John Hayakawa Torok, "Finding the Me in LatCrit Theory: Thoughts on Language Acquisition and Loss," *University of Miami Law Review* 53 (1999): 1019–1036.

3. Gilles Deleuze and Felix Guattari, *Kafka: Toward a Minor Literature* (Minneapolis: University of Minnesota Press, 1986).

4. W. H. Auden, *The Dyer's Hand and Other Essays* (New York: Random House, 1956), 160.

5. Eldridge Cleaver, *Soul on Ice* (New York: McGraw-Hill, 1968), 58.

6. Marc Galanter, "Why the Haves Come Out Ahead: Speculations on the Limits of Legal Change," *Law and Society Review* 9, no. 1 (1974): 95–160, at 124.

7. Martin Luther King Jr. made a similar observation about the African American community in the South, who "accepted [segregation] without apparent protest. . . . Their minds and souls were so conditioned to the system of segregation that they submissively adjusted themselves to things as they were." Martin Luther King Jr., *Strive toward Freedom* (New York: Harper, 1964), 21–22.

8. We might go so far as to wonder whether a judge—the ultimate insider—would feel himself an outsider if drawn into the legal process as a party. In this regard we can recall Judge Learned Hand's confession that "I must say that as a litigant I should dread a lawsuit beyond almost anything else short of sickness and death." In Fred Shapiro, *The Oxford Dictionary of Legal Quotations* (New York: Oxford University Press, 1993), 304.

9. Colin Wilson, *The Outsider* (New York: J. P. Tarcher, 1987).

10. Hanna Fenichel Pitkin, "Rethinking Reification," *Theory and Society* 16, no. 2 (1987): 263–293, at 273.

11. Scott Turow, *Personal Injuries* (New York: Farrar, Straus, & Giroux), 3.

12. Scott Turow, *Innocent* (New York: Grand Central Publishing, 2010) 10–11.

13. Franz Kafka, *The Trial*, trans. Breon Mitchell (New York: Schocken Books, 1998), 3.

14. Alexis de Tocqueville, from *Democracy in America*, reprinted in *Gale Encyclopedia of American Law*, 3rd ed. (Detroit: Gale, 2011): 541–544.

15. Ibid.

16. David Hume, "Of the First Principles of Government," in *Essays: Moral, Political, and Literary* (New York: Cosimo, 2007) 28.

17. Franz Kafka, "The Problem of Our Laws," in *The Complete Stories*, 438.

18. Deleuze and Guattari, *Kafka: Toward a Minor Literature*, 45.

19. Joseph Heller, *Catch-22* (New York: Simon & Schuster, 1994), 419.

20. Matt Taibbi, *The Divide* (New York: Spiegel & Grau, 2014), xvii.

Chapter 7: Modern Law Inverts Punishment So That It Predates the Crime

1. Franz Kafka, "In the Penal Colony," in *Franz Kafka, The Complete Stories*, ed. Nahum Glatzer, trans. Willa and Edwin Muir (New York: Schocken Books, 1995), 145.

2. Lewis Carroll, *The Annotated Alice: 150th Anniversary Deluxe Edition*, ed. Martin Gardner (New York: W. W. Norton, 2015), 233.

3. Philip K. Dick, "The Minority Report," in *Selected Stories of Philip K. Dick* (New York: Houghton Mifflin, 2013), 224–225.

4. Alexander Volokh, "n Guilty Men," *University of Pennsylvania Law Review* 146, no. 1 (1997): 173–216, at 174.

5. Gideon, "The Presumption of Guilt," *A Public Defender*, April 4, 2010, http://apublicdefender.com/2010/04/04/the-presumption-of-guilt/.

6. Monica Davey, "Chicago Police Try to Predict Who May Shoot or Be Shot," *New York Times*, May 24, 2016, A11.

7. US Department of Justice, "Jail Inmates at Midyear 2014," Bureau of Justice Statistics, NCS 248629 (June 2015), 4: "At midyear 2014, about 6 in 10 inmates were not convicted but were in jail awaiting court action."

8. See Complaint in *Trowbridge v. Cuomo*, Civil Action 16 CV 3455 (US District Court for the Southern District of New York). See also para. 97, alleging that a misdemeanor defendant who asks for a jury trial will typically have to wait 827 days.

9. Allen Cone, "Feds Accessing Medical Records without Warrants," United Press International, June 11, 2016, http://www.upi.com/Top_News/US/2016/06/11/Feds-accessing-medical-records-without-warrants/9691465654445/.

10. Janet Reitman, "Inside Gitmo: America's Shame," *Rolling Stone* 1252 (2016): 52.

11. Ibid., 56.

12. Ibid., 51. See also http://www.miamiherald.com/news/nation-world/world/americas/guantanamo/article127473314.html

13. Franz Kafka, *The Trial*, trans. Willa and Edwin Muir (New York: Schocken Books, 1992), 4, 228.

14. Robert Jackson, "The Federal Prosecutor," Address at the Second Annual Conference of United States Attorneys (Apr. 1, 1940), quoted in *Morrison v. Olson*, 487 U.S. 654, 728 (1988) (Scalia, J., dissenting).

15. Franz Kafka, *The Castle*, trans. Mark Harmon (New York: Schocken Books, 1998), 63.

16. John Lechte, "Kafka," in *Fifty Key Contemporary Thinkers* (New York: Routledge, 1994), 272 (emphasis mine).

17. Andy Kroll, "This Is How Private Prison Companies Make Money Even When Crime Rates Drop," *Mother Jones*, September 19, 2013, http://www.motherjones.com/mojo/2013/09/private-prisons-occupancy-quota-cca-crime.

18. Yale Law School, *The Avalon Project: Documents in Law, History, and Diplomacy*, http://avalon.law.yale.edu/18th_century/rightsof.asp.

19. See Ritchie Robertson, Introduction, in *Franz Kafka, The Metamorphosis and Other Stories* (Oxford: Oxford University Press, 2009), xxx (quoting Kafka's letter to Kurt Wolff of October 11, 1916).

20. William O. Douglas, "The Dissent, a Safeguard of Democracy," *Journal of the American Judicature Society* 32 (1948): 104–107.

21. *Utah v. Strieff*, 136 S. Ct. 2056, 2069 (2016) (Justice Sotomayer, dissenting).

22. The court file is *Litowitz v. Abetova*, 07 F 699 (Lake County, Illinois).

23. Mary Neiswender, "Manson Tells Why He Has a Swastika," *Long Beach Press-Telegram*, March 12, 1971, 5.

Chapter 8: Modern Law Fails to Accept the Ambiguity of Texts

1. *General Civil Code for All the German Hereditary Provinces of the Austrian Monarchy* (1811 version), trans. Joseph Chevalier (Vienna: Rudolf Lechner, 1866).

2. Peter Goodrich, *Legal Discourse: Studies in Linguistics, Rhetoric and Legal Analysis* (New York: St. Martin's Press, 1987), 7.

3. Bayless Manning, "Hyperlexis and the Law of Conservation of Ambiguity," *Tax Law* 36 (1982): 9.

4. Jacob Gershman, "Judge Posner Is 'Very Bothered' by Legal Jargon," *Wall Street Journal*, Law Blog, May 19, 2016, http://blogs.wsj.com/law/2016/05/19/judge-posner-is-very-bothered-by-legal-jargon/.

5. *US v. Dessart*, 823 F.3d 395, 405 (7th Cir. 2016) (Judge Posner, Concurring).

6. Nicholas Horn, "T(r)op(ic)ology: Law, Interpretation, Power," *Griffith Law Review* 5 (1996): 125–144.

7. Franz Kafka, *Letter to His Father*, trans. Ernst Kaiser and Eithne Wilkins (New York: Schocken Books, 1966), 3.

8. In *Letter to His Father*, Kafka says that all of his writing is ultimately about his father: "My writing was all about you; all I did there, after all, was to bemoan what I could not bemoan upon your breast." Ibid., 83.

9. Jerzy Kozinski, *Passing By: Selected Essays 1962–1991* (New York: Grove Press, 1995), 239.

10. Franz Kafka, *The Castle*, trans. Willa and Edwin Muir (London: Vintage, 2005), 303.

11. Walter Benjamin, *Reflections: Essays, Aphorisms, Autobiographical Writings*, ed. Peter Demetz (New York: Schocken Books, 1986), 205.

12. Milan Kundera, "Kafka's World," *Wilson Quarterly* (Winter 1998): 88–98.

13. T. S. Eliot, "Burnt Norton," in *Four Quartets* (New York: Harcourt, 1971), at line 149.

14. Franz Kafka, *The Castle*, trans. Anthea Bell (Oxford: Oxford University Press, 2009), 21–22.

15. Ibid.

16. Ritchie Robertson, "Introduction," ibid., xxvi.

17. Franz Kafka, *The Castle*, trans. Mark Harman (New York, Schocken, 1998), 8.

18. Kafka, *The Castle*, trans. Anthea Bell, 12.

19. Ibid., 316.

20. Ibid.

21. Jacques Derrida, "Before the Law," in *Acts of Literature* (New York: Routledge, 1992), 181–220.

22. Franz Kafka, *The Trial*, trans. Willa and Edwin Muir (New York: Schocken, 1992), 217.

23. Derrida, "Before the Law," 208.

24. Ibid., 197.

25. Horn, "T(r)op(ic)ology: Law, Interpretation, Power," 125–144.

26. Panu Minkkinen, "The Radiance of Justice: On the Minor Jurisprudence of Franz Kafka," *Social & Legal Studies* 3 (1994): 349–363.

27. Kafka, *The Trial*, 120–121.

28. Roberto Unger, *The Critical Legal Studies Movement* (Cambridge, Mass.: Harvard University Press, 1986), 119.

29. Erich Fromm, "Marxism, Psychoanalysis, and Reality," trans. Florian Nadge (1966), 6, *Marxists Internet Archive*, http://www.marxists.org/archive/fromm/works/1966/psychoanalysis.htm.

30. Pierre Bourdieu, *Pascalian Meditations*, trans. Richard Nice (Stanford, Calif.: Stanford University Press, 2000), 178.

31. Theodor Adorno, "Notes on Kafka" in Theodor Adorno, *Prisms*, trans. Samuel and Shierry Weber (London: N. Spearman, 1967), 246.

Chapter 9: Modern Law Is Comic and Carnivalesque

1. Franz Kafka, *Letters to Milena*, trans. Philip Boehm (New York: Schocken Books, 1990), 213.

2. Franz Kafka, *Letters to Family, Friends, and Editors*, trans. Richard and Clara Winston (New York: Schocken Books, 1977), 41.

3. Franz Kafka, *The Blue Octavo Notebooks*, ed. Max Brod, trans. Ernst Kaiser and Eithne Wilkins (Cambridge, Mass.: Exact Change, 1991), 13.

4. Franz Kafka, *Letters to Felice*, ed. Erich Heller and Jurgen Born, trans. James Stern and Elisabeth Duckworth (New York: Schocken Books, 2006) 145–146.

5. Ibid.

6. This is consistent with Auden's comment that Kafka wrote about situations instead of people, in the sense that his humor is built around situations instead of discrete jokes. W. H. Auden, *The Dyer's Hand and Other Essays* (New York: Random House, 1956).

7. Simon Critchley, *On Humor* (London: Routledge, 2002).

8. For example, Ted Cohen, *Jokes* (Chicago: University of Chicago Press, 1999).

9. David Foster Wallace, "Laughing with Kafka," *Harper's Magazine*, July 1998, 26–27.

10. Fyodor Dostoevsky, *Notes from Underground*, trans. Richard Pevear and Larissa Volokhonsky (New York: Vintage, 1994), 35.

11. Franz Kafka, *The Castle*, trans. Mark Harman (New York, Schocken, 1998), 63.

12. Ibid., 89.

13. Franz Kafka, *The Trial*, trans. Willa and Edwin Muir (New York: Schocken, 1992), 40.

14. Michael Newton and Michael Scharf, *Enemy of the State: The Trial and Execution of Saddam Hussein* (New York: St. Martin's Press, 2008), 108.

15. Mary Douglas, "Jokes," in *Rethinking Popular Culture*, ed. Chandra Makerji and Michael Schudson (Berkeley: University of California Press, 1991), 296.

16. Milan Kundera, *The Joke*, trans. Michael Henry Heim (New York: Harper Collins, 1992), 34.

17. Ibid., 288–289.

18. Michel Foucault, *Madness and Civilization: A History of Insanity in the Age of Reason*, trans. Richard Howard (New York: Vintage Books, 1988), 288.

19. Mikhail Bakhtin, *Rabelais and His World*, trans. Helene Iswolsky (Bloomington: Indiana University Press, 2009), 10.

20. Ibid., 123.

21. Ralph Nader, "Touching Letters from Barack Obama," *The Nader Page*, June 28, 2012, https://blog.nader.org/2012/06/28/touching-letters-from-barack-obama/.

22. See "New Hedge Fund Buys Barclay's Toxic Assets with $12.6 Billion Loan from Barclays," *FINalternatives*, September 17, 2009, http://www.finalternatives.com/node/9113; *Forbes*, "The Barclay's Hedge Fund Shuffle," September 16, 2009, http://www.forbes.com/2009/09/16/barclays-cayman-fund-markets-banks-risk.html.

23. Matt Levine, "Apollo Paid Itself Some Fees and Gave Itself Some Loans," *Bloomberg*, August 23, 2016, https://www.bloomberg.com/view/articles/2016-08-23/apollo-paid-itself-some-fees-and-gave-itself-some-loans.

24. Gretchen Morgenson, "Enron's Collapse: The Letter," *New York Times*, January 17, 2002.

25. Reece Ristau, "Lebanon Man Spends $1,000 to Deliver 300,000 Pennies to Lebanon DMV," *Bristol Herald Courier*, January 16, 2017.

26. David Cay Johnston, "Tax Law Was Cited in Software Engineer's Suicide Note," *New York Times*, February 18, 2010; Harvey J. Shulman, "Our Low-Tech Tax Code," *New York Times*, February 20, 2010.

27. Franz Kafka, *The Castle*, trans. Willa and Edwin Muir (New York: Vintage Books, 2005), 54.

28. Ibid, 70.

29. *Securities and Exchange Commission v. Fuqi International, Inc. and Yu Kwai Chong*, Civil Action No. 1:13-cv-995 (US District Court for the District of Columbia) (imposing deregistration of the company and fines against its CEO for fraud), https://www.sec.gov/litigation/complaints/2013/comp22739.pdf; *In the Matter of Philip Cory Roberts and Bay Peak LLC*, Securities and Exchange Commission Release No. 77099, February 9, 2016 (banning the promoters of Fuqi International from activities in the securities industry).

30. The source of all quotes from Kelly that are unattributed are from private conversations between myself and Mr. Kelly, who has authorized my written account to be published in this book.

31. *Kelly v. Fuqi International Inc.*, Civil Action No. 6797-CVG, Delaware Court of Chancery, Memorandum Opinion dated January 2, 2013, 2013 WL 1356663 (Glasscock, Vice Chancellor). The matter was resolved more fully in *Rich ex. Rel. Fuqi International v. Yu Kwai Chong*, 66 A.3d 963 (Delaware Court of Chancery, 2013).

Conclusion: Was Kafka Correct about Modern Law?

1. Robin West, "Authority, Autonomy, and Choice: The Role of Consent in the Moral and Political Visions of Franz Kafka and Richard Posner," *Harvard Law Review* 99 (1985): 384–428; Richard Posner, "The Ethical Significance of Free Choice: A Reply to Professor West," *Harvard Law Review* 99 (1986): 1431–1448. Posner's

comments also appear in the revised version of his book *Law and Literature* (Cambridge, Mass.: Harvard University Press, 1998). West's reply: "Submission, Choice, and Ethics: A Rejoinder to Judge Posner," *Harvard Law Review* 99 (1986): 1449–1456.

2. Christine Bell, "Teaching Law as Kafkaesque," in *Tall Stories? Reading Law and Literature*, ed. John Morison and Christine Bell (Aldershot, UK: Dartmouth Press, 1996), 11. See also, for example, Austin Sarat, ed., *The Social Organization of Law* (New York: Oxford University Press, 2007); John Bonsignore et al., *Before the Law: An Introduction to the Legal Process* (New York: Houghton Mifflin, 2005).

3. Martha Robinson, "The Law of the State in Kafka's *The Trial*," *ALSA Forum* 6 (1982): 127–147, showing how Kafka recognized, followed, and commented on the reality of the criminal law and theory of his day; and Lida Kirchberger, *Franz Kafka's Use of Law in Fiction* (New York: Peter Lang, 1986), using an approach that she describes as "philological," looking at the German terms that Kafka employed in key texts about law.

4. Theodore Ziolkowski, *The Mirror of Justice: Literary Reflections of Legal Crises* (Princeton, N.J.: Princeton University Press, 1997), seeing Kafka's writings on law as a reflection of tensions within the legal system of Austro-Hungary.

5. See, for example, J. P. Stern, "The Law of *The Trial*," in *On Kafka: Semi-Centenary Perspectives*, ed. Franz Kuna (New York: Harper & Row, 1976).

6. Carol Weisbrod, "Family Governance: A Reading of Kafka's Letter to His Father," *University of Toledo Law Review* 24 (1993): 689; L. G. Cleland, "Medical-Legal Iatrogenesis: A Kafkaesque Analysis," *Adelaide Law Review* 12 (1989): 225–229; Martha Dragich, "Justice Blackmun, Franz Kafka, and Capital Punishment," *University of Missouri Law Review* 63 (Fall 1998): 853–923.

7. Alison Flood, "Kafkaesque: A Word So Overused It Has Lost All Meaning?" *Guardian*, May 18, 2016, https://www.theguardian.com/books/booksblog/2016/may/18/kafkaesque-a-word-so-overused-it-has-lost-all-meaning.

8. Parker Potter Jr., "Ordeal by Fire: Judicial References to the Nightmare World of Franz Kafka," *Pierce Law Review* 3 (2005): 195–330.

9. Anna Dehavenon, "Charles Dickens Meets Franz Kafka: The Maladministration of New York City's Public Assistance Programs," *N.Y.U. Review of Law & Social Change* 17 (1989–90): 231–254. See, for example, James Harrington, "Texas' New Habeas Corpus Procedure for Death Row Inmates: Kafkaesque—and Probably Unconstitutional," *St. Mary's Law Journal* 27 (1995): 69, using the term "Kafkaesque" without attribution; Harold Ticktin, "A Tale of Kafka's That Is Based upon His Many Years as a Lawyer in Prague," *National Law Journal*, August 6, 1984, 17, seeing Kafka's work as a critique of bureaucracy.

10. Scott Finet, "Franz Kafka's *Trial* as Symbol in Judicial Opinions," *Legal Studies Forum* 12 (1988): 23–35.

11. Frederick DeCoste, "Kafka, Legal Theorizing and Redemption," *Mosaic* 27 (1994): 170.

12. David Von Drehle, "Two Days That Changed America," in *The Supreme Court: Decisions That Changed America* (New York: Time Books, 2016): 10–15.

13. Bruno Latour, *We Have Never Been Modern*, trans. Catherine Porter (Cambridge, Mass.: Harvard University Press, 1993).

14. Franz Kafka, *The Blue Octavio Notebooks*, ed. Max Brod, trans. Ernst Kaiser and Eithne Wilkins (Cambridge, Mass.: Exact Change, 1991), 52.

15. Max Brod, *Franz Kafka* (New York: Da Capo Press, 1995), 85 ("Not that Kafka ever took any active part in political movements. But his reflective interest was claimed by any efforts that aimed at improving the lot of man"). For more on Kafka's political involvement, see Lee Baxandall, "Kafka as Radical," in *The Kafka Debate*, ed. Angel Flores (New York: Gordian Press, 1977), 121. Note that as a state employee Kafka had to undergo a screening to ensure that he was not a member of any radical or subversive organization. He passed the vetting process.

16. Friedrich Engels, "Socialism: Utopian and Scientific," in Friedrich Engels, *The Communist Manifesto and Other Writings* (London: Wordsworth, 2008) 354.

17. Ibid., 357.

18. Georg Lukács, "Against a Misplaced Realism," in *The World of Franz Kafka*, ed. J. P. Stern (New York: Holt, Reinhart, 1980), 182.

19. George Lukács, "Franz Kafka or Thomas Mann," in *Realism in Our Time*, trans. John and Necke Mander (New York: Harper & Row, 1964), 76.

20. Georg Lukács, *Theory of the Novel* (Cambridge, Mass.: MIT Press, 1971), 22.

21. Arpad Kadarkay, *Georg Lukács: Life, Thought, and Politics* (London: Basil Blackwell, 1991), 435.

22. Christine Sypnowich, *The Concept of Socialist Law* (Oxford: Clarendon Press, 1990); Morton J. Horwitz, "The Rule of Law: An Unqualified Human Good?" *Yale Law Journal* 86 (1976–77): 561–566, reviewing E. P. Thompson, *Whigs and Hunters: The Origin of the Black Act* (New York: Pantheon Books, 1975).

23. Christian Goodden, "The Prospect of a Positive Existential Alternative," in *The Kafka Debate*, ed. Angel Flores (New York: Gordian Press, 1977), 102.

24. Michel Carrouges, quoted in Georges Bataille, *Literature and Evil*, trans. Alastair Hamilton (New York: Penguin Books, 2002), 166.

25. Friedrich Nietzsche, *Beyond Good and Evil*, trans. Walter Kaufman (New York: Vintage Press, 1989), 91 (aphorism 157).

26. Quoted in Walter Benjamin, "Franz Kafka: On the Tenth Anniversary of His Death," in *Illuminations*, ed. Hannah Arendt, trans. Harry Zohn (New York: Schocken Press, 2007), 144.

27. *Miller v. State*, 124 A.D.3d 997, 1000 (N.Y. App. Ct. 2015), awarding damages for false imprisonment to a man who was detained after his release date due to a "Kafkaesque" mix-up by the correctional institution.

28. Marc Galanter, "The Modernization of Law," in *Modernization*, ed. Myron Weiner (New York: Basic Books, 1966), 153–165.

29. See Heidi Libesman, "Between Modernity and Postmodernity," *Yale Journal of Law and the Humanities* 16, no. 2 (2004): 413–423; reviewing Santos's book, *Towards a New Legal Common Sense: Law, Globalization, and Emancipation* (London: Reed Elsevier, 2002).

30. *Manuel v. City of Joliet*, 580 US ______ (2017).

31. Ritchie Robertson, "Introduction," Franz Kafka, *The Castle* (Oxford: Oxford University Press, 2009), xx.

INDEX